Partners for Peace
edited by George J. Lankevich

1. *The United Nations under Trygve Lie, 1945–1953* by Anthony Gaglione, 2001.
2. *The United Nations under Dag Hammarskjöld, 1953–1961* by Peter B. Heller, 2001.
3. *The United Nations under U Thant, 1961–1971* by Bernard J. Firestone, 2001.
4. *The United Nations under Kurt Waldheim, 1972–1981* by James Daniel Ryan, 2001.
5. *The United Nations under Javier Pérez de Cuéllar, 1982–1991* by George J. Lankevich, 2001.
6. *The United Nations under Boutros Boutros-Ghali, 1992–1997* by Stephen F. Burgess, 2001.

Source: United Nations

The United Nations under Trygve Lie, 1945–1953

Anthony Gaglione

Partners for Peace, No. 1

The Scarecrow Press, Inc.
Lanham, Maryland, and London
2001

SCARECROW PRESS, INC.

Published in the United States of America
by Scarecrow Press, Inc.
4720 Boston Way, Lanham, Maryland 20706
www.scarecrowpress.com

4 Pleydell Gardens, Folkestone
Kent CT20 2DN, England

British Library Cataloguing-in-Publication Information Available

Library of Congress Cataloging-in-Publication Data

Gaglione, Anthony, 1934–
    The United Nations under Trygve Lie, 1945–1953 / Anthony Gaglione.
       p. cm.—(Partners for peace ; no. 1)
    Includes bibliographical references and index.
    ISBN 0–8108–3698-X (alk. paper)
       1. Lie, Trygve, 1896–1968. 2. United Nations—Biography. 3. World
    politics—1945–1955. I. Series.
    D839.7.L5 G34 2001
    341.23′09′044—dc21   2001031052

DEDICATION

To Beverly, Jim-David, Brian, and David who make all things possible. Also to Dr. Margaret MacKrell Gaglione, Marie E. Gaglione, Joseph Anthony Gaglione, Caitlin Gaglione, Karen Weber, Frances Forlenza Gaglione, Dr. Abraham Yeselson, Dr. Steve and Connie Arianas, Kristian and Doris Eshelman, Herb and Julie Weber, Myron and Ditty Ehrlich, Carolyn and Shepp Bross, and Wilma and Joel Pittman.

Areas of Interest during Trygve Lie's Term

Contents

Preface   ix

1   Wartime Origins of the United Nations   1

2   Cold War: The Dream Fades   19

3   Trygve Lie: Man in the Middle   43

4   The Palestine Partition Plan   49

5   The Dream Revisited   75

6   SUNFED   93

7   A Matter of Perspective   109

8   The Case of Indonesia   113

Chronology   131

Appendix A   United Nations Members   207

Appendix B   Excerpt from the Charter of the United Nations   209

Bibliography   211

Index   223

About the Author   233

Preface

This book traces the events and personalities that led to the creation of the United Nations and analyzes the period spanning the tenure of its first secretary-general, Trygve Lie. Because these early years—1945–1953—coincide with the complete breakdown in East–West relations, this is also, in part, a book about the Cold War. I have attempted to show that the end of great power cooperation prevented the United Nations from taking an active role in promoting international cooperation, and that, instead, it became an arena for some of the most dangerous confrontations between the Soviet Union and the West. With cold-war politics penetrating virtually every organ of the world body, public confidence was severely shaken and, as the period covered in this book drew to a close, there was every reason to fear that the United Nations itself would become a casualty of the Cold War.

The United Nations survived these turbulent years only to face new challenges. The political and economic agendas of the third world replaced the Cold War as the dominant focus of the organization. The various organs of the United Nations became the scenes of attacks against rich nations by third world members who believed that insufficient attention was being given to the problems of economic development, colonialism, and racism. No longer able to control events within the world body, the major powers abandoned the United Nations in favor of more traditional diplomatic channels. Public interest in the UN diminished, as the organization increasingly was viewed as a "talking machine" that accomplished little. And with the growing impression within the academic community that the United

Nations had become irrelevant, the outpouring of scholarly interest
that accompanied the early years also slowed to a trickle.

Today the United Nations is the object of renewed interest, after
decades of relative neglect. Events in the Persian Gulf pushed the UN
to the forefront of public attention, restoring the confidence that
many had placed in it as the one great hope for fulfilling the persis-
tent human desire for peace and a world community based on the
principles of justice and prosperity. This book serves its purpose if it
satisfies a desire on the part of the reader to examine the origins of
that dream. It is also hoped that the treatment of the events depicted
here will help the reader strike a balance between optimism and reality. For while the issues that divide nations today have changed, conflict remains a constant feature of world politics, and the propensity
of countries to use the United Nations for the satisfaction of their narrow interests continues.

1

Wartime Origins of the United Nations

When the League of Nations failed to respond to Axis aggression in the 1930s, many statesmen became convinced that national survival depended on self-reliance and military power rather than the principles of collective security and international law. The failure of a single world community, envisioned by the League covenant, to challenge the fascist deification of the nation-state helped bring about the war. Yet, despite the powerful influence that national sovereignty exerted on the thinking and actions of all leaders, the impulse to bring order and civility to the world through international organization did not die around the globe. In the United States, whose failure to join the League was widely considered the League's major weakness, planning for a new organization proceeded even as Japanese, Italian, and German armies were extinguishing the last glimmer of hope that had been invested in the League. For both idealists and practical visionaries, the League ideal remained a vital link between the disaster they were witnessing and the dream of a peaceful earth. Not surprisingly, the organization that emerged from the ashes of World War II closely resembled its ill-fated predecessor both in theory and structure.

In the summer of 1939, while Hitler prepared to invade Poland, the Commission for the Study of Peace was formed under the direction of James T. Shotwell, a former president of the League of Nations Association. Leading scholars in the fields of international law and politics were enlisted and produced what to this day remains the most thoughtful exposition of the principles and problems associated with international organization—a study that assumed that a fresh start was necessary to avoid the League's image of failure. As Hitler's armies conquered Scandinavia, the Low Countries, and France, it was also evident that any new world body depended on an Allied victory. There was in this a deep and abiding irony since the global aspirations of the American peace movement were now submerged in the broader effort to defeat the Axis powers, a goal that ultimately depended on U.S. participation in the war.

An alliance was quickly formed between internationalists and groups that favored American entry into the war. The League of Nations Association joined forces with the newly formed Committee to Defend America by Aiding the Allies (CDA) to support President Franklin D. Roosevelt's efforts to break the hold of isolationism on the American mind. By the time Germany invaded Russia in June 1941, the neutrality legislation of 1936–1937 had been revised, lend-lease was operating, and the administration was about to adopt a "shoot-on-sight" policy to protect merchant shipping in American "defensive waters." The United States had become, in the words of the CDA's William Allen White, "an unbelligerent unneutral." Roosevelt readily embraced the idealism of the peace movement, for it allowed him to impart a moral tone to administration policy. His masterful "Four Freedoms" speech of January 1941 offered lofty goals even as it depicted isolationists as givers of aid and comfort to the enemies of democracy. The president's personal views of international organization were at this time unformed and uncommitted to any specific program of postwar cooperation. Yet proponents of international organization cheered his words. They shared Roosevelt's interest in breaking the grip of isolationism on American attitudes and knew that the success of their plans depended on his moral and political leadership. They also believed that the practical effects of Roosevelt's statements would eventually catch up with his rhetoric.

Such logic did not apply to Secretary of State Cordell Hull, an ardent internationalist whose devotion to that cause had persisted over a lifetime. Hull understood that internationalist ideals expressed in the midst of a great crusade would quickly dissolve in the inevitable collision of sovereign interests and partisan debate that would follow the end of hostilities. His opening-of-the-year statement on January 1, 1940, argued that it was in America's self-interest to use its influence to create a stable "world order under law." With the approval of the president, Hull established within the State Department the Advisory Committee on Problems of Foreign Relations, whose task it would be to develop the government's policy on international organization.

Thus, during the war the State Department became a clearinghouse for studies from private groups and foreign governments on the problems to be overcome before the establishment of a lasting peace.

The Atlantic Charter of August 1941 merged the practical and ideal elements of U.S. policy. Meeting at Placentia Bay, Newfoundland, aboard the U.S. cruiser *Augusta*, Roosevelt and Prime Minister Winston Churchill agreed that one aim must be the creation of a postwar organization for peace. Churchill welcomed the opportunity to cement ties between the two countries and to initiate joint planning for war. The president desired a statement of goals that depicted wartime collaboration as more than an alliance. Neither leader was yet committed to any specific concept of world organization. The president was especially opposed to an explicit U.S. commitment because of continuing bitterness over the League fight. It was at the urging of presidential adviser Harry Hopkins and Undersecretary of State Sumner Welles that the president joined in a pledge to seek a peace based on the disarmament of the aggressors until a permanent security system could be established. This vague promise became the most widely publicized outcome of the conference.

On January 1, 1942, just days after the Japanese attack on Pearl Harbor, an anti-Axis coalition was formally announced with the signing of the Declaration of the United Nations in Washington. Because it pledged the signatories to a joint effort against a common enemy and gave mutual assurances against a separate peace, the declaration's main purpose was war. Yet because the declaration linked the joint undertaking to the "purposes and principles" of the Atlantic Charter, internationalists lost little time in characterizing this connection as implicit support for the creation of a world body.

Soon after the president's speech, the Commission to Study the Organization of Peace announced the publication of its third report, titled "The United Nations and the Organization of Peace."

By early 1942 support for U.S. participation in a new organization for peace surfaced through public statements from the State Department. In a radio address on March 1, 1942, Assistant Secretary of State Adolph Berle described Allied efforts as a "people's war," a cause "vastly different from a war of politicians or governments." The vision of decent people united against evil leaders who glorified national sovereignty was a powerful one, and three months later, the Memorial Day speech of Sumner Welles put flesh on the image. "The United States [would become] the nucleus of a world organization," he said, that would "undertake the maintenance of an international police power in the years after the war to ensure freedom from fear to peace-loving peoples." Welles led a committee that was to study the problems associated with the creation of a permanent system of collective security at the end of the war. On July 23, 1942, Secretary of State Hull publicly divulged the nature of the system that the United States envisioned—one that would keep the peace among nations, by force if necessary. By the following summer, the Welles committee had produced a draft constitution for an international organization that would eventually form the basis for the Dumbarton Oaks proposals of 1944.

Early interest in the development of a global system of security was largely an American preoccupation. The British and Russians did not share American faith in the efficacy of such schemes, nor did they completely trust U.S. motives. Hull's approach at the State Department was designed to avoid the Wilsonian fallacy of equating the statement of aspirations with the achievement of goals, and in this Hull succeeded. He refused to allow strategic contingencies to complicate the secret dialogue on international organization. Neither was he distracted by sharp differences that existed among the Allies on postwar territorial adjustments, economic restructuring, and colonialism. His aim was to build consensus for a dream that could become real only after victory. In August 1943, at the First Quebec Conference, Hull obtained the tentative agreement from British Foreign Secretary Sir Anthony Eden that a joint Allied declaration at the upcoming Moscow Conference of Foreign Ministers would endorse an organization to maintain "international peace and security." Hull viewed Soviet agreement to the proposal as vital to its success. With the declaration on international organization the first item on his agenda, and at the advanced age of seventy-two, the secretary of state boarded an airplane for the first time in his life, and flew to Moscow.

PLANNING A PEACE ORGANIZATION

The Moscow conference opened on October 19, 1943, in an atmosphere of cooperation and triumph. The campaign for North Africa had been won; Italy was about to surrender; the tide of battle was about to shift on the Russian front; and some months before, the Allies at Casablanca had agreed on the principle of unconditional surrender. Military affairs dominated; the Soviets wanted to discuss measures to hasten the end of the war, particularly the opening of a second front in France, while the British were mainly interested in securing Russian agreement to enter the war in the Far East. Vyacheslav Molotov, the Soviet foreign minister, had failed to even include the matter of international organization on the agenda, and only the urging of Secretary of State Hull obtained it a position. Yet, when the conference concluded, the United States, the United Kingdom, the Soviet Union, and China declared, for the first time, their intention to establish a permanent organization to maintain peace and security at the conclusion of the war.

On November 18, 1943, Hull addressed a joint session of Congress—the first such invitation extended to a secretary of state—a happy man. He reported that much had been accomplished at Moscow including preparation for the upcoming meeting of the "Big Three" at Tehran, but the conference was crowned by the Four-Power Declaration on future organization of the peace. Congress had already proven receptive, the Fulbright Resolution of the House of Representatives and the recent passage of the Connally Amendment in the Senate put both houses on record as favoring American participation in a new world organization.

For Hull, the Moscow conference ended a long personal struggle to secure the blessings of peace for his countrymen. He understood, of course, that the task ahead would not occur in this rarified air of optimism, for the Allies were deeply divided. And while Pearl Harbor had severely crippled the influence of old-line isolationism, domestic criticism of any scheme that threatened to embroil the United States in the affairs of Europe was fully anticipated. Yet, in the afterglow of Moscow, Washington initiated an exchange of proposals on a prospective charter for the new organization. Invitations were issued to Britain, the Soviet Union, and China to participate in private, preliminary conversations at Dumbarton Oaks, an estate in the Georgetown section of Washington, D.C. Owing to Soviet neutrality in the Pacific war at the time and to the ambiguous status of China as a sponsoring power, the talks were conducted in two phases. The first, from August 21 to September 28, 1944, included the United States, Britain, and the Soviet Union. From November 29 to October 7, China met separately with the United States and Britain.

The atmosphere of the talks was cordial and agreement was quickly reached on the main structure of the organization. Membership would be open to all states, based on the principle of foreign equality and so all states would be represented in a General Assembly. The proposals also provided for a Secretariat, an international court, and "such subsidiary agencies as may be found necessary." As a major concession to American wishes and the concerns of the smaller powers that the organization not be devoted exclusively to security, an Economic and Social Council to promote social, economic, and humanitarian programs was approved. But the heart of the world body was the Security Council where the Great Powers exercised exclusive responsibility on matters dealing with peace and security. Despite the illusion of cooperation conveyed to the public, Churchill and Soviet Premier Joseph Stalin did not share with the internationalists in the State Department an equal attachment to a global order under covenant and law. Churchill favored a return to a more traditional system of military alliances based on the creation of blocs in Europe to balance the menacing power of the Soviet Union. For Stalin, safety depended on secure frontiers and friendly governments on the borders of the Soviet Union. Neither leader envisioned the new organization as an independent force in international politics. In this regard, the Soviet attitude was at once more realistic than the American and less cynical than the British. Continued cooperation among the Great Powers might enable the organization to function; in the absence of cooperation, no amount of legal fine-tuning could save it.

The Dumbarton Oaks proposals were, as Prime Minister Herbert Evatt of Australia described them, "a Great Power production." The British insisted and the United States agreed to exclude the small powers from the talks despite the objections of Cordell Hull and the opportunity this offered to Republican leaders to depict the discussions as a large-power conspiracy. Consensus emerged for a system of collective security that stressed the exclusive responsibility of the Great Powers to suppress war through organized force. Power was concentrated in a Security Council where agreement among permanent members was required prior to any collective action. Britain and the Soviet Union emphasized the limited character of the responsibilities of the General Assembly, a forum in which their interests remained relatively exposed. Finally, no agreement was possible at Dumbarton Oaks on the issue of trusteeship, a matter of special significance to the small nations and one whose importance the United States had stressed since the earliest deliberations of the Welles committee.

Understandably, voting rules as they applied to decisions of the Security Council—the organ in which the vital interests of the major powers were most likely to intersect—were of critical importance, and controversy quickly developed. The United States preferred that, on decisions concerning the pacific settlement of disputes, any party to a dispute be required to abstain. The Soviets insisted that the veto apply to all matters that came before the Council. There existed, however, mutual understanding among the Big Three concerning the desirability of the veto itself, and Hull had earlier told leading members of the U.S. Senate that the veto was an indispensable pre-condition for American participation in the organization. Without it, the administration would invite the spurious but effective criticism that congressional authority over war and the president's power to direct the use of American troops had been surrendered. Hull was satisfied that the paralyzing effect of the veto would be minimized through the "broad cooperative spirit" that led to "the creation of the UN," and that the major powers would exercise restraint in its use. But the veto controversy did encompass more than procedural dif-ferences; it symbolized the basic distrust that existed among the Big Three and satisfied each one's need to preserve a capacity to frustrate hostile action within the organization when and if vital national interests were threatened. It allowed suspicion to co-exist with hope in an experiment whose consequences were as yet uncertain.

Between February 4 and February 11, 1945, Roosevelt joined Churchill and Stalin at Yalta for what was to be their final meeting. It is one of the more unhappy ironies of the Yalta Conference that the war leaders removed the main obstacles to the creation of the world body while making agreements that would severely limit the organi-zation's ability to function. Stalin accepted the American formula on the veto, thus removing the principal item of contention at Dumbar-ton Oaks. He also dropped a demand for a seat for each of the sixteen constituent republics, accepting instead an offer by Roosevelt and Churchill to sponsor seats for the Ukraine and Belorussia at the impending general conference. It was further agreed that original membership in the United Nations would be extended to any nation that had declared war on Germany by March 1, 1945. This was a major concession on the part of the Soviet Union since it would admit a number of Latin American governments and hence add to the influ-ence of the West in the General Assembly. Finally, a major gap in the Dumbarton Oaks proposals was filled with the agreement to create a trusteeship system. The unusual display of harmony on these matters at Yalta, owing largely to the fact that the Allies met Soviet demands for territorial adjustments in Eastern Europe and the Far East, was capped by a Big Three agreement to sponsor a general United Nations Conference to open on April 25, 1945, in San Francisco.

HOPE FOR PEACE RISES ABOVE DISCORD

The choice of San Francisco reflected the shift in the center of global diplomacy from Europe to the New World. Also, President Roosevelt believed that holding the conference on American soil before the end of hostilities would ensure that the United States would not, for the second time in a generation, reject its own offspring. Although Roosevelt died on April 12, the new president, Harry S. Truman, immediately announced that the conference would open on schedule on April 25. It did so in a blaze of favorable publicity and amid optimism and expectancy. Discord among the sponsoring powers, however, was apparent when the Soviet Union refused to accept the permanent presidency of Secretary of State Edward Stettinius. Moreover, the absence of a delegation from Poland—due to a dispute over the credentials of the Lublin or London factions of the Polish government—was a pointed reminder of the cracks that were already visible in the Yalta agreement. External events quickly pressed on in the deliberations when the Soviets announced on the first day that the Red Army had surrounded Berlin.

Much of the drama at San Francisco centered on the conflict between the Great Powers—who defended their dominance as a reflection of their role in winning the war and their future responsibilities as the policemen of the world—and the smaller nations who justified limitations on the influence of the Great Powers as a vindication of the ideals in the Atlantic Charter. Led by the delegations of Australia and New Zealand, the smaller powers mounted an attack on the veto, the great symbol of political inequality in the organization. They submitted a lengthy list of questions seeking clarification of the scope of the veto but failed utterly to budge the Big Three. Instead the major crisis of the conference erupted when the Soviet Union reverted to the position that it had consistently favored, namely that the veto apply to all matters before the Security Council including the threshold question of whether to include an item on its agenda.

Reportedly, the charter itself was saved only through the personal diplomacy of Harry Hopkins in Moscow, who persuaded Stalin to accept the Yalta formula. Assured that the veto prevented the weight of hostile majorities in the General Assembly from threatening their vital interests and under constant pressure from the Latin American and Pacific delegations, the sponsoring powers did agree to a significant liberalization of the powers of the larger and more democratic body. Article 10 empowered the General Assembly to "discuss any questions or any matters within the scope of the . . . Charter." Many believed that the lifting of restrictions on what the General Assembly could discuss significantly enhanced the prospects for peace since even Great Powers would be reluctant to defy the weight of world opinion. History would determine whether this was more than wishful thinking. At the least, the Great Powers would not have their national policies exempted from public scrutiny and under certain circumstances, might even be expected to defend their actions before the world body.

Largely, but not exclusively, on the initiative of the smaller powers, the pursuit of "peaceful and friendly relations among nations" was linked in the charter with "the solution of economic and social problems" and with "universal observance of human rights." An Economic and Social Council (ECOSOC) was established as a principal organ of the United Nations to promote international cooperation in various social, economic, and humanitarian fields. Finally, the charter advanced the principle that nations responsible for administering non-self-governing territories undertake, as a "sacred trust," to promote the well being of the inhabitants and the progressive advancement of such territories toward the goal of self-government.

Herbert Evatt, who along with Peter Fraser of New Zealand and Jan Smuts of South Africa had led the challenge to the principle of "great power hegemony," dared to hope that with these additions, old ideas of sovereignty were changing. But this ideal fell short of the significance that the sponsoring powers attached to the charter's pious expressions of concern for the hungry and infirm. Stettinius reported to the president with obvious satisfaction that the Economic and Social Council was not to have "any coercive powers." Similar attitudes were expressed regarding dependent peoples in the colonies.

The sponsoring powers insisted that the core purpose of the conference was to devise a system to prevent future wars. Guided by the past, they wrote a charter stressing reliance on the whole gamut of practices developed under the Hague Conference system and later incorporated into the League: "enquiry, mediation, conciliation, arbitration and judicial settlement." Conceptually, however, global responsibility for the maintenance of peace under the charter differed sharply from the theory, if not the actual practice, of the League. Under Article 10 of the League covenant, members undertook "to respect and preserve as against external aggression the territorial integrity and existing political independence" of each other's nations. This "scout's oath" principle, manifested in the equation that "an attack on one was an attack on all," presupposed the existence of an international community that would honor the pledge against a common threat. The failure of such a community to materialize in the face of Japanese and Italian aggression together with the experience of World War II convinced the framers of the charter to confine the responsibility for peace to those powers whose combined might was winning the war.

Therefore, while the principle of international community finds expression throughout the charter, the maintenance of peace rests on the presence of a smaller community of organized force within the larger one. The major powers occupy the dual roles of peacemaker and policeman, a proposition that implicitly separates the problem of peace from the broader concerns of the international organization. Because of the veto, no enforcement measures could be taken against a permanent member of the Security Council or, for that matter, a smaller nation that enjoyed the support of one of the permanent members. But the charter failed to provide an adequate response to a breakdown in cooperation among the permanent members of the Security Council. Peacekeeping success rested entirely on the willingness of the members of the Grand Alliance, primarily the United States and the Soviet Union, to agree to use force against an aggressor.

Cordell Hull had been especially concerned over the restoration of traditional military alliances that, to his mind, were a major cause of two world wars in less than a half century. The Dumbarton Oaks proposals, owing largely to the influence exerted by Hull, subordinated the activities of regional agencies to the paramount authority of the Security Council. The need to balance the competing tendencies of alliance politics and collective security surfaced when the charter recognized the role of regional organizations in the maintenance of peace and security. At San Francisco, many nations favored granting a broader scope of responsibility to regional arrangements. The Latin American delegation feared that the charter might jeopardize final Congressional approval of hemispheric defense plans under the recently signed Act of Chepultapec. Australia and New Zealand contemplated similar plans in the South Pacific as did the Arab states in the Middle East. All the smaller nations shared the apprehension that in the event of a falling out among the permanent members, they would not be adequately protected.

Among the Great Powers, interest in loosening the grip of the veto on strategic planning was no less keen. The United States and Britain accepted a Soviet amendment that freed regional pacts aimed at the unlikely resurgence of German or Japanese aggression from the supervision of the Security Council. In theory, this left the Soviet Union free to militarize Eastern Europe without violating the Security Council's primary authority for collective security and left similar defensive arrangements in the West subject to a Soviet veto. A compromise was reached through a proposal by Harold Stassen, a member of the U.S. delegation, that would "guarantee" to all members the right of "individual or collective self-defense," and the wording became part of Article 51 of the charter. While Article 51 does not explicitly mention regional organizations, the sweeping nature of the guarantee implies an almost unlimited scope for the formation of autonomous security arrangements. Ironically, this article of the charter prepared the ground for the militarization of the entire globe.

When the delegates at San Francisco finished drafting the charter, they hoped the United Nations could inaugurate a period of international cooperation and peace. These sentiments were especially strong in the United States where the new organization had been vigorously promoted by both private and government actions. Congress responded to overwhelming public support by ratifying the charter on July 28, 1945, in a landslide vote of 89–2, a far different response than Woodrow Wilson met on his return from Versailles.

Hope was necessary for men like Lord Halifax, for even as the grand coalition neared completion of its victory over the Axis, there was little basis for optimism that sufficient political will existed among the Great Powers to implement the charter's concept of collective security. Discord among the Allies over the shape of peace in Europe and growing ideological distance between the Soviet Union and the West limited the potential utility of the organization as an instrument of conflict resolution. Thus, while the United Nations came into being out of widespread revulsion for war and faith in international cooperation, it faced a future filled with novel perils. It remained to be seen if governments could summon the political will of which Lord Halifax had spoken. Would the United Nations preserve the peace and foster social, economic, and humanitarian progress?

SETTING UP SHOP

Once the charter was signed, certain steps were required before the organization could function. For example, the charter had no legal force until it was ratified by a majority of the signatories. Further, provisional arrangements had to be made for the upcoming opening of the first General Assembly in London. There was also the matter of a permanent home for the United Nations, a question that had not been settled at San Francisco. To see to these and other details, the signatories on June 26, 1945, established a Preparatory Commission consisting of one delegate from each signatory state.

Meeting in London, the Preparatory Commission completed its first task when ratifications were deposited by the three Soviet republics and Poland on October 24, 1945 (UN Day). By December 24, the commission had also adopted operating procedures and an agenda for the first General Assembly, which was scheduled to open on January 10, 1946. It also drafted rules of procedure for each of the other organs of the United Nations. It is a tribute to the diligence of the commission that the pattern it established in setting up the first General Assembly would continue to serve all future assemblies.

Selecting the First Secretary-General

The most pressing matter before the first General Assembly was to select the first man to lead the United Nations. At San Francisco, the sponsoring powers had insisted that the veto apply to the selection of the secretary-general, which for practical purposes meant that the identity of the first secretary-general rested entirely on the agreement of the Big Three. Each power had a favorite who was unacceptable to at least one of the other two. Trygve Lie was Washington's second choice and number three on the list of candidates prepared in Moscow. He was also strongly supported by the United States and the Soviet Union for the prestigious post of president of the General Assembly. When the Soviet Union publicly endorsed Lie for the presidency of the General Assembly against his old friend Paul-Henri Spaak, the foreign minister of Belgium, the election of Spaak was virtually assured, thus preserving the availability of Lie for the more important post of secretary-general. Informed privately by Andrei Gromyko that Lester Pearson of Canada, the first choice of the United States and a popular candidate among many delegates, was unacceptable to Moscow because he was a North American, Secretary of State Edward Stettinius moved to nominate Lie. The nomination was accepted by the Security Council and approved in the General Assembly by a vote of 46–3 on February 1, 1946.

The feeling that Stettinius had been finessed by the Soviets into nominating Trygve Lie, coupled with the public endorsement of Lie by the Soviet Union, led unfairly to the claim that the new secretary-general was "Moscow's man." Actually, Lie represented the ideal compromise. He was from Norway, a smaller nation that enjoyed friendly relations with both the Soviet Union and the West. He was a respected politician with a fine war record; a socialist since his youthful entry into Norwegian politics, he had a solid history of opposition to communism and a strong devotion to Western democratic ideals. On a more personal level, Lie had been described as an emotional man, "given to fretting," loyal in his personal relationships (as his behavior toward his top level staff at the UN would later attest), and intensely devoted to his family.

Biography of Trygve Lie

Trygve Lie was born on July 16, 1896, in a working-class suburb of Oslo, Norway, to Hulda and Martin Lie. He enjoyed none of the early advantages that would have prepared him for the international stature he would later achieve. When Lie was a small boy, his father died, leaving his mother to manage the family's affairs as the proprietor of a boarding house. Through the kindness of the boarding house residents, Lie obtained his first job as a clerk at the Norwegian Labour Party Headquarters in Oslo, marking the beginning of a lifelong association with the Norwegian labor movement. In 1911, at age fifteen, Lie joined the Norwegian Trade Union Youth Organization, becoming president of the organization's local office at Aker the following year.

Educated at the University of Oslo, Lie received a law degree in 1919. Soon after, he began a legal practice while maintaining his political ties to the Labour Party. In 1921, Lie married Hjordis Joergensen and together they raised three daughters. Lie rose rapidly through the ranks of the Labour Party. In 1919, he became assistant to the secretary of the Norwegian Labour Party, a position he held until 1922, when he began a thirteen-year career as general counsel to the National Trades Unions Federation. By 1926, Lie had risen to the position of executive secretary of the Labour Party, a post he held concurrently with his duties as general counsel for one year.

In 1935 Lie, then thirty-nine years old, sought national office and was elected to parliament. Lie continued his ascent to a leadership role within the ruling Labour Party. Between 1935 and 1939, he served as Minister of Justice. In 1939, he became Minister of Trade, Industry, Shipping, and Fishing. In that capacity, Lie was credited with saving the Norwegian merchant fleet for the Allies when he ordered 25,000 seamen to avoid Norwegian ports following the Nazi invasion of Norway in 1940.

With the German occupation of Norway, Lie became foreign minister of the Norwegian government-in-exile in London, his first real exposure to international politics. Throughout the war years, Lie ably conducted his country's foreign policy, but the experience, he later admitted, did not prepare him for the unique challenges of conference diplomacy. In April 1945, Lie was appointed to head the Norwegian delegation to the San Francisco conference on international organization. There he served briefly as chairman of the committee that drafted the articles pertaining to the Security Council in the United Nations Charter.

When World War II ended, the Norwegian government-in-exile was dissolved and Lie resigned as foreign minister. He was reelected to parliament in Norway's first postwar elections and was once again appointed foreign minister in the new Labour government that took power in October 1945. In January 1946, Lie led the Norwegian delegation to the first United Nations General Assembly in London.

On February 1, 1946, Trygve Lie was elected by the General Assembly to be the first secretary-general of the United Nations, after losing a close election for the less important post of president of the General Assembly to Paul-Henri Spaak, the foreign minister of Belgium. Lie's public record in Norway was marked by conspicuous political success and general respect for his competence and record of achievement. The world in which he was now to function was in a real sense filled with unique possibilities and insurmountable obstacles, a dark landscape only partially illuminated by the experience of his League of Nations predecessors. This world would quickly introduce the new secretary-general to the novel experience of failure.

Lie was immediately faced with the task of helping to secure the removal of Soviet troops from northern Iran, the first of many crises that would mark his years at the UN. With the proclamation of the state of Israel in 1947, Lie tried unsuccessfully to find a diplomatic solution to the Arab–Israeli conflict that followed. From 1948 until he left office, he made little headway in resolving the India–Pakistan dispute over Kashmir. Lie's failed attempt to ease the Berlin crisis of 1948, to that point the most dangerous of many East–West confrontations, convinced him that the Cold War was severely weakening the United Nations.

In 1950, Lie launched his famous "Twenty-Year Peace Plan," a comprehensive proposal that stressed international cooperation to solve outstanding global problems and greater reliance by the nation-states on the United Nations. His widely heralded "peace mission," a twenty-seven-day tour of the world's major capitals, failed to persuade the leaders of the Great Powers to accept the plan.

By the end of his first term in 1950, Lie had lost the confidence of both sides in the Cold War: Washington resented his efforts to secure a seat for Communist China in the Security Council following the Chinese revolution in 1949, and the Soviet Union was outraged by his handling of UN intervention in Korea. On November 1, 1950, after the Soviet Union vetoed Lie's reelection in the Security Council, the General Assembly—without a formal election—extended his term for three years. Faced with Moscow's refusal to recognize him as secretary-general, Lie's usefulness as an intermediary in the Cold War was at an end. On November 10, 1952, Lie resigned as secretary-general.

Lie spent the remaining years of his life writing his memoirs and serving his country in a number of important appointed posts. In 1954, *In the Cause of Peace,* memoirs of his years at the United Nations, appeared. Between 1955 and 1958, Lie published three additional volumes: *Live or Die, Norway at War* (1955), *With England in the Front Line: A History of the War Years* (1956), and *Homeward Bound* (1958), personal reflections on his life in Norway. Between 1955 and 1963, Lie was governor of Oslo and Akershus and, as chairman of the Foreign Industry Committee from 1959 to 1963, he helped promote foreign investment in Norway. Two brief appointments to national office followed: he was minister of industries (1963–1964) and minister of commerce (1964–1965). In 1959, Lie tried unsuccessfully to mediate the border dispute between Ethiopia and Italian Somaliland, his only diplomatic activity after leaving the United Nations. Trygve Lie died in Geilo, Norway, on December 30, 1968, at age 72.

In what might have been a fitting epitaph, Lie concluded about his years as secretary-general that it was not an easy job. He once observed that the most satisfying accomplishment of his years at the United Nations was his role in overseeing the planning and construction of the permanent headquarters at Turtle Bay on the east side of New York.

CHOOSING THE SITE

The Preparatory Commission quickly narrowed the choice of a permanent home for the United Nations to a locale either in Europe or in the United States. Although there was strong sentiment in favor of Europe as a cultural center of a large part of the world and concern about locating the United Nations in the territory of a major power, the Preparatory Commission chose the United States by the narrow vote of 25–23–2, an outcome influenced in part by vigorous Soviet opposition to a European location. Later the choice was narrowed to the eastern seaboard and finally to the New York area.

The second half of the first session of the General Assembly opened in the autumn of 1946 in cramped quarters at Hunter College in New York City. By year's end operations were moved to more spacious temporary quarters at two sites on Long Island. The Security Council and the offices of the Secretariat were housed in an unused portion of the Sperry arms factory at Lake Success, twenty-five miles from Manhattan. The General Assembly meetings took place ten miles nearer to Manhattan at Flushing Meadows, in a building constructed for the 1939 World's Fair.

The search for a permanent headquarters was quickly mired in controversy. Secretary-general Lie favored the construction of a forty-square-mile United Nations village in affluent Westchester County, but the plan collapsed amid protests from local residents who feared the disruption of their bucolic existence and the opposition of many delegations that preferred the more cosmopolitan environs of nearby Manhattan. New York's city fathers, anxious to get the headquarters, but with no available space within the city, offered the world's fair site at Flushing Meadows, only to be turned down. And when the General Assembly met on November 5, 1946, to consider the matter, the competition over which American city would become the "capital of the world" was wide open again. President Truman offered the Presidio naval base in San Francisco, but the idea was opposed by many delegations because of the great distance from

Europe. By early December, with New York apparently out of the picture, the field had been narrowed to Philadelphia, the cradle of American democracy.

The loss of the United Nations from the New York area was a blow to the prestige of the city as well as a disappointment to Trygve Lie, who enjoyed the city's cultural amenities. The situation appeared hopeless when in December came the dramatic announcement of an $8.5 million gift from the Rockefeller family to purchase seventeen acres of abandoned warehouses and run-down tenements along the East River. An additional $26 million was quickly committed by the city of New York to improve the approaches to the UN complex and to "bury" six blocks of First Avenue. The project became a reality with the offer of a $65 million interest-free loan by the United States delegation to the United Nations.

The construction of the headquarters took nearly six years to complete and was, for Trygve Lie, a "labor of love." The interiors were designed and decorated by artisans from the member states, and $50,000 in dimes was collected from American schoolchildren to construct a fountain at the entrance of the Secretariat, a spectacular building overlooking the East River and containing 5,400 large windows. In October 1952, the General Assembly moved into its new home.

2

Cold War:
The Dream Fades

The early days of the United Nations were days of great expectation. World War II had excised the ghost of the League of Nations and the delegates at San Francisco had done their work well, producing a charter that not only established conditions for a peaceful world but also addressed the pressing social and humanitarian issues of the age. Reporters from around the globe flocked to Lake Success and later to Turtle Bay to observe the new organization tackle the great problems of peace, human rights, social justice, and economic progress.

Naturally, the most attention was focused on the Security Council, which met in continuous session, often twice a day and sometimes on Saturday. Here the five Great Powers, together with six rotating nonpermanent members, would attempt to prevent aggression and seek alternatives to the use of force in settling international disputes. The anxious eyes of the world were on the Big Five: would they be able to cooperate to control international violence or was the world about to enter yet another era of disappointment? It is to that question that we now turn.

The opening of the UN coincided with the disintegration of the Grand Alliance. Barely freed from the bloody grip of World War II, the victorious Allies faced each other across a chasm of fear and distrust. Yalta and Potsdam revealed with painful clarity that when it came to mapping out the future, the men who had combined so brilliantly to defeat a brutal enemy were operating at cross-purposes. The West's desire to restore prewar order in Europe and to reassert colonial ties in other parts of the globe conflicted with Soviet demands for security that, among other things, included the creation of friendly regimes in Eastern and Central Europe. Under the best circumstances, resolution of these competing aims demanded skillful and patient diplomacy and, above all, trust. Instead, attitudes in the Soviet Union and the West on all outstanding issues were quickly dominated by the rigid political and ideological imperatives of a new and pervasive struggle—the Cold War.

While the roots of the Cold War lay in decades of distrust, which did not abate even during the period of closest wartime collaboration, it was Winston Churchill who revealed the inner logic of the struggle. The aging war leader, recently dismissed from office by the British electorate, accepted a U.S. invitation to deliver an address on international relations on March 5, 1946, at Westminster College in Fulton, Missouri—President Truman's alma mater. From his opening words, Churchill made it clear that he saw an ominous future: "Opportunity is here now," he declared, "clear and shining for both our countries. To reject it or ignore it or fritter it away will bring upon us all the long reproaches of the aftertime. . . . The Stone Age may return on the gleaming wings of science. . . . Beware, I say. Time may be short."

The challenge, as Churchill saw it, was that "an iron curtain" had fallen across the continent. He went on to describe the tyranny that the Soviet Union had forced on the peoples behind the curtain and voiced his belief that the leaders in Moscow intended to spread their hegemony to the West. Churchill urged an alliance of English-speaking peoples as the surest way to curb Soviet ambitions. Although the British Labour government and the U.S. State Department quickly disavowed official connection with the former prime minister's remarks, Churchill's sentiments were certainly in line with those of Truman, who was on record as "being tired of babying the Russians." Truman had also read and approved the address before it was delivered. If nothing else, Churchill's Fulton speech gave the West its most enduring symbol in the Cold War and revealed the vital core of Western Cold War policy: the containment of communism.

Stalin lost little time in taking up the challenge when, one week later in a *Pravda* interview, he charged his former comrade-in-arms with "slander, discourtesy and tactlessness." Then he bluntly promised to "thrash" Churchill and "his friends" in the event of another war.

The Cold War quickly destroyed any expectation that the United Nations could function as an instrument of collective security. The charter explicitly recognized the special responsibilities of the Great Powers to maintain the peace, but Security Council action in dealing with threats to or breaches of the peace depended on the agreement of the permanent members; it was they who were authorized to negotiate the creation of military forces to implement decisions of the Security Council. The success of the system depended on the United States and the Soviet Union, but they could find virtually nothing to agree on, severely impairing any collective enforcement measures.

Obviously a breakdown of this magnitude was devastating; it need not, however, have proven fatal if the superpowers had resisted the temptation to draw the organization itself into the emerging global discord. The choice lay between a Security Council that would not function if confronted by a hostility between the Soviet Union and the West, and a council that considered many divisive issues that it was powerless to settle and that exposed its impotence. The first alternative would reflect an understanding of the link between Great Power harmony and the aims and success of the Security Council. Where agreement was missing, issues would not be placed on the agenda. Little business would come before the council, but the record would reveal that the Great Powers were honoring the spirit in which the council was created. In fact, the first option was adopted. Beginning in 1946 with the first complaint to come before the Security Council, that forum became the scene of bitter combat between the superpowers, with each side seizing every opportunity to embarrass and condemn the other. The Soviet Union was outnumbered and isolated within the UN, and the West, at little cost in blood or treasure, used the organization to register its own righteousness and the evil intent of its communist rivals.

On January 19, 1946, just two days into the first session of the Security Council, Iran complained that the refusal of the Soviet Union to remove its troops from Iran's northern provinces was a threat to international peace. The genesis of the dispute lay in the decision by Britain and the Soviet Union early in 1942 to move troops into Iran to prevent the strategically vital and oil-rich land from falling to the Axis. Both Allies promised to respect the "territorial integrity of Iran" and to withdraw all forces no later than six months after the end of the war, an understanding that was reaffirmed by the Big Three at Tehran.

It was widely known that Stalin, ever suspicious of British intrigue, was alarmed over a joint exploration agreement signed in late 1944 between the Anglo-Iranian Oil Company and Standard Oil, and that he desired a similar deal with the Iranian government, to exploit oil reserves in the north. However, reports reaching Washington and

London from the U.S. and British embassies in Tehran in the last months of 1945 were also filled with speculation that Moscow's actions were aimed at annexing the Iranian province of Azerbaijan. The ultimate aim, as feared by Wallace Murray, U.S. ambassador to Iran, was to bring the whole country into the Soviet sphere of influence.

Western diplomatic pressure on the Soviet Union during 1945 proved of no avail. Secretary of State James Byrnes, in Moscow to attend a meeting of the Council of Foreign Ministers in December, was sharply rebuked by Stalin over the double standard the West was applying to Iran, one that reserved for itself the right to protect vital global interests but denied the same privilege to the Soviet Union. Stalin piously assured Byrnes and British Foreign Minister Ernest Bevin that the Soviet Union had no territorial or political designs on Iran; that Russian troops remained in the country to contain local disorders and Kurdish unrest caused by many years of neglect and exploitation by the Iranian government. To allow 1,500 Iranian troops to reenter the area, Stalin said, would further inflame the situation and, given the local hostility of the Iranian leadership, pose a serious threat to the oil fields in Baku.

Soviet resolve was viewed by Bevin as a threat to British oil and strategic interests. With the fainthearted backing of Byrnes, Bevin suggested the creation of an Anglo-Soviet-American Commission to aid the Iranian government in restoring civil authority in Azerbaijan. But the Iranian prime minister, reluctant to invite permanent Russian interference in Iranian affairs, rejected the plan. Instead, he preferred to take his chances at the United Nations, a move the U.S. government had made known it approved.

The Iranian complaint introduced a novel and potentially dangerous element to the East–West equation. By forcing the Soviet Union to publicly justify its Iranian policy, a new dimension was added to the conflict itself. The Soviet delegate was outraged and characterized the Iranian charge as baseless, a gratuitous attempt by Iran with the complicity of the West to embarrass the Soviet government. Russia, he added, continued to favor bilateral negotiations as called for under Article 33 of the charter, and it was Iran, not the Soviet Union, that had interrupted negotiations under way since November 1945.

Not content with a simple defense of its Iranian policy, the Soviet Union fired off a propaganda volley of its own against the West. Two days later, on January 21, the Ukrainian Soviet Socialist Republic (SSR) complained to the Security Council about the presence of

British troops in Indonesia, and Russia charged in both the Security Council and the General Assembly that the presence of British forces threatened the political independence of Greece. The war of words and nerves that would mark UN history had begun.

A Security Council resolution on January 30, which urged Iran and the Soviet Union to renew talks, was soon followed by a personal visit to Moscow by the new Iranian Prime Minister Ahmed Ghavam to dicker with Stalin over the terms of a settlement.

There seemed, at first, a willingness by all parties to minimize the political fallout from the original complaint, but on February 28, 1945, Secretary of State Byrnes, speaking before the Overseas Press Club, announced the United States' intention to keep the Iranian matter before the UN independent of any progress made by talks in Moscow. "We must make plain that the United States intends to defend the charter," he said. "We will not and we cannot stand aloof if force or the threat of force is used contrary to the purposes and principles of the Charter." Byrnes's attitude further stiffened when Moscow ignored the March 2 deadline for the withdrawal of all foreign troops from Iran. On March 5, while Churchill was speaking at Fulton, he sent a stern note to Moscow demanding the immediate withdrawal of Russian forces from Azerbaijan and then, without waiting for a Soviet reply, released the contents of the note to the press.

In the days that followed, unconfirmed reports reached Washington that a large Russian force was advancing on Tehran. Despite Soviet insistence that the reports were unfounded, Byrnes threatened to take the matter to the Security Council, even if Iran refused to do so. On March 18, with the encouragement of the United States and despite a warning from Moscow that it would consider a complaint to the Security Council an "unfriendly act," Iran requested that the council take up the issue of Russian troop movements.

UN MUST PROVE ITSELF

When the Security Council debate opened on March 27, it was in an atmosphere of unrestrained East–West hostility. That same day it was announced in the Soviet press that all Soviet troops would leave Azerbaijan by early April. Andrei Gromyko, the Soviet ambassador to the UN, confirmed this and requested a postponement of the Security Council debate until April 10.

Russia's move was supported by Lie, who believed that debate "would probably intensify rather than ease the dispute." But Washington would have none of it. Truman insisted that the "UN must prove itself on this first try" and sent Byrnes to New York to personally make the American case before the Security Council. The secretary argued against postponement, insisting that the Security Council could be satisfied with nothing less than the unconditional withdrawal of Soviet troops from Iran. Faced with what amounted to an ultimatum, Gromyko stormed out of the council chamber, vowing not to return until Iran's complaint against the Soviet Union was withdrawn.

On March 29, with Gromyko absent from his seat, the Security Council adopted a resolution by Byrnes requesting that Iran and the Soviet Union inform the council on the status of negotiations. The Soviet press denounced the action as unfair and a violation of the charter. Nevertheless, on April 4, Prime Minister Ghavam and the Soviet ambassador to Tehran, Ivan Sadchikov made public an exchange of notes that ended the crisis. The Soviet Union pledged to remove all troops from Iran by early May and to recognize the exclusive authority of the Iranian government to bring about reforms in the province of Azerbaijan. A combined Soviet–Iranian oil company was to be formed with the Soviet government the major stockholder, but here, it appeared, Ghavam had hoodwinked the normally wily Soviet leader. The agreement included a clause that required the Iranian parliament's final approval of the venture in seven weeks. When the time came, the parliament refused. On April 15, Iran informed the president of the Security Council that it was withdrawing its complaint against the Soviet Union.

It is difficult to know if the embarrassment suffered by the Soviet Union in the Security Council led to its willingness to evacuate northern Iran. More likely, given Stalin's contempt for world opinion on other issues, Soviet aims in Iran were limited. Even the eventual Iranian renege on the oil deal provoked no protest from Moscow, leading some experts on the period to conclude that Stalin had used the oil project mainly to stir Iranian opposition to British interests in the country. Truman, however, was delighted with the Security Council debate; the Soviets had "backed down," lending credence to his judgment—one which would develop more fully later on—that Moscow responded only to firmness. Moreover, the ambivalence in American opinion—some critics favored appeasement of the Soviet Union while others counseled a less confrontational policy—was significantly overcome. Cold War mentality had triumphed and Soviet popularity in the United States, said Byrnes, "was completely dissipated." As for the claim that the administration was soft on communism, Byrnes concluded, "This period has passed."

But while officials in Washington celebrated, the effect of the Iranian complaint on the UN was shattering. Great Power rivalry had intruded into the very citadel of the world body, adding the weight of a public rupture in East–West relations to the difficulties that the Security Council already faced in fulfilling its main objective. Russian Ambassador Gromyko, stung by the U.S. attack, responded to Iran's withdrawal of its complaint with an impassioned, face-saving denunciation of Western motives and demanded that the issue be removed from the council's agenda. But even this fig leaf was denied him. Led by U.S. and British opposition, the Iranian issue was retained on the agenda where it remains to this day. When Lie tried to repair the damage by circulating a legal brief supporting removal of the issue from the agenda, Secretary of State Stettinius dressed him down. In Washington, where the secretary-general's intervention was openly resented, sources leaked that Lie was "Moscow's man."

Within days, the implications of the Iranian issue for the function of the Security Council became painfully clear, when a dispute over the failure of France and Britain to withdraw forces from Lebanon and Syria provoked the first of many Soviet vetoes. Since no direct threat to Russian national interests existed and the matter was essentially settled, the veto can only be explained by Soviet bitterness over the discrepancy in treatment received by it and by the Western nations on essentially similar complaints before the Security Council.

The Soviet use of the ultimate Great Power weapon—the veto— where there was no direct threat to Russian national interests, was an ominous sign of things to come. By using the veto to register general opposition to Western interests, the Soviet Union had deliberately violated an implicit understanding among the Great Powers that the veto would be used only as a last resort, as a shield against the Security Council's becoming an alliance against one of the permanent members. More important, it demonstrated a loss of confidence in the ability of the Security Council, acting through the harmony of the Big Five, to enforce the peace. Henceforth, the veto would become the symbol of East–West hostility. The Soviet Union continually used this prerogative to thwart Western attacks on its policy, and the West pointed to the mounting number of Soviet vetoes as proof that Russia lacked respect for the charter.

The politics of the Cold War also immediately embroiled nations seeking admission to the organization. At Yalta, it will be recalled, original membership had been restricted to nations that were on the winning side in the war. The charter extends membership to "other peace-loving nations" provided they are "able and willing" to carry out their obligations under the charter. New applicants would be admitted by a majority vote of the General Assembly, following a recommendation by the Security Council, which meant that the veto would apply on all membership applications.

The admission of new members was of obvious, even pressing, importance since twenty nations with a total population of 300 million, including thirteen of the twenty-six European states, remained outside the UN a year after its founding. Superficially, the debate over which of these could be admitted centered on theoretical differences regarding the principle of universality as well as the fitness of individual applicants to participate in the work of the United Nations. In fact, few issues offer more striking proof of the effect of cold war than the membership issue because, unlike other political disputes, the mere existence of the organization was the only prerequisite needed for discord.

In August 1946, the Security Council met to consider the applications of Afghanistan, Albania, Iceland, Ireland, the Mongolian People's Republic, Portugal, Sweden, and Jordan. Officially the United States acted as the champion of universality and offered a "package deal" that would have admitted the favorites from both sides. Gromyko rejected the offer, insisting, instead, that each application be judged on its own merits. He then vetoed the applications of Ireland, Jordan, and Portugal, claiming that the Soviet Union did not have diplomatic relations with Ireland and Portugal, and that there were serious questions regarding the true nature of Jordan's independence. Albania and Mongolia failed to obtain the required seven votes in the council; Albania, according to the United States, because of its wartime collaboration with the Axis. Actually, the preferred legalisms on both sides were irrelevant. There were tangible benefits for the West. For example, by forcing repeated Russian vetoes of a particular applicant, say Italy, the West could argue that the Soviet Union was denying that country its rightful place in the world community. But the deadlock over membership had largely become part of the overall pattern of cold war gamesmanship.

In 1946 only Afghanistan, Iceland, Sweden, and Thailand stayed the course. The following year, eight more nations applied, including the former enemy states of Bulgaria, Finland, Hungary, Italy, and Romania, with which peace treaties had been concluded. Now the Soviet Union was prepared to accept a deal in which it would agree to admit Italy and Finland in exchange for Western approval of Bulgaria, Hungary, and Romania. But the West refused. Instead it sought an advisory opinion from the International Court of Justice, which supported the West's view that the admission of one state could not be dependent on the admission of another.

Despite a mounting backlog of rejected applicants, the established pattern of mindless opposition continued for years. A few states were admitted—Pakistan and Yemen in 1947, Burma the following year, and in 1949 and 1950, Israel and Indonesia, which were essentially creations of the United Nations. For the most part, the West relied on the Communists' lamentable human rights record to disqualify Soviet-sponsored applicants, and the Soviet Union retaliated with various legal arguments to reject Western favorites. By the time the issue was finally settled in 1955, ironically by Western acceptance of a "package" deal that resulted in the admission of sixteen new members, the Soviet Union had cast fifty-one vetoes, six on Italy alone.

COLLECTIVE SECURITY:
IDEAL VERSUS REALITY

During the period between the world wars, there had been widespread agreement among students of the League of Nations that the omission of automatic sanctions against aggression was a principal weakness of its covenant. The creation of an independent military force under the control of the organization itself was not seriously considered at San Francisco, although this approach remains dear to the hearts of ardent internationalists. Instead, Article 42 of the charter empowers the Security Council to "take such action by air, sea, or land forces as may be necessary to maintain and restore international peace and security." Under Article 43 members undertake, through individual agreements, to provide the Security Council with troops and military facilities in the event that collective military action is required. The charter also provides in Article 47 for the creation of a Military Staff Committee, consisting of the chiefs of staff of the permanent members, to advise the Security Council on matters relating to its "military requirements" and to assume command of military operations. Although the Security Council lost no time in setting up the Military Staff Committee, it was quickly apparent that the debate on Article 43 would reflect the tensions between the Soviet Union and the West. On the surface, talks broke down over technical differences. In general, the West favored a large UN force with contributions based on the size and special circumstances of each power. Britain and the United States would thus supply air and sea units and the Soviet union, the bulk of the ground forces. The Security Council could deploy these on a flexible basis even prior to a crisis. The Soviet Union insisted on equal contributions and refused to relinquish control over its own forces prior to the passage of a Security Council resolution that identified a specific target. As to the size of the force, Russia saw no need for a large one—if there were no intention to use it against a permanent member.

After a year of Great Power negotiations, during which agreement was reached on a number of minor matters, the Military Staff Committee reported (April 30, 1947) that no agreement was possible on the terms under which member states would provide the Security Council with military forces. Article 43 became a dead letter by July 1948, when the committee, with uncharacteristic candor for a deadlocked United Nations committee, admitted that no progress was possible. From the deliberations of the committee and from the debate that followed in the Security Council, it was evident that cold war suspicions had destroyed any hope that the major powers could agree on a UN strike force.

The failure of the Great Powers to reach agreement on the establishment of a permanent military force struck at the heart of the concept of collective security envisioned by the founders of the United Nations. That concept rested on the continued solidarity of the wartime alliance, the willingness, to use an often repeated phrase, of the major powers to act as the "policemen of the world." By failing to meet the basic requirements of that joint responsibility, the Great Powers forced the world to retreat to more traditional approaches to deal with aggression. As in the past, safety would depend on self-help, military alliances, and, most unfortunately, the buildup of armaments. And while the charter makes little more than passing reference to the link between arms reductions and a more peaceful world, disarmament has always been a vital part of that equation.

In contrast to the Covenant of the League of Nations, which urged members to reduce armaments "to the lowest level consistent with national safety," arms control under the UN Charter is tied to the belief that peace depends on the availability of sufficient military power to resist aggression and on the exclusive responsibility of the permanent members of the Security Council in this area. Article 26 does invite the Military Staff Committee to formulate "plans for the regulation of armaments" but it does not commit the United Nations to a specific program of disarmament, or for that matter, as under the League, render any judgment on the intrinsic merits of an arms-free world. It should be noted that at San Francisco, this ironic convergence of aims was not seriously disputed. Even the smaller powers, who vigorously attacked the veto and argued for broader political responsibilities for the General Assembly, did not quarrel with the proposition that the management of force rested exclusively on the collaboration and consent of the Big Five.

In light of the nuclear age, however, confidence in the Great Powers to manage a rational armaments policy was being severely shaken. Disarmament became a pressing concern of the international community along with the widespread conviction—one that lingers to this day—that atomic weapons were by their very nature different from conventional armaments. Many states demanded that the awesome power of the atom be harnessed to peaceful purposes under an effective system of international control, thrusting the United Nations into the dangerous arena of atomic diplomacy.

While the destruction of Hiroshima and Nagasaki removed all doubt about the military importance of atomic energy, the political implications of the bomb were less certain. In 1945, the balance of power in the world appeared to be dramatically altered in favor of the West since, theoretically, it was possible for the West to extort important concessions from the Soviets in Eastern Europe, Germany, and elsewhere. But while Truman anticipated an improvement in the West's bargaining position, he was unwilling to use the bomb to, as Sen. Edwin C. Johnson (Colorado) put it, "compel mankind" to adopt a lasting peace. At the first Conference of Foreign Ministers in London during September 1945, Secretary of State Byrnes refused to respond to Soviet demands with nuclear blackmail.

Most experts agree that, in any case, the Western monopoly was temporary. As early as September 1945 Canadian Prime Minister Mackenzie King revealed that a Soviet espionage ring operating in Canada and the United States had transmitted atomic secrets to the Soviet Union. In general, scientists supported growing liberal sentiment to "internationalize" the bomb, fearing that the suspicions engendered through exclusive U.S. control would lead to a potentially deadly arms race with the Soviet Union. What this meant to hard-liners in the administration and Congress was that the United States would be handing the immense potential of the atom over to an unproven body, or worse, that the West would give away its most effective weapon in its war against communism. U.S. Secretary of the Navy James C. Forrestal, whose sentiments echoed those of newly appointed Secretary of War Robert P. Patterson and the Joint Chiefs of Staff, was opposed to trusting the Russians. The only form of international control that Forrestal would accept was a U.S. trusteeship over the bomb under UN auspices, a policy that would add the sanction of the international community to the monopoly already enjoyed by the United States. Republicans in Congress, led by arch anti-Bolshevik Sen. Arthur Vandenberg (Ohio), also favored a tough stance toward the Soviets.

Faced with such diverse pressure, it is not surprising that the Truman administration's nuclear policy in the days immediately after the war was in disarray. On October 3, Truman publicly adopted the internationalist line renouncing the use and development of the atomic bomb. Delay, he said, would foster a "desperate arms race." Criticism from the right was swift, and within days, the president was forced to reconsider his position. In his press conference on October 8, Truman assured Americans that the United States was prepared to discuss with other nations only the scientific principles of atomic energy; the secret of the bomb itself would remain in U.S. hands, as a "sacred trust."

Appealing as the notion of a sacred trust was to most Americans, it only seemed to spur criticism of U.S. policy from the left. In the liberal press, the president was accused of "conducting American foreign policy . . . according to the principles of Theodore Roosevelt and St. Francis of Assisi." Eleanor Roosevelt wondered out loud how "we can hold this secret and expect others to trust us when we apparently do not trust anyone else." Truman also encountered pressure from the British and Canadians, America's partners in the Manhattan Project, which was responsible for developing the atomic bomb. Prime Ministers Clement Attlee and Mackenzie King, both under domestic pressure to seek a plan for international control, impressed on Truman the need to formulate an atomic energy program prior to the opening of the General Assembly in London in January 1946. Convinced that the opening session's success depended in no small measure on the major powers' willingness to reassure the world about the dreaded new weapon, Attlee and King agreed to come to Washington to help draft a joint statement of policy.

Events moved rapidly. Truman, Attlee, and King issued a declaration on November 15 calling for the creation of a United Nations commission on atomic energy, which would work to ensure that the atom was put to peaceful uses. The commission would also seek to eliminate "from national armaments . . . atomic weapons and all other major weapons adaptable to mass destruction." One month later, at the second Council of Foreign Ministers meeting in Moscow, a conference otherwise mired in controversy, Molotov agreed to the Western plan. He insisted only that the commission report directly to the Security Council, and so on January 24, 1946, the General Assembly unanimously approved the creation of the twelve-member United Nations Atomic Energy Commission.

Early in January 1946, the plan that the United States would place before the United Nations began to take shape. Under the direction of Undersecretary of State Dean Acheson and David E. Lilienthal, chairman of the Tennessee Valley Authority (TVA), a public power project in the southeastern United States, a team of State Department people and outside consultants created a proposal that met the growing demand for international atomic controls yet, at the same time, safeguarded U.S. interests. The Acheson-Lilienthal plan recommended the creation of an Atomic Development Authority that, following a worldwide survey of existing atomic resources, would exercise control over an international monopoly covering all aspects of atomic energy: exploitation, research, development, and ownership. Following the progressive integration of all nations into the plan, existing stockpiles of weapons would be destroyed and the making of bombs would be banned. But until the Atomic Development Authority was operating fully, the United States would remain free to build and stockpile weapons as it saw fit.

The Acheson-Lilienthal proposal was a conscious blend of wishful thinking and political realism. Its success rested on the willingness of nations to design and sign the agreements necessary to progressively bring the international monopoly to life. Acheson believed that five or six years would be needed for the plan to fully take effect, but deliberately avoided setting time limits or stating political conditions for moving through the various stages. Although many believed that an international system of inspection and control was ultimately needed, Acheson, largely at Lilienthal's urging, agreed that sanctions for cheating were unnecessary; unauthorized use of fissionable materials by a country—say, the Soviet Union—would mean the beginning of World War III.

Attempting an Atomic Energy Policy

By March 1946, when the Acheson-Lilienthal proposals were made public, foreign policy in Washington and Moscow was dominated by the logic of the cold war, even if the consequences included the horror of nuclear warfare. The Soviet Union viewed U.S. support for international controls as a pretext for preserving the existing strategic imbalance and feverishly pursued its own atomic energy program. In the United States, the debate over international control of the atom was quickly overtaken by a heightened sensitivity to any breach of security that threatened America's monopoly. With the demobilization of U.S. armed forces proceeding at the rate of more than one division a day, the bomb was viewed as the only counterbalance to the threat posed by the huge Red Army in Eastern and Central Europe.

The inevitable consequence of perceiving atomic weapons as a reasonable substitute for standing armies, mortars, and tanks was erosion of much of the mystique and terror surrounding the bomb. U.S. policy was forced to balance its public stance in favor of international control with the need to preserve, and even expand upon, its advantage over the Soviet Union's nuclear technology. The man Truman chose to advance these conflicting aims at the United Nations was Bernard Baruch, a wealthy businessman and adviser to presidents.

The plan that Baruch placed before the UN on June 14, 1946, was consistent with the unyielding attitude of the Truman administration toward the Soviet Union. Baruch, with the approval of the president and over the opposition of Acheson, modified the Acheson-Lilienthal proposals in two important, and ultimately fatal, respects. First, the United States refused to exchange technical information, halt production of bombs, or destroy existing stockpiles until the establishment of a system of inspection and control. For the Soviet Union this meant accepting international penetration of its closed society and exposing its own secret atomic program in exchange for nothing of value. Moreover, the plan contained the very real prospect of an even larger strategic advantage for the West in the interim. Second, Baruch also insisted that, with regard to the United Nations' sanctions in the event of cheating, there be no veto to protect countries who decide to develop atomic energy "for destructive purposes."

Baruch had to be aware that tying his atomic energy proposal to a modification of the veto would ensure the proposal's defeat. The Soviet position on the principle of Great Power unity was well known: the veto applied to all matters of substance before the Security Council—without exception. A possible explanation for Baruch's unusual demand was that Washington was more interested in publicly exposing the Soviet Union's abuse of the veto power than in achieving an agreement on the issue itself, an improbable outcome in any event. If anything, Baruch's dramatic and widely reported challenge to the Soviet Union to play by the rules—"Punishment must be swift and condign," he thundered—could only deepen Soviet suspicions that the United Nations had become an arm of Western policy.

On June 19, Gromyko presented the Soviet response to the Baruch plan and, with it, opened an unbridgeable gulf between the Soviet Union and the West. Gromyko called on all nations to agree immediately to prohibit production of atomic bombs and to destroy within three months all existing stockpiles of atomic weapons. On the matter of applying sanctions for cheating, the most controversial feature of the Baruch plan, Gromyko proposed that each nation enact legislation to ban production and use of atomic weapons and assume responsibility for punishment of violations. This last proposal was significantly similar to the approach to violations originally favored by Acheson and Lilienthal. Like Acheson, Gromyko stressed that the success of any atomic ban agreement depended more on mutual trust than on a system of inspection to police it. But while Gromyko agreed on the establishment of an international control agency, this could occur only after the fulfillment of all pledges and with the understanding that each of the major powers would retain its veto power over any recommendations that such an agency might make.

In the months that followed, the USSR continued to insist that nuclear weapons be outlawed prior to the creation of an international authority and that the veto was inviolable. There was no hope that the Great Power positions might be reconciled since Truman believed with Baruch that acquiescence to the atomic ban treaty was an invitation to the Soviets to acquire the bomb through stealth. The Soviets, meanwhile, refused to budge and behaved in public as if the bomb didn't matter. By early fall an impasse had been reached; each side was locked in a battle for moral leadership on an issue neither believed in.

Early in November, the Truman administration concluded that the edge the West had initially enjoyed in the propaganda war was slipping away and that the time had come to bring the UN phase of the debate over atomic energy to a head. The choice had come down to the complex and unworkable U.S. plan and the equally implausible, but appealing Soviet proposal to rid the planet of the dreaded new weapons. While Molotov thundered, with more than a little truth, that the U.S. plan was little more than a ruse "motivated by a desire to bring forth USSR vetoes," the smaller nations were quickly losing interest in the arguments of both sides.

In these circumstances, Baruch, with Truman's approval, decided to put the U.S. plan to a vote in the Atomic Energy Commission, despite the inevitability of a Soviet veto later in the Security Council. On December 31, 1946, with Poland and the USSR abstaining, the Atomic Energy Commission approved the Baruch plan. Proclaiming that the United States had achieved a "complete victory," Baruch immediately returned to private life. Passing through Washington in January on his way to Hobcaw, his lavish plantation in South Carolina, Baruch said he could "see no reason why the United States should not continue to make atomic bombs."

When the Baruch plan came before the Security Council in February 1947, Gromyko at first offered amendments, but quickly retreated to the original Soviet position. In July he cast the anticipated Soviet veto and ended any UN role in nuclear disarmament. Meanwhile, the United States was stockpiling atomic weapons in sizes up to twenty-five times the force of the Hiroshima bomb and in numbers that quickly outstripped the safeguards in the Baruch plan. In August 1949, only four years after Hiroshima, the Soviet Union heralded the start of a forty-year arms race with the explosion of an atomic bomb of its own.

To concerned observers, the failure of the United Nations to moderate the attitudes of the superpowers was distressing. In reality Soviet and U.S. leaders simply did not trust each other enough to accept the United Nations, or any forum, as a venue for negotiation.

Baruch himself seemed unperturbed by the dangerous consequences of the impasse.

Given the equally rigid stance of the Soviet Union, it appeared that Washington and Moscow were prepared with equanimity to add a deadly arms race to the complex ideological struggle that was being waged around the globe.

TRUMAN'S FOREIGN POLICY
ESCALATES COLD WAR

During the spring of 1947, while the debate on atomic energy was raging at the UN, the Cold War entered a new and more dangerous phase. The enunciation of the Truman Doctrine in March marked the apparent willingness of the United States to back the vivid images of Churchill's "Iron Curtain" speech with a broad commitment of U.S. resources, including military force. Ostensibly a request for $400 million dollars in economic aid to Greece and Turkey, the president's message to Congress elaborated a U.S. foreign policy of global scope.

One of the principal aims of U.S. policy, Truman announced, was to be able to work out a way of life "free from coercion." The world, he continued, was faced with two choices: one was a way of life based on freedom; the other relied on "terror and oppression" to forcibly impose the will of a minority upon the majority.

Beneath the president's militant rhetoric there lurked an even more disturbing message. The vision of a diverse but peaceful community of nations looking to the United Nations for the settlement of its disputes was replaced by one in which the organization itself was to be enlisted on one side of a struggle. No room for compromise existed. Henceforth, Western opposition to communist expansionism would wrap itself in the language of the Charter. The UN would assume a major role in Western efforts to expose Soviet shortcomings and to legitimize Western policy, a process already under way with regard to the main focus of the president's doctrine—the Balkans.

Since December 1946, the Security Council had been investigating the Greek government's charge that armed guerrilla bands from Albania, Bulgaria, and Yugoslavia were aiding the rebels in Greece's civil war. The incursions, Greece charged, threatened peace and security in the region and on December 19, the council adopted a U.S. proposal to create a Balkan Commission of Investigation. The commission's report issued in May 1946 supported the Western charges of communist interference in the affairs of a democratic state. Yugoslavia was cited as the principal offender, although "to a lesser degree," Albania and Bulgaria were also held responsible for supporting "guerrilla warfare in Greece." Albania, Bulgaria, and Yugoslavia were accused of training, recruiting, and dispatching Greek refugees for action in guerrilla units in Greece and of allowing their territory to be used as a sanctuary for guerrillas fleeing Greek government forces. Bulgaria and Yugoslavia were also cited for encouraging a separatist movement in Macedonia with the goal of detaching that area from Greece. The commission recommended that Albania, Bulgaria, and Yugoslavia desist from frontier violations and that they enter into direct negotiations with the government of Greece to settle their differences.

Having made its case against the Soviet satellites and, by implication, the Soviet Union itself, the United States, on July 29, introduced a resolution in the Security Council that incorporated the substance of the commission's report. The draft was promptly vetoed by the Soviet Union and four more vetoes of Western initiatives effectively blocked all Council action. Finally, the issue was removed from the Council's agenda; all documents and records were sent to the General Assembly where, free of Soviet vetoes, Western charges continued to be registered until 1954.

Following the Balkan investigation, all that stood in the way of complete integration of the Security Council into Western containment policy was the Russian veto. American and British spokesmen accused Russia of abusing that charter privilege, "defying the will of the majority," and "paralyzing" the Security Council. Demands were heard to "eliminate the veto" and even to expel the Soviet Union from the United Nations. On September 17, 1947, U.S. Secretary of State George Marshall proposed a way around Soviet vetoes—creation of a "Little Assembly" (Interim Committee on Peace and Security) that the General Assembly would establish as a "continuous body" to carry matters forward in the event of a Soviet veto in the council.

Although the Little Assembly never functioned as intended, the fact that the West was willing to destroy the very foundation of the organization to achieve cold war victories sharply etched the shape of things to come. The Soviets, of course, responded in kind and on September 18, the day after Marshall made his radical proposal, UN Representative Andrei Vishinsky retaliated with a slashing attack on Western "warmongers." He then submitted a resolution in the

General Assembly (an unusual move since the Soviet Union was opposed in principle to the assembly's competence) asking the UN "to condemn the criminal propaganda for a new war, carried on in reactionary circles in a number of countries." Over initial U.S. objections, the General Assembly eventually passed a diluted version of the Soviet proposal, which condemned warmongering but without naming names. While debates on "war propaganda" and the veto reflected deep-seated antagonisms between East and West that seriously weakened the Security Council, they were really only preliminary sparring matches. The "main event" came in the aftermath of the Czech coup in February 1948. The "loss" of Czechoslovakia, a country that exemplified Western democratic ideals, to communism was a particularly bitter defeat in the West. The coup itself was rooted in communist-led wartime resistance, the liberation of the nation largely by Soviet forces, and Czechoslovakia's precarious geographical location. In the country's one free postwar election, the Communist Party had won 38 percent of the vote, which, while denying the Party a parliamentary majority, secured for its leadership strategic levels of power, especially in the Ministry of the Interior, which controlled the public and secret police.

Czech President Eduard Benes and Foreign Minister Jan Masaryk had tried to keep Czechoslovakia free of cold war antagonisms. But in the context of Western resolve to roll back the Iron Curtain, Moscow was determined to exile or liquidate non-communist leaders and to impose subservient communist regimes on the nations of Eastern and Central Europe. On February 29, Benes, faced with extreme communist agitation at home and the Red Army massed on the border of Czechoslovakia, accepted the resignations of the non-communist members of the cabinet and the formation of a communist government.

The coup was swift and nearly bloodless; nothing could be done to save Czechoslovakia. Still the West was determined to publicly indict the Soviet Union for its complicity in the takeover. On March 10, 1948, Jan Papanek, the deposed Czech government's permanent representative to the United Nations, transmitted a letter to the secretary-general in which he charged that the independence of Czechoslovakia had been threatened with the use of force by the Soviet Union. Papanek asked that the Security Council investigate the situation in Czechoslovakia as "one which threatened the maintenance of international peace and security." Since the complaint came from a "private person," the secretary-general was unable to act on the request. But Chile, acting as a surrogate for the Western powers, placed the matter before the Security Council, over bitter Soviet complaints that the council was interfering in the domestic affairs of Czechoslovakia.

The ensuing debate marked a new high in cold war vituperation. Soviet leaders were accused of running a monstrous totalitarian state, bent on destroying the dignity and freedom of peace-loving peoples. Moscow was charged with having directed the coup and of sending Valerian Zorin, a deputy foreign minister of the Soviet Union, to Prague to personally give the orders to key Czech communists. Soviet army maneuvers on Czechoslovakia's borders, it was charged, were timed to facilitate the coup and to intimidate its opponents. The United States accused the Soviet Union of enslaving Czechoslovakia and of extending its tyranny over the rest of Eastern Europe.

The Soviet delegate denied all charges, asserted that the new government of Czechoslovakia had come to power through constitutional means, and then launched a vicious attack of his own. The delegate depicted Chile's representative as a "puppet of Wall Street," doing the dirty work of the United States, which controlled the economy and foreign policy of Chile. The real issue, said the Soviet delegate, was American, not Soviet, imperialism; the United States was seeking vengeance for the refusal of the Czech people to be drawn into the "Marshall Plan" and, thus, become enslaved to American monopolies.

Events in Czechoslovakia had, of course, foreclosed any role for the Security Council. Nevertheless, the United States, insisting that the veto did not apply to the Security Council's investigative powers, demanded that the council investigate Russian participation in the coup. The Soviet Union countered that, according to a four-power agreement reached at San Francisco, the determination of whether a matter was procedural, and thus not subject to the veto, was itself a substantive question. It then cast two vetoes, one to declare the American request for an investigation to be a substantive issue, and another to prevent the investigation itself. Following the Soviet vetoes, which should have ended the matter, France and the United Kingdom made clear their intention to bring to the Security Council statements by Czech exiles concerning the coup.

The Security Council debate on Czechoslovakia confirmed the most pessimistic appraisals of the intentions of the Soviet Union and the West. The unrestrained quality of the debate demonstrated that the superpowers had abandoned any desire to preserve the Security Council as an impartial and collegial forum. Aware that nothing could be done for Czechoslovakia, the United States nevertheless pressed the matter of an investigation, thereby contributing to the image of the Security Council as a failure. Furthermore, the Czech coup revealed the part that the United Nations would play in implementing one of the more ambitious and dangerous aims of the Truman Doctrine. By that doctrine the president had implicitly committed the United States to the liberation of the enslaved nations behind the Iron Curtain, a policy whose success depended on American willingness to use force to dislodge the Soviets from their empire. Given the unacceptable risks of this option, the Security Council represented an ideal substitute for bullets and atomic bombs. Soviet vetoes thus became the measure of Western victories.

Cold War Heats Up in Berlin

As the tragic memory of Czechoslovakia receded, the most dangerous episode of the Cold War began to unfold in Berlin. Total cold war was triggered by the failure of the victorious Allies to implement wartime agreements on Germany. By the spring of 1948 the occupation zones agreed upon in 1945 became spheres of influence, with each side setting up institutional frameworks to enhance benefits and control. Had the divisions been neat, the dangers would have been great enough, but the status of Germany was made more perilous by an agreed Western presence in Berlin, inside the Soviet zone. Any attempt by either side to modify this precarious situation could precipitate a major war.

Agreements on common Allied policy toward Germany reached at Potsdam (July 1945) provided, among other things, that Germany be treated as a single economic unit. By 1948, negotiations to implement this and other arrangements had broken down. Meetings of the Council of Foreign Ministers and near riotous sessions of the Allied Control Council in Berlin failed to save the situation from further deterioration. Finally, Secretary of State Marshall proposed that the Western Allies adopt an integrated policy for the development of West Germany. Meeting in London from March until early June, the Western powers agreed to merge Western zones in Germany as a prelude to the creation of a federal republic. West Germany should be brought into the Marshall Plan and represented on a newly established international commission on the Ruhr Valley industries, from which the Soviet Union would be excluded. And, on June 18, as part of overall Allied coordination of economic policy, currency reforms were announced for the new Western zones.

From the perspective of the Soviet Union, these actions could only be understood as an attempt to consolidate the Western position in West Germany and to exclude Soviet influence from that area. If Russia were to achieve a similar result in the East, it would require that the West be expelled from Berlin. Therefore, charging that the currency reform violated the Potsdam agreement, Marshall Vasili Sokolovsky, the Russian representative on the Four Power Control Council, announced on June 19 that measures would be enforced in Berlin to prevent the "disruption of economic life" in East Germany. The Berlin blockade was on. War was an immediate risk if the West insisted on maintaining its position in Berlin. Militarily, the Soviet Union held a vast superiority in conventional forces, while the United States still enjoyed its atomic monopoly. If either side miscalculated, Europe could be overrun by Russian forces or, worse, devastated by atomic bombs. Aware of the risks, Truman's response, on June 27, was typically blunt: "We [are] going to stay—period!" Without abandoning the possibility of a military option, a British-American airlift began supplying the city of 2.5 million people with the necessities of life.

As preparations went forward to expand the airlift, Western diplomats appealed in vain to Molotov and Stalin to lift the blockade. By September, all these efforts were at an impasse. The Soviet Union published its version of these talks and the West answered by presenting its side and announcing that the matter would go before the Security Council.

The move by the Western powers on September 29 to bring the Berlin blockade to the United Nations was consistent with the tough stand adopted by Truman. Britain and France supported the initiative, but with misgivings about the dangers inherent in the decision. Prior to the complaint, Secretary of State Marshall had received a personal cable from Foreign Minister Bevin, expressing his wish to avoid a complete breakdown in diplomatic negotiations that "would send the issue to the United Nations." Bevin, according to Marshall, kept referring to the fact that "we're on the front line."

Diplomatic escalation to the Security Council seemed to foreclose further attempts at negotiation. With winter approaching, uncertainty about the airlift's ability to continue to fuel and feed West

Berliners increased the risk of a military showdown. Truman's policy to maintain the presence of the West in Berlin would therefore be legitimized at the UN by justifying current or contemplated measures—including war—to enforce that decision. The only forums that the Soviets accepted as suitable for talks about Germany were those institutions created by the Allies specifically for that purpose: the Council of Foreign Ministers and the Allied Control Council. The Russians opposed as illegal the adoption of the issue on the UN agenda and, when their protest failed, withdrew from the debate. With a virtual monopoly over the proceedings, the West convened the Security Council five times during October and wrapped Western policy in the ideals of the Charter while portraying the blockade as an act of Soviet aggression.

It appears that making this record was the sole purpose of the Western initiative. If, as a logical extension of diplomatic efforts already under way, the Western powers had brought the matter to the Security Council under the peaceful settlement provisions of Chapter VI, the three sponsoring members and the Soviet Union, as parties to the dispute, would have been prevented from voting on the adoption of the agenda. With the Ukrainian SSR certain to support the Soviet Union, the West would have failed to obtain the required seven votes to sustain the debate. Instead, despite the fact that no shots had been fired, the matter was brought under the enforcement provisions of Chapter VII, which ensured that the West would make its case. Further, Western claims were helped along by a Soviet veto of a resolution sponsored by the nonpermanent members of the Security Council that called on the Soviet Union to end the blockade and to resume talks among the Big Four on the currency dispute in Berlin.

The Soviet veto was predictable since Russia rejected the Security Council's jurisdiction and because the resolution asked that the Soviets give up the blockade in exchange for little more than further talking. Still, the veto helped the West to assert the legal and moral superiority of its Berlin policy.

The Berlin debate was a startling victory for the West. With the memory of World War II still fresh, the people of Western Europe and the United States were being psychologically prepared for a new war, one that would usher in the atomic age with untold millions of casualties.

But war did not come. With one plane landing every two minutes in West Berlin and the city receiving nearly as much fuel and food as before the blockade, the airlift was a dazzling success. The Soviet retreat was signaled on January 27, 1949, when, in an interview with J. Kingsbury Smith, European manager of International News Service, Stalin neglected to mention the currency issue, the ostensible cause of the crisis. Informal talks between Phillip Jessup and Jacob Malik, the U.S. and Russian delegates to the United Nations, confirmed that the omission was deliberate. Wider negotiations later succeeded in ending the blockade on May 12, 1949.

From a broader perspective, the Berlin crisis ended all hope that the Security Council could function as a vehicle for global negotiation. It could neither prevent nor resolve conflicts between great states or act as a tool of collective coercion against aggression. By seeking to legitimize actions, including the use of force, against a permanent member, the Western Big Three had moved beyond the already dangerous implications of the Czech coup. In 1948, rage and impotence were reflected in a debate whose sole purpose was to embarrass the Soviet Union over a policy that the West was unable to directly affect. Western use of the UN could be compared to the cocking of a gun: if the Soviet Union surrendered, war would be averted; if not, the gun was ready to go off.

At the height of the Berlin crisis, Secretary-General Trygve Lie extended his good offices to the protagonists. According to his memoirs, Lie was skeptical about the desires of either side to accept a UN solution and offered to mediate the dispute largely out of a sense of duty. Since the Iranian complaint, Lie had become increasingly alarmed over the toll that the Cold War had taken on the UN and often appealed in vain for a return to "the spirit of Yalta and San Francisco." In September 1947, the secretary-general had said, "The very cornerstone of the UN, Big Power cooperation, and understanding is being shaken. . . . The peoples of the world, and many governments as well, are shocked, frightened, and discouraged. Fear breeds hate and hate breeds danger." Throughout his troubled tenure, but especially after the Berlin crisis, Lie threw himself and the prestige of his office into the fight to salvage the dream of world order. It is to that effort that we now turn.

3

Trygve Lie:
Man in the Middle

For Trygve Lie, the Berlin crisis marked a turning point in his approach to his role as secretary-general and, ultimately, in his personal fortunes. During the first two years of the UN's existence, Lie continued to hope that some version of Great Power harmony might enable the organization to enforce the peace. Deeply stung by Western criticism of his stand on the Iranian complaint, Lie remained cautious in asserting his own powers. He seemed to state his opinions on political trouble spots only through legal memoranda prepared by the Secretariat staff or in his annual reports to the General Assembly.

In 1948, a string of shattering events forced Lie to alter his thinking about the potential UN role in maintaining peace. Even more directly, he began to reassess the place he had reserved for himself in easing world tensions. At first, Lie had stressed mediation and conciliation as the only feasible alternatives for the United Nations in the face of Great Power disharmony. Such a stance would permit the UN's programs for social, humanitarian, and economic progress to grow and remain free of cold-war politics. But by 1949, Lie's inhibitions began to dissolve, due largely to the Berlin crisis and intensified by fear that Soviet demands over the seating of Communist China could threaten the existence of the organization. During the spring of 1950, Lie launched his famous Twenty-Year Peace Plan, a bold political initiative that offered the superpowers a way out of the Cold War through reliance on the facilities and procedures of the United Nations. But before the plan could be adequately tested, Lie's usefulness in mediating East–West differences came to an end with his support of the United Nations' action in Korea. That decision would have a lasting impact on the role of the secretary-general and would inhibit each of Lie's successors.

Before taking up the details of Lie's political conversion, we must examine the historical antecedents for the role of secretary-general and the charter as it relates to the office. The office of secretary-general is rooted firmly in the experience of the League of Nations and particularly in the personality of its first secretary-general, Sir Eric Drummond.

Drummond, a British career civil servant with a background in the Foreign Office, deliberately played down the political potential of his position and emphasized the "silences of the Covenant." He promoted the image of the League Secretariat as an efficient, truly international civil service. A bold administrator, he skillfully avoided making concessions to the host of pressure groups in Geneva. His advice was sought by many diplomats, but he preferred to cloak this role in caution and anonymity, a style that earned him the respect and trust of the world community. And while Drummond's annual reports were models of clarity and factual detail, they never included personal political judgments. So deeply are Drummond's footprints planted in the history of international organization that all future consideration of the office of secretary-general would begin from the style he epitomized.

Among those who had reason to consider the office was President Franklin Roosevelt. In his early career, Roosevelt fully supported the League of Nations, yet he understood its flaws and envisioned a new type of secretary-general for the United Nations. This sentiment was shared by the delegates at San Francisco, and they directly combined the major aims of the organization with the political functions of the secretary-general. Under Article 99, "The Secretary-General may bring to the Security Council any matter which in his opinion may threaten the maintenance of international peace and security."

In addition to this special privilege, there is a unique symbolic resonance, not to mention a wide range of implied political prerogatives, that flows from the language of Article 99. To quote the report of the Preparatory Commission in 1945, "The Secretary-General, more than anyone else, will stand for the UN as a whole. In the eyes of the world . . . he must embody the principles and ideals of the Charter." Moreover, the secretary-general may investigate the causes of international unrest, and actually propose measures to the members for the settlement of disputes.

In addition to his initiating functions, the secretary-general is instructed by Article 98 to "make an annual report to the General Assembly on the work of the organization." Although little political importance was attached to this provision at San Francisco, the annual report quickly became a vital tool for advancing the image of the secretary-general as the principal spokesman for the international community; Trygve Lie used the report to express personal attitudes and offer recommendations on important political matters.

LIE TRAVELS THE MIDDLE ROAD

Trygve Lie's "middle road" soon became a personal minefield. He attempted to avoid becoming identified with one or the other side in the Cold War, while working to enhance the prestige and influence of the United Nations. In his first annual report to the General Assembly, a document that serves as a yearly "State of the Union" message to the world on the organization, Lie chided the member nations for not doing enough to "capture the imagination and harness the enthusiasm of the peoples of the world" on behalf of the United Nations. He reminded them that the UN was "no stronger than the collective will of the nations that support it." As the prime spokesman for the new world body, Lie preached his vision in innumerable speeches and press conferences. In contrast to Drummond, Lie quickly became the advocate of a United Nations as an independent political and moral force in the world.

Governments, however, inevitably equate support for charter principles with satisfaction of their narrow political and ideological interests. Lie learned this painful lesson early when, on April 16, 1946, he boldly—and correctly—advised by way of a legal memorandum, removal of the Iranian issue from the agenda of the Security Council. Since Iran had withdrawn its complaint against the Soviet Union, the secretary-general took the unprecedented step of defying the majority of the council (only the USSR, France, and Poland supported him). Opposing the West for its cold war attitudes, Lie would later say, "The United Nations . . . should aim to settle disputes, not inflame them." It served no useful purpose, by Lie's assessment, to have the Iranian matter appear "year after year" on the council's agenda. The repetition served only to widen the rift between the Soviet Union and the West, and weakened the UN itself.

While the furor caused by Lie's memorandum was out of proportion to whatever influence it might have had on the Iranian issue, it was a striking reminder of the ambiguous response that Lie might expect whenever he chose to defend the charter. The superpowers would always perceive that he was taking sides. However, in 1946 Andrei Gromyko, delighted by Lie's intervention, fervently held a broad constitutional interpretation of the secretary-general's powers, citing Article 99. He said the secretary-general has the right to comment on "various aspects of questions submitted to the Security Council." (Korea, of course, was still fully two and one-half years off.) Secretary of State Byrnes, on the other hand, publicly criticized Lie for exceeding his powers. Dean Acheson, assistant secretary of state with little fondness for multinational diplomacy and perhaps even less for the United Nations, was more candid: "Iran is no stronger than the United Nations and the United Nations, in the last analysis, is no stronger than the United States." Acheson, like Gromyko, would also experience a change of heart as a result of the Korean affair.

Although Lie lost his fight for a sensible outcome to the Iranian complaint, he prevailed on the broader constitutional issue. On June 6, 1946, the Security Council unanimously adopted a rule that permits "the secretary-general or his deputy acting in his behalf [to] make either oral or written statements to the Security Council concerning any question under consideration by it." However, in a setting where constitutional principles remained valid only as long as they lent support to narrow national interests, Lie could derive cold comfort from a victory that threatened further exposure to hostile criticism. As he would later observe, there emerged a pattern wherein he was "within his rights and a good fellow besides," when his intervention supported a national position; when he dared to differ with a Great Power, he "exceeded his authority" and his "motives may be suspect."

From 1946 to 1948, Lie grew increasingly concerned over the consequences that the Cold War was having on the organization itself. He was alarmed by the provocative tenor of debates, which he described on one occasion as "clearly designed to draw blood." There was also the dangerous tendency, especially in the West, to ignore the UN in the evolution of foreign policy. Lie was critical of Truman's decision to circumvent the UN in announcing unilateral aid to the Balkans in 1947. Although Lie would later praise the economic features of the Marshall Plan, he believed it to be part of the same dangerous trend furthered by Churchill's Iron Curtain speech, the Truman Doctrine, and the military alliance system that was soon to develop. Lie correctly predicted that the "open invitation" presented to the West to align its policies with the charter through the automatic voting majorities it enjoyed would only deepen the self-imposed isolation of the communist world.

Nevertheless, Trygve Lie continued to press his unpopular views concerning the charter. In 1947, on the grounds that the failure of members to implement UN resolutions impaired the organization's prestige, he urged the General Assembly to force compliance with a resolution that recommended withdrawal of diplomatic personnel from Franco's Spain. The assembly not only refused to honor this request, but also refused to reaffirm the original resolution. The same year, Lie wrote a legal opinion supporting the Security Council's authority to implement the terms of the Italian peace treaty as they related to the Free Territory of Trieste. Under the treaty, competing Italian and Yugoslav claims were resolved by assigning to the Security Council the responsibility for the administration and territorial integrity of Trieste. Despite the reluctance of the West to invite Soviet interests into the region, the Security Council unanimously approved Lie's legal position. The plan, however, quickly became a casualty of the Cold War since the Soviet Union and the Western powers failed to agree on a governor. A final settlement was not achieved until 1954, when Italy and Yugoslavia agreed to a division of territory that gave Italy the city of Trieste and awarded to Yugoslavia the adjoining area on the Adriatic Sea.

Less than a year later, Lie argued with even greater vigor, but similar results, in favor of the Security Council's authority to enforce the General Assembly's plan of partition for Palestine. No doubt encouraged by the support that partition had received from the United States and the Soviet Union, Lie assured the UN Palestine Commission on January 9 that the Security Council would not fail to exercise the powers entrusted to it by the charter. The pledge, under heavy fire from Arab nations, proved empty when U.S. Ambassador Warren Austin insisted that the Security Council had no legal power to enforce political settlements, and the General Assembly decided instead to appoint a UN mediator for Palestine.

Finally, when the United States appeared to back away from the plan itself, Lie made the remarkable suggestion to Austin that they both resign in protest, a step that, ironically, Andrei Gromyko helped to dissuade the secretary-general from taking.

4

The Palestine Partition Plan

Palestine, only the size of Vermont, has historically been an arena of conflict because its location has attracted the geo-political interests of the major European powers, and its barren lands are sacred to three of the world's great religions. No other place so well illustrates the political force and historical importance of ideas as the heritage of colonialism and the clash of competing nationalisms combined to make Palestine a "hot spot" for three generations.

British diplomacy during World War I made incompatible promises to the Arab majority, which hoped that the war would bring an end to 400 years of Turkish rule, and to the Zionist movement, which sought a national home for the Jews. The Balfour Declaration of 1917 pledged British support for a "national home for the Jewish people of Palestine" with assurances that the civil and religious rights of the non-Jewish communities of Palestine "would not be prejudiced." This ambiguous document was inserted in the mandate agreement for Palestine and approved by the League of Nations following the defeat of the Central Powers. As postwar Jewish immigration to Palestine increased, the British government struggled unsuccessfully to contain the bitter rivalries that developed between Arabs and Jews. In 1936, following widespread bloodshed, the Foreign Office was forced to conclude that the conflicting national aspirations in Palestine could not be settled within the terms of the mandate. In a white paper of 1939, Britain reaffirmed to Arab critics that Palestine would not become a Jewish state, but the pace of Jewish immigration continued to increase. Only World War II postponed this escalating clash of nationalisms.

For Britain, victory over the Axis brought imperial decline and economic collapse. Palestine once again became the scene of deadly armed conflict between Arab and Jewish militias. British efforts to involve Washington in the search for a solution there failed when the Truman administration, out of genuine sympathy for the victims of the Holocaust, tied U.S. willingness to guarantee British interests in Greece and the Balkans to the admission of an additional 100,000 refugees to Palestine. Faced with irreconcilable national differences in Palestine and disappointed by Washington, British Foreign Secretary Ernest Bevin announced in February 1947 his government's intention to abandon the mandate for Palestine and "to submit the problem to the judgment of the United Nations."

Accordingly, on May 15, 1947, the first special session of the General Assembly created the UN Special Committee on Palestine (UNSCOP) to investigate issues "relevant to the problem." Zionist leaders welcomed the UNSCOP investigation as an opportunity to focus international attention on the Jewish refugee problem and to publicize its case for a Jewish state in Palestine. However, Arab leaders objected to linking Nazi persecution of Europe's Jews with the political status of Palestine, claiming that such a merger of issues could only prejudice the rights of the "Arab population of Palestine." Since these rights were "self-evident" and not properly a subject for UN investigation, the Arab Higher Committee, the main spokesman for the Arab side, refused to meet with UNSCOP representatives and demanded instead the immediate transfer of sovereignty to the Palestinian people.

Reflecting these irreconcilable forces, the UNSCOP report of August 31, 1947, unanimously recommended that Britain's mandate be terminated. Independence would be granted to Palestine after a short transitional period during which the United Nations would guarantee access to the Holy Places and provide a mechanism to impartially settle disputes. A majority of UNSCOP endorsed a plan of partition wherein two states, one Jewish and one Arab, would coexist within a broader economic union. An additional 150,000 Jewish immigrants would be allowed to enter the Jewish zone and Jerusalem, including the city of Bethlehem, would constitute a *corpus separatum* under United Nations trusteeship. A minority plan, submitted by India, Iran, and Yugoslavia, proposed a single federated republic with Jerusalem as its capital.

Although the majority plan of the ad hoc committee offered a release from the tensions of a multinational state, it was totally unacceptable to the Arabs, who opposed the creation of any Jewish state in Palestine. Jewish leaders, for their part, were equally opposed to federation, as a betrayal of the immense sacrifices they had endured in the cause of independence. The British helpfully announced they would not support any plan that was not acceptable to both Arabs and Jews. While both world superpowers supported partition, there was no likelihood that the United States would participate in any plan of enforcement that increased Soviet influence in the Middle East. Prospects for compromise, therefore, appeared to be dim. Nevertheless, the General Assembly acted quickly on the positive recommendation of the ad hoc committee. On November 29, it adopted the majority's slightly altered plan (33–13–10) and created a United Nations Partition Commission to supervise the orderly transfer of authority from Britain to the new states. The UNSCOP plan established a Jewish state comprising the upper Galilee, the Jordan and Baison valleys, a coastal strip from Acre to just south of Tel Aviv, and the greater portion of the Negev. The Arab state included western Galilee, most of the west bank of the Jordan River, and the Gaza Strip. While boundaries were based in part on the ethnic distribution of the population, about 45 percent of the approximately one million inhabitants of the Jewish state were Arab. Within the Arab state, Jews constituted a 2 percent minority in a total population of about 750,000, and in the neutral enclave of Jerusalem, the Jewish and Arab populations were roughly equal. Despite the fact that the suggested partition resulted in a Jewish Palestine state about one-eighth the size of the "national home" envisioned in the Balfour Declaration, Zionist leaders quickly embraced the assembly resolution. Members of the Arab League, however, left the assembly chamber in protest following the vote on partition, and Palestinian Arabs vowed to oppose it, if necessary, with blood.

On January 21, the British announced that the termination of the mandate would end abruptly on May 15, 1948. The Palestine commission would not be authorized to enter Palestine more than two weeks prior to that date, nor would it be allowed to supervise the formation of armed militia units to preserve order in vacated Jewish and Arab areas. The Foreign Office agreed to honor the current monthly quota of 1,500 Jewish refugees, but refused to evacuate a seaport or portions of the interior to ease the refugees' resettlement. On the surface, these actions accorded with the United Kingdom's policy of neutrality yet, in practice, they seemed calculated to court favorable Arab opinion. London appears to have decided that in the absence of outside help, the infant Jewish state could not survive. Arms flowed into Palestine and terrorism escalated as Jews and Arabs fought for control of areas vacated by the British. On February 18, 1948, the Palestine Commission reported to the Security Council that Palestine would be the scene of much warfare unless an international army takes "prompt and effective action."

The Security Council convened to consider the report of the Palestine Commission against the background of the Czech coup and Soviet-supported revolutionary movements in China, Korea, Iran, and Greece. The weight of the Cold War was, therefore, added to the considerable burden that British intransigence had already placed on prospects for a peaceful partition. Among the permanent members of the Security Council, only the Soviet Union favored the Palestine Commission's recommendation for UN force, although Lie, who believed that the credibility of the United Nations was at stake, lobbied vigorously for armed intervention by the Security Council. However, Warren Austin, the American delegate, insisted that the council was not empowered under the charter to enforce decisions of the General Assembly. After a month of inconclusive debate, and while the U.S. delegation at the United Nations was still officially promoting partition, Austin made the startling proposal that the council request a second special session of the General Assembly to discuss the creation of a temporary UN trusteeship over Palestine. He also proposed the creation of a truce commission to supervise observance of a ceasefire. Whatever the motivations for this apparent shift in U.S. policy— partition was supported by both political parties, a majority of Congress, and the president—the immediate result was to limit the Security Council's role to one of conciliation and to shift implementation back to the General Assembly. The UN had reached an impasse. The fate of partition was essentially left to the battlefield and by April, Palestine was engulfed in civil war. Safed, Acre, Tiberius, and the new city of Jerusalem fell to the Haganah, now the Jewish army, even before the Arab League announced its intention to eradicate the Jewish state. The General Assembly predictably failed to act on the U.S. trusteeship proposal and, on May 13, suspended the functions of the Palestine Commission. On May 15, 1948, as the Union Jack was folded in Haifa for the last time and Zionist leader David Ben Gurion proclaimed the state of Israel, armed forces from Egypt, Iran, Jordan, Lebanon, and Syria invaded Palestine. The war quickly spread. Israeli and Arab forces moved rapidly in areas that were outside the partition boundaries, and as they did, opened one of the more tragic chapters of the war as countless civilians fled their homes before the advancing armies.

On May 20, the Security Council appointed Count Folke Bernadotte, president of the Swedish Red Cross, to mediate the Palestine fighting. On June 9, after the Arab states had ignored several Security Council requests to end hostilities, Bernadotte arranged a temporary truce, but fighting soon resumed when the Arabs rejected an extension of the cease-fire. Washington, which had opposed collective action, now apparently experienced a change of heart. On July 15, the Security Council approved a U.S. resolution that declared for the first time that "the situation in Palestine was a threat to international peace and security." The Great Powers were unable to agree on specific actions to be taken if hostilities continued.

While events drifted at UN headquarters, Bernadotte proposed a comprehensive political agreement that called for resettlement of Arab refugees in Palestine, preservation of religious rights in the Holy Land, and adjustments in the territorial provisions of the partition plan that favored the Arabs. The Bernadotte plan was rejected by everyone, but especially by Israeli leaders who opposed further reductions of the partition borders. The war had added to Israel's territory; by mid-July, Israeli forces occupied much of western Galilee, a broad corridor from Jerusalem to Tel Aviv, and the city of Jerusalem as well as most of the territory assigned to the Jewish state in the UNSCOP plan. Undoubtedly, Israeli leaders, who now proclaimed these gains to be vital to the integrity of the state of Israel, approached Bernadotte's intervention with suspicion.

On September 17, while the Security Council was taking up his report, Bernadotte was assassinated by members of the Stern Gang, an extremist Jewish paramilitary organization. Bernadotte's death ended UN influence on political and military events in Palestine. Since neither Israel nor the United States was willing to accept modifications in the partition plan, the Bernadotte plan was abandoned. Meanwhile, the Arab military position rapidly deteriorated; by the end of October, the armies of Syria and Iraq were no longer a factor in the war, the 5,000-man Arab Liberation Army had been defeated on the Lebanese frontier, and Israeli forces had broken through Egyptian lines in the Negev. On November 16, the Security Council issued a desperate call for a permanent demarcation line based on the military situation on July 15, but the Israelis, now on the verge of total military victory, refused to comply. Appeals to the Security Council by acting UN mediator Ralph Bunche for an international police force to contain the spreading violence also went unheeded, and by December 29, when the Security Council declared a final cease-fire, the Arab military campaign had collapsed.

Despite the fact that the Security Council had long before lost control of events in Palestine, it now instructed Bunche to secure armistice agreements between Israel and its warring neighbors. After six weeks of tense negotiations, Bunche arranged an armistice between Israel and Egypt at Rhodes on February 24, 1949, and later similar armistice agreements were concluded with the other Arab states. Their stated objective was to restore permanent peace to Palestine, although the lines of demarcation were not to be regarded as permanent political or territorial boundaries. They, like all provisions of the armistice agreements, were not to prejudice "the rights, claims, and positions" of the signatories in connection with the settlement of "the Palestine question." For his skillful and patient diplomacy, Bunche earned the Nobel Prize for Peace.

It is tempting to conclude that the effort of the United Nations to design a political solution for Palestine was a failure that has led to decades of conflict. Actually, its partition scheme arose from the British decision to abandon the mandate and turn the issue over to the United Nations. Accepting responsibility for Palestine was consistent with charter provisions dealing with matters of trusteeships and non-self-governing territories, and partition seemed a reasonable way to satisfy competing demands for national identity in Palestine. But it was utopian to expect that in the atmosphere of cold war, the United Nations could enforce the plan. Once war began, the Security Council's efforts were confined to futile appeals for cease-fires.

After the Israeli victory, Bunche's conclusion of armistice agreements was a significant achievement, but armistice left the underlying political causes of the conflict no closer to permanent solution. As a result of the war, the size of the new state of Israel was greater by one-third than that allotted it under partition, while the Arab state disappeared within the borders of Egypt and Jordan. The United Nations was left with the difficult task of supervising the armistice agreements, and assigned the task to the UN Truce Supervision Organization in Palestine (UNTSO) established in 1949. Peace treaties were not signed and Israel and its neighbors settled into a limbo of no peace, no war. As a tragic aftermath of the war, perhaps 900,000 Arab refugees became the permanent wards of the United Nations Relief and Works Agency for Palestine Refugees in the Near East (UNRWA). The bitterness of the failed partition plan persists to this day and the issues that divide these two peoples seem no closer to resolution.

Actually, Trygve Lie was being squeezed by forces beyond the capacity of any one man to control. This was the dawning of the "golden age" of U.S. support for the United Nations. In Washington, Western interests and the principles of the charter had become synonymous, and it followed that any deviation by the secretary-general from the Western line was a betrayal of approved norms of international conduct and morality. Lie derived little comfort from the periodic support his views received from the Soviet Union, which, in any event, manifested a cynical disregard for the charter whenever it suited Russian interests. In fact, by the time of the Czech coup, Lie had become convinced that Stalin placed little value on the United Nations and, insofar as Eastern Europe was concerned, was bent rather on setting up a system of satellites.

The Berlin crisis confirmed that the United Nations was of little value in direct superpower confrontations. Lie suddenly understood that neither giant power would sacrifice vital interests for the sake of strengthening the organization. Following the Soviet veto of the "six neutrals" resolution, Lie privately proposed to his friend Phillip Jessup, the United Nations delegate to the General Assembly, that the Secretariat might develop a mutually acceptable plan to end the blockade. Lie secretly dispatched his legal counsel, Abraham Feller, and Assistant Secretary-General Arkady Sobolov to "sound out" official reaction to his plan in Washington and Moscow. Although Moscow somewhat unexpectedly encouraged the secretary-general to pursue the study, the United States, and particularly Britain, refused to consider any settlement to the crisis on other than Western terms. Bevin accused Lie of meddling where he did not belong and directed the secretary-general to address his inquiries to the Soviets who were "after all, responsible." A joint statement by Lie and Herbert Evatt, president of the General Assembly, urging the superpowers to take all necessary steps toward resolving the Berlin situation was also turned aside.

It is difficult to assess the significance of Lie's efforts to associate the United Nations with a settlement of the Berlin crisis, either through the office of the secretary-general or in the broader context of the UN's role in world affairs. Broadly speaking, the secretary-general's authority to employ the resources of his office to mediate international disputes was strengthened since Lie's interventions were not directly challenged.

However, on more than one occasion, the West criticized his involvement, and settlements were reached as if the UN did not exist. By Lie's own account, none of the measures undertaken by the United Nations in these years "brought immediate results." They were instrumental, however, in focusing attention on the issues that divided the superpowers and in voicing the desire of "ordinary people" for peace.

In his concluding address before the General Assembly on May 18, 1949, Lie characterized the peaceful resolution of the Berlin crisis as the United Nations' "way to peace." But it soon became evident that the crisis had produced a fundamental change of heart in Lie regarding the role of the United Nations in the Cold War. A year earlier, the secretary-general had exhorted the superpowers to consider bringing the Berlin crisis to the UN only if it were "done in the spirit of a genuine attempt to reach a settlement," a theme to which he now returned. Clearly distressed by the West's use of the UN to legitimize its Berlin policy, Lie urged the Great Powers to speedily settle the remaining issues of wartime agreements, a major cause of the Cold War and the reason for the withdrawal of public confidence in the world body. Lie's own confidence in the UN's ability to function as the world's policeman had been severely shaken. He, therefore, stressed the organization's role as mediator of conflicts and as an organizer of a movement to reduce injustice and to protect human rights.

For the remainder of 1949, Trygve Lie strayed little from this more cautious line, the one major exception being a controversial proposal for a UN guard force. Lie continued to believe that the lack of a permanent UN force was a major cause of the organization's failure to save lives, especially in places like Palestine and Indonesia where East–West interests did not clash directly. He launched his idea at the June 10, 1948, Harvard commencement, the same occasion that, one year earlier, had been used by Secretary of State George Marshall to announce the Marshall Plan. The proposal, Lie said, envisioned a small guard force, different from a striking force. This distinction was, no doubt, aimed at avoiding the experience of the Military Staff Committee when it had earlier failed to create a permanent UN force.

Lie's proposal drew wide public attention and, at his press conference one week later, the details of the plan began to emerge. The force would consist of 1,000 to 5,000 men, recruited by the secretary-general. Later in the year Lie specifically identified its uses—guard duty at UN missions, the protection of UN supervised plebiscites, and the administration of truce terms—and added that the force might also be used by the Security Council to "prevent the aggravation of a situation threatening the peace."

The Soviet Union strongly opposed the plan, publicly citing the Security Council's exclusive constitutional powers in the use of force. Diplomats suspected there was lingering Russian resentment over the failure of the secretary-general to include Communist bloc observers in the UN Truce Supervision team that had been sent to Palestine. But in Washington, Lie's proposal ran into the deepening commitment to Western strategic unity, and was greeted with equal displeasure. By the time the General Assembly got around to considering the guard force in April 1949, Lie had become thoroughly discouraged by the scope of opposition he had encountered, and was prepared to accept what he could get. Finally, on June 16, Lie told the General Assembly his plan represented "nothing new"; it was only an "administrative and technical" facility required "to discharge the functions connected with field missions." The UN guard now became a technical field service of 300 uniformed but normally unarmed men to provide land and air transport, radio communications, custodial care for records, and security for property and personnel at various UN missions. It would perform no political or military functions in connection with any operations authorized by the Security Council or General Assembly. In the prevailing cold war atmosphere, the failure of Lie's original plan was foreseeable. Lie himself, with some irony, noted that an internationally recruited police force was too radical an idea for many governments. And when, on November 22, 1949, the General Assembly approved the watered-down proposal to create a UN field service, it was over the continued opposition of the Soviet Union.

By the end of 1949, Trygve Lie's public activities increasingly reflected the breakdown in Great Power consensus and the low public esteem and political influence that the UN now generated. Lie's annual report to the General Assembly in July 1949—shortly after the April signing of the North Atlantic Treaty—barely hid his annoyance with the Great Powers for abandoning the United Nations. Lie avoided direct reference to the North Atlantic Treaty Organization (NATO) or to the network of Soviet-sponsored alliances in his July message, but his views were well-known. In Norway for his annual holiday the previous year, Lie had delivered an address at Bergen that criticized regional defense pacts and attacked the claim that they were authorized under Article 51 of the Charter. Lie now warned that regional security arrangements like NATO, while they "may sometimes redress the balance of power in the world," contributed to a "false conception of the role of the United Nations." In the "long range," Lie emphasized, the real security interests of the Great Powers rested on strengthening the United Nations and not on the immediate strategic advantages sought through alliances and arms races.

To Lie, a committed internationalist, the Cold War distorted global priorities by drawing the entire world into the narrow scheme of political and strategic needs of the Great Powers. Lie had singled out the creation of the state of Israel as an "epic" event of history that represented the end of 2,000 years "of sorrow." More people, Lie pointed out, lived in India, Pakistan, and Indonesia, where the UN had saved many lives, than in the whole of Europe, where much attention had been directed since the end of the war.

SEATING OF COMMUNIST CHINA
THREATENS UN

Following the Communist takeover of mainland China in October 1949, the United Nations became once more the scene of bitter cold war confrontation. Lie, who had planned to retire to his beloved Norway when his term expired, found himself again at the center of the struggle, his retirement further off than he could possibly guess. On November 18, Chou En-lai, prime minister of the People's Republic of China, cabled the secretary-general and the president of the General Assembly to protest the seating of the Nationalist Chinese delegation in the various UN organs. On December 29, 1949, while secret talks were being held in Moscow between Chinese Communist and Soviet officials, the Soviet delegate defended the Chinese position in the Security Council. Nothing came of the Soviet action and, on January 8, the Security Council received a second cable from Chou En-lai, this one demanding the ouster of the "Chinese Kuomintang [official ruling party of the Republic of China] . . . clique" from its seat on the council. The Soviet Union now introduced a resolution to expel the Nationalist delegate from the council. This action, Lie would later recall, took place while he was preparing a New Year's message to the world that expressed confidence in a "thaw in the Cold War" during the coming year. On January 13, the council defeated the Soviet proposal by a vote of 6–3 (India, USSR, and Yugoslavia) with two abstentions (United Kingdom and Norway). Jacob Malik, the Soviet delegate, then shocked the council by announcing that the USSR would boycott future council meetings while the Nationalist Chinese delegation illegally occupied the Chinese seat. He further declared that the USSR would cease to recognize the legality of any council decisions in which the "representative of the Kuomintang group" had participated. The Soviet walkout, joined by all other Communist bloc countries except Yugoslavia, soon spread to all UN organs in which Nationalist China was represented.

Lie was filled with foreboding over the capacity of the struggling organization to survive this latest crisis. The Soviet walkout threatened a complete breakdown in communication between East and West. Lie publicly denounced the Soviet action, but he was equally concerned that the United States would use the issue of Chinese representation to test American influence in the UN. Faced with a weak legal case and the opposing sentiments of many noncommunist governments— including Great Britain, India, New Zealand, Israel, and all the Nordic countries—the United States might well demand strict solidarity on pro-Western resolutions. To Lie, this cold war attitude, regardless of the effect it might have on the national policies of the nations involved, could only hurt the UN. The secretary-general's gloomy assessment was ultimately proven right.

Although it is difficult to know what he had hoped to achieve by intervening, Lie acted upon the one glimmer of hope that penetrated the impasse—the fact that most members, including the United States, considered the seating of the competing Chinese delegations a procedural matter. As such, it was not subject to a veto by one of the permanent members of the Security Council, and might be set-tled independently of cold war attitudes. Lie's campaign to seat Communist China in the Security Council began on January 21 with a quiet visit to Washington where he hoped to convince Secretary of State Dean Acheson that the continued absence of the Soviet Union posed a grave threat to the United Nations. Acheson showed mild interest in the secretary-general's analysis of the Soviet Union's intentions but he refused to budge on U.S. recognition of the com-munist regime or on replacing the Nationalist delegation at the UN. He also opposed calling a special session of the General Assembly to consider the issue of Chinese representation.

Lie's strategy, however, depended less on influencing U.S. policy than it did on persuading seven members of the council to accept the credentials of China's Communist government. Because five members of the Security Council—the USSR, Norway, Yugoslavia, the United Kingdom, and India—already recognized the Peking government, Lie's success rested on convincing two additional members to separate the issue of recognition from a decision to admit Communist China to the United Nations. France, Lie believed, might be swayed since its refusal to recognize the new government was based largely on the fact that Peking had sided with the Viet Minh, the Vietnam Federation of Independence, against the French-sponsored government in Indochina, not on fundamental opposition to the new leadership in Peking. If France shifted, then Egypt, Cuba, and Ecuador—the remaining members of the council who did not recognize Peking—might be convinced to vote in favor of seating Communist China in the Security Council.

Some members opposed seating Communist China on the grounds that they had not recognized the new regime. While this was largely an irrelevant legal defense of what was entirely a political position, Lie, nevertheless, prepared a legal memorandum that argued in favor of separating the issues of recognition and representation. Recognition, Lie argued, was a "unilateral act," which one government might freely extend to or withhold from another. Since membership in the United Nations or its various organs involved a nation in the collective decisions of the organization, the proper test for UN membership was whether a government was "able and willing" to carry out its obligations as required by Article 4 of the charter.

Although the memorandum made a powerful case for seating Peking, Lie had done little more than align himself with traditional international law. An advisory opinion of the International Court of Justice had declared that diplomatic recognition could not be made a condition for membership in the United Nations. The memorandum, in fact, confirmed existing policy at the UN where members consistently voted for admission of states with which they did not enjoy diplomatic relations. Moreover, most members agreed with the secretary-general's basic political argument: Nationalist claims that the Mao regime would soon collapse were unfounded.

Despite Lie's intense lobbying of the delegations of France, Cuba, Egypt, and Ecuador, he failed to pry loose the two votes needed to seat Peking. Chiang Kai-shek made the most of his U.S. ties through the so-called China lobby and, according to the secretary-general, at least one

Latin delegation that had begun to waver was pressured back into line by the U.S. State Department. Meanwhile, the contents of the Lie memorandum were leaked to the press, effectively ending the initiative that depended on quiet diplomacy for success. On March 8, Lie somewhat apologetically made the memorandum public, but the damage to his reputation was severe. He was widely accused of exceeding the authority of his office and of being an "appeaser" who had "surrendered to the Soviets." Matters were only made worse by the wave of anticommunist hysteria sweeping the United States in the wake of the House Un-American Activities Committee investigations into communist subversion in the United States.

LIE'S TWENTY-YEAR PEACE PROGRAM

Western criticism and the near certain futility of further attempts to seat Communist China over the continued opposition of the United States did not stop Lie's efforts. He undertook a personal campaign to convince the superpowers that the United Nations was an indispensable forum for East–West negotiations and to break the deadlock over the issue of Chinese representation. Lie launched his plan during a Washington speech to the B'nai B'rith on March 21, 1950, when he announced, "What we need, what the world needs, is a twenty-year program to win the peace through the United Nations." The address attracted widespread and generally favorable attention from the press, the public, and leading world figures. James Reston of the *New York Times* wrote that the secretary-general "has now demonstrated publicly that he is going to act in what he believes to be the best interests of the United Nations, even if [the Great Powers] do not like it, and that is something of an innovation." From Albert Einstein came a personal note of encouragement: "May your concrete proposals succeed in showing us a way out of the present tension, occasioned as it is more by emotional factors than by material causes."

Within weeks, Lie's Twenty-Year Peace Plan was shaped into a ten-point memorandum that the secretary-general proposed to discuss privately with each of the Big Four. While there was little that was new in the plan, its broader political implications were nothing short of spectacular, for Lie had undertaken to personally mediate an end to the Cold War. The memorandum was withheld from the public until the secretary-general had held discussions with Truman,

Stalin, British Prime Minister Clement Attlee, and French Premier Georges Bidault.

The boldest and most innovative provision in Lie's memorandum called for holding periodic top-level meetings of the Security Council away from UN headquarters, a suggestion that would transform the council into a semipermanent system of summit diplomacy. To further strengthen this concept, Lie requested that the superpowers seek agreement on modifying the veto power and on improving existing UN machinery for settling international disputes. Lie suggested a renewed effort to achieve international controls of atomic energy, now that the U.S. atomic monopoly had been ended. The Baruch plan was dead, Lie believed, serious negotiations between Washington and Moscow were remote, and only a fresh initiative through the international organization could avert a deadly atomic arms race. Lie also argued that failure to make headway in the regulation and reduction of conventional arms contributed to the atmosphere of tension in the world and, therefore, strongly advised direct negotiations on arms reductions even prior to settlement of outstanding political issues.

Lie pointed out that fourteen states were being denied membership in the United Nations because of cold war politics. He argued for the acceptance and rapid application of the principle of universality of membership in the UN. Germany and Japan, he stressed, should also be admitted upon conclusion of peace treaties as should all nations that soon might achieve independence. The real issue, of course, was seating the representatives of the Peking government.

Lie believed that the "dangers and costs of the cold war" were increased by the failure of the Great Powers to address a host of social, economic, and humanitarian issues. He suggested that the member governments make more vigorous use of the specialized agencies. He called for the creation of an active program of technical assistance for worldwide economic development and encouraged broad-scale capital investment to raise the standards of living in underdeveloped countries.

Lie completed his comprehensive survey of the world's needs by calling for a more vigorous development of the United Nations in the field of human rights, the peaceful advancement of dependent peoples toward a status of political equality, and the active and systematic development of international law.

Between April 20 and May 29, the secretary-general journeyed to the Big Four capitals to promote his peace plan. He was warmly

received everywhere and was pleased to discover that his sugges-
tions were not being lightly dismissed. But the key members of the
UN ultimately were unwilling to accept the Lie memorandum as a
structure for negotiating outstanding East–West differences. Neither
did they desire a broader reliance on the organization in the formation of foreign policy.

In Moscow, Stalin and Molotov naturally welcomed Lie's stand on
universal membership and hinted that the Soviet Union might be
willing to inaugurate periodic meetings of the Security Council away
from New York, provided Peking were seated. But the Kremlin leaders, almost certainly in the advanced stages of planning for the
Korean War, were not anxious to ease tensions with the West. Lie
could not have known this and was deeply offended when he was
rudely accused by Stalin of offering a program that reflected an
"American point of view." The secretary-general was, after all, still
reeling from the pounding he had taken in the Western press over the
seating of Communist China. He reminded Stalin that his indigna-
tion and that of the UN was the rationale for the plan itself.

The reactions of the West's Big Three proved even less encouraging.
In Washington, where the newly signed North Atlantic Treaty had
become the cornerstone of Western military and political opposition to
Soviet expansionism, Lie's initiative was an embarrassment. It could
only impede efforts to rally public support for rearmament and the fulfillment of other commitments under the alliance. Moreover, the U.S.
position of January 1950—that Chinese representation in the UN was a
"procedural question" to which the veto did not apply—remained
unchanged. Truman opposed allowing the Soviet Union to bully the
United Nations into seating Peking. Foreign Minister Ernest Bevin
supported the president, adding that the secretary-general was, in fact,
sapping Western resolve by confusing the "common people" with
dangerous and unrealistic appeals for disarmament. Turning to the
matter of Decolonization (point 9 in the memorandum), the ailing
British statesman rebuked Lie for contributing to the "ill-tempered and
unpleasant" attacks on British colonial policy that had become common in the UN. Only in Paris was there genuine sympathy for Lie's
legal argument on behalf of seating Peking. But while Bidault also
agreed in principle to holding periodic summit meetings within the
Security Council system, France could ill afford a break with the West
at a time when U.S. arms were urgently needed for the struggle against
Ho Chi Minh's forces in Vietnam.

Trygve Lie had undertaken his peace mission with few illusions about the willingness of the superpowers to give up their "immediate struggle for power" in favor of UN solutions to their problems. Still, in early June, Lie continued to hope that the two votes needed to seat Communist China might be found, the Soviet walkout would then be ended, and the Security Council revived as a forum for Great Power negotiations. The North Korean attack across the thirty-eighth parallel on June 25, 1950, shattered this hope and ended Lie's career as an impartial broker in the Cold War.

CONFLICT IN KOREA TRIES
LIE'S IMPARTIALITY

At the Cairo Conference in 1943, Prime Minister Churchill and Generalissimo Chiang Kai-shek had agreed that Korea, which had endured more than forty years of brutal Japanese occupation, would "in due course" achieve its political independence. At Yalta two years later, Stalin, who had not been present at Cairo, joined in this pledge. At the Moscow meeting of the Council of Foreign Ministers in December 1945, the Big Four agreed that Korea would be administered under a joint United States–USSR trusteeship for five years after which free elections would take place and ruling power would be transferred to a new unified Korean government. This arrangement quickly failed, and the thirty-eighth parallel, the temporary dividing line between U.S. and Soviet occupation zones, became a permanent political border. On each side of the line, rival governments were sponsored by the occupying powers and separate administrations were set up, artificially splitting the social and economic structure of the country.

Unhappy with this arrangement, Washington submitted the issue to the United Nations. At its second session in 1947, the General Assembly passed an American resolution that called for elections to be held under UN supervision, to be followed by the reunification of Korea. A nine-member commission was created and sent to Korea to watch over the scheduled elections for reunification. Moscow bitterly opposed the move and predictably refused to allow the UN commission to function north of the thirty-eighth parallel. Nevertheless, in May 1948, elections took place in South Korea under the commission's supervision, and the government of the Republic of Korea was formed with Syngman Rhee as its first president. In keeping with

U.S. wishes, the General Assembly at its Paris sessions of 1948 and 1949 declared the Rhee government the "only freely elected government" in Korea, and established the UN Commission on Korea.

Meanwhile, the Soviet Union refused to recognize the South Korean government and announced the formation of the Democratic People's Republic in the North. Although Soviet troops were withdrawn, their departure was followed by a rapid military buildup. By early 1950 the communist regime in Pyongyang, now boasting a well-equipped army of 200,000 men, talked openly of unifying Korea by liberating the South from foreign occupation. Two governments thus existed, one backed by the Soviet Union and the other supported by the United States, each claiming to represent the people of Korea. The stage was set for armed conflict.

Shortly before midnight on June 24, 1950, Assistant Secretary of State for UN Affairs John C. Hickerson awakened Lie with the news that North Koreans had attacked across the thirty-eighth parallel. Lie immediately requested Executive Assistant Andrew Cordier to cable the UN Commission in Seoul for confirmation of the report and made preparations for an emergency meeting of the Security Council the following afternoon. Actually, the call from Hickerson was part of a White House effort to integrate U.S. and UN policy. Upon learning of the attack, Secretary of State Acheson had approved a plan whereby part of the overall U.S. response would include a request for an urgent meeting of the Security Council and a request for an immediate cease-fire. At 3 a.m., Lie was again awakened, this time with a request from UN Ambassador Ernest Grass to call the council into emergency session the next day.

The invasion presented the United States with unpleasant choices. To allow superior North Korean forces to overrun the South would damage U.S. containment policy and deepen domestic opposition to a government already under attack for having "lost" China. A second choice—providing material and logistical support to South Korea—might prove insufficient to repel the invasion and could lead to an even deeper commitment later on. Finally, the United States could go to war immediately and face the risks associated with fighting a land war in Asia, weakening the Western alliance, and potentially escalating the battle into World War III.

Truman did not hesitate. At Blair House, the temporary presidential residence, on the evening of June 25, 1950, the president, along with his top advisers, decided that immediate military steps must be taken. Gen. Douglas MacArthur would be requested to provide air and sea cover for retreating South Korean forces; the Seventh Fleet would be moved into the Formosa Straits; preparations would be started to move U.S. occupation forces from Japan to the battle zone.

Legitimization of these actions at the UN was already under way. That afternoon (Sunday, June 25), the emergency session of the Security Council, by a vote of 9–0 (Yugoslavia abstaining), passed a U.S. resolution that charged North Korea with "breaking the peace"; it ordered an immediate cease-fire and withdrawal of North Korean forces from the South. All members were urged to help the UN and to refrain from giving assistance to the North Korean authorities. A suggestion by Yugoslavia to invite the North Koreans to participate in the debate (South Korea was seated) was defeated. The council would deal exclusively with one issue, North Korean aggression, and would do so without hearing from the accused.

On June 26, Truman, who had assumed correctly that the North Koreans would ignore the Security Council's cease-fire order, announced that the United States would support the council's efforts to end this "serious breach of the peace." However, since the June 25 resolution did not explicitly authorize the use of force, the president's statement clearly anticipated further actions by the UN. Acheson, therefore, recommended to the president that on June 27, the United States propose a "new resolution calling on the members of the United Nations [to] furnish such assistance to the Republic of South Korea as may be necessary to repel the armed attack and to restore international peace and security in the area." Naturally, Acheson did not intend by this action to allow the UN to dictate U.S. policy. Even the sudden return of the Soviet Union to the Security Council, always a possibility, would have no effect on the ability of the United States to act unilaterally. About this possibility, Acheson later wrote, "If Malik [the Soviet delegate] returned to the Security Council and vetoed the resolution, we would have to carry on under the existing one." For the Soviet Union, continued support for Peking appeared to outweigh the importance of casting what amounted to a meaningless veto in the face of U.S. plans to respond militarily in Korea. Malik did not return and the Security Council passed the resolution by a vote of 7–1 (Yugoslavia) with India and Egypt abstaining.

In a real sense, U.S. initiatives in the Security Council freed Trygve Lie from having to take sides immediately in what was shaping up as a trial of strength between the United States and the Soviet Union.

Whether the secretary-general could have maintained his neutrality on a matter of such critical importance to the United States is open to question. Widespread international sympathy for South Korea made it difficult for Lie to avoid expressing public disapproval of the clear-cut North Korean aggression. In any event, Lie had abandoned his normal caution and, against the recommendation of close advisers, asked to be the first speaker in the emergency meeting of the council on June 25. Without directly invoking Article 99, Lie nevertheless described the military actions of North Korean forces as a "direct violation" of a resolution in the General Assembly, as well as "a violation of the principles of the charter." The Security Council, he continued, had the "clear duty . . . to take steps necessary to re-establish peace." Two days later, following the council's general appeal for assistance to South Korea, Lie cabled all member governments requesting "early information" about the "type of help" they could furnish. Strangely, Lie ignored his customary habit of consulting with member delegations prior to undertaking an important political initiative. His initiative, in fact, drew criticism from a number of member governments who were troubled by the fait accompli that Truman had laid before the council.

For months, Trygve Lie had engaged in painstaking personal diplomacy aimed at moderating East–West tensions. Now he abandoned this approach and adopted "administrative neutrality" and a strong defense of the charter. "The Secretary-General is the executive for the decisions by the legislative organs of the United Nations," Lie later wrote, "and this was my role in the Korean conflict." Responding to criticism that he had acted in advance of instructions from the political organs of the United Nations, Lie defended his action: "I accordingly anticipated and associated my office and myself with the most determined effort to give reality to the principles of collective security."

But this was not the conception of collective security the Great Powers had agreed to at San Francisco. As the Soviet Union quickly pointed out, Lie had aligned himself with the war aims of one permanent member against the strategic interests of another. This undermined the political understanding on which the principle of collective action rested. He had also, according to Andrei Gromyko, played an "unseemly role" in the gross violations of the charter on the part of the United States.

The resolutions of June 25 and 27 were possible, of course, only because of the Soviet boycott of the Security Council. Within a matter of days, the Soviet Union, Czechoslovakia, and Poland cabled Lie to question the legality of all council actions regarding Korea. They argued that the council was not empowered to act on a matter of substance in the absence of two permanent members—the Soviet Union and the "legal" government of China. In addition, the council's actions constituted an unlawful "interference into the domestic affairs of Korea," and further, because U.S. military operations preceded the June 27 resolution, it was the United States, and not North Korea, that was guilty of aggression.

In the prevailing political climate, Soviet bloc charges of illegality carried little weight with the members of the council, and were registered more for the record than anything else. Jean Chauvel, the French representative in the Security Council, captured the mood of the council when he opined, "By abandoning the Security Council," the Soviet Union had "abandoned the Charter." When the Soviet Union returned to both, he continued, "it would recover its right of speech, of criticism, and of veto." The U.S. State Department had also prepared a lengthy reply to the Soviet charges, which it presented to the council on June 30. The brief argued that a series of precedents had established that an abstention by a permanent member of the Security Council "did not constitute a veto." The "voluntary absence of a permanent member from the Security Council," the United States contended, was "clearly analogous to abstention." The U.S. statement also refuted the Soviet claim regarding the seating of Peking. The Security Council had the final word in all disputes over credentials and, since the council had not withdrawn its accreditation of Nationalist China, votes cast on the June 25 and 27 resolutions by its representatives were the official votes of China.

For reasons that remain unclear, the secretary-general had also requested that the legal department of the Secretariat prepare the memorandum, "Legal Aspects of Security Council Action in Korea," which Lie circulated among key delegations with the expressed intention that it be passed on to the Soviet delegation. Substantially similar in content to the State Department brief, the Secretariat memorandum only deepened Moscow's distrust of Lie and confirmed its belief that he was subservient to the West.

But for Lie this "loss of confidence," although it had a shattering effect on his usefulness as an international civil servant, appeared an acceptable price to pay to resist North Korean aggression. The secretary-general was firmly convinced that the hostilities had been abetted by the Soviet Union, a belief he held until his death.

Sensitive to Soviet charges that Security Council resolutions were little more than a cover for U.S. military policy, Lie did make every effort to "internationalize" the UN response in Korea. Upon his vigorous urging, sixteen nations would eventually place military units under UN command but this was, in sum, a meager response. The main burden would rest with the South Koreans themselves, who contributed about 40 percent of the ground troops, and the United States, whose contributions amounted to more than half the ground troops and virtually all the naval and air forces. Lie's failure can be traced in part to the reluctance of many governments to become involved in what was essentially an American war, but was due mainly to the refusal of the Pentagon to share control over military operations with the United Nations.

When Lie suggested the creation of a UN Committee of Coordination to stimulate and coordinate offers of assistance from member governments under the terms of the June 27 resolution, the American mission at the United Nations firmly turned him down. Theoretically, that resolution formed the basis for the first genuine collective security action in history; all member states were free to furnish whatever assistance they could, and it was the duty of the secretary-general to encourage the broadest international participation. In fact, the United States refused to permit any use of the resolution that did not accord with its broader policy considerations. It was the United States alone, for example, that refused an offer by Chiang Kai-shek to send 33,000 troops to Korea. Any remaining doubt as to control was removed on July 7 when the Security Council recommended that all military assistance be made available to a "unified command under the United States," asked the United States to appoint the commander of UN forces, and authorized the unified command to fly the United Nations flag. When the Security Council adjourned, Trygve Lie presented U.S. Ambassador Warren Austin with the UN flag that had been flown by Count Bernadotte, the martyred UN mediator in Palestine.

In the ensuing weeks as UN troops tried desperately to maintain a defense perimeter around the port city of Pusan at the southern tip of the Korean peninsula, Lie was subjected to a blistering attack in the Soviet press. In New York he was prodded by journalists to explain the apparent contradiction between his Twenty-Year Peace Plan, which Andrei Gromyko now denounced as having been written in Washington, and his pro-U.S. stand on Korea. During a July press conference, Lie maintained, "There is no change in my position: there is no contradiction." But despite his insistence, the plan was dead and with it, his own suitability as a go-between. Lie did place the plan before the fifth regular session of the General Assembly where the pro-Western majority approved it over Soviet opposition in November 1950. Its proposals never were implemented, and the plan became another casualty of the Cold War.

Jacob Malik, the Soviet delegate, returned to the Security Council on August 1, the day the Soviet Union was scheduled to assume the presidency of the council. Malik's presence meant that any further U.S.-supported resolutions would be vetoed. As matters stood, however, it was too late for the Soviet Union to influence ongoing United Nations military operations. But dramatic changes in the course of the war would soon require a change in the existing identification of the UN with Western policy.

On September 15, General MacArthur made his dazzling amphibious landing at Inchon. North Korean forces, caught by surprise, retreated rapidly to the North and within two weeks, United Nations forces had achieved total victory below the thirty-eighth parallel. Exhilarated by this happy turn of events, but also alarmed over the prospect of a wider war, Trygve Lie on September 30 drafted a working paper of "Suggested Terms of Settlement of the Korean Question." Lie called for an immediate cease-fire and the demilitarization and withdrawal of North Korean forces from the South. The North Korean authorities would be required to accept UN-supervised elections within one year, and the eventual unification of Korea was contemplated. Should Pyongyang refuse these terms, the General Assembly would recommend a resumption of military operations with the "objective of eliminating the North Korean authorities."

The secretary-general's terms were hardly generous to North Korea. Still, they were unwelcome in Washington, where Truman had already authorized MacArthur to invade North Korea with the intention of unifying the entire country militarily. Existing Security Council resolutions, however, did not authorize UN military operations north of the thirty-eighth parallel. Since recourse to the Security Council for this purpose was not possible because of the presence of the Soviet delegate, the West turned to the General Assembly. And on October 7, with MacArthur's forces having already entered North Korea, the assembly acted. By a vote of 47–5 with 7 abstentions, the General Assembly authorized the UN command to take "all appropriate steps" to ensure stability throughout Korea, including the holding of elections for the establishment of a "unified, independent, and democratic government in the sovereign state of Korea."

Despite the fact that the aims endorsed by the General Assembly resolution directly coincided with Western interests, Trygve Lie joined in what he would later describe as the "elation" of "having put aggression to flight." "This was Korea," he declared, "not Manchuria; this was the United Nations, not the League of Nations." Lie also defended Western policy against Soviet charges that the General Assembly had acted illegally in authorizing the use of force in North Korea. He stressed that United Nations actions under the June 25 and 27 resolutions were simply recommendations, not commands; the General Assembly, was, therefore, free to make similar recommendations and might have authorized all United Nations' actions in Korea if circumstances had not been different.

Trygve Lie's stance on Korea was a tribute to his courage and sense of duty; he would later describe it as "the best justified act of seven years in the service of peace." However, the association of Lie's office with Western-sponsored UN initiatives also contributed to the Soviet Union's most humiliating diplomatic defeat in the United Nations. In addition, it seemed that the secretary-general personally sided with Western interests in the most serious crisis of the Cold War. Understandably, the Soviet Union vented its bitterness and frustration on Lie.

SUPERPOWERS CONSIDER
LIE'S REAPPOINTMENT

On October 9, just two days after the General Assembly approved the widening of United Nations operations in Korea, the Security Council met to consider the reappointment of Trygve Lie. In December 1949, Lie had announced to the press, "I am not a candidate for reappointment."

Lie had become convinced that the Cold War had ended all hope that the United Nations could function as a league to enforce the peace. The crisis over Chinese representation and the subsequent Soviet walkout appeared to deepen Lie's resolve to leave. "The whole thing is a mess," he wrote to Norwegian Foreign Minister Halvard Lange. "I have no desire to be sitting here with the sole responsibility, should the United Nations collapse." The secretary-general's impartial defense of the charter in Iran, Czechoslovakia, the Balkans, and elsewhere had occasionally drawn the anger of the

Great Powers, but there had been no significant loss of confidence in Lie by Washington or Moscow. Indeed, early in 1950, Soviet Foreign Minister Vishinsky, no doubt influenced by Lie's stand on Peking, publicly favored an extension of Lie's term. "It seems to me," Lie wrote to his family, "that I've done my duty, and I'll be completely satisfied if I can get through this final year with my whole skin." But by the fall, Moscow was determined to punish Lie for his support of Western interests in Korea, and the secretary-general who had only recently decided "to quit while the quitting was good," was equally determined not to be "run out of town." The United States, perhaps more out of concern for continuity in its UN policy than for the beleaguered secretary-general, led the fight to extend Lie's term.

In the Security Council, Andrei Vishinsky promptly vetoed Lie's nomination and then mounted a monthlong campaign in support of a successor. Britain and France, which were known to be wavering on the reappointment, were pressured by the Soviet Union to adhere to the principle of Great Power unity for the sake of a smooth-running Secretariat. Moscow publicly endorsed candidates with pro-Western leanings, including Sir Benegal Rau of India, Charles Malik of Lebanon, and Gen. Carlos P. Romulo of the Philippines, hoping that their rejection would prove embarrassing to the West. It did not matter much what the Soviet Union's private feelings were about a candidate's abilities, so long as he was someone other than Trygve Lie; Vishinsky had said earlier, "When you hear the voice of General Romulo, you hear the sound of empty barrels."

The United States was as determined to support Lie as the Soviet Union was to oppose him. Britain and France were convinced by Washington that abandoning Lie would support Soviet charges of illegality regarding the UN's involvement in Korea. In addition, the way was prepared with other delegations to move the issue of Lie's appointment into the General Assembly in the event that the Council became deadlocked. By the end of October, with the Soviet veto of Lie and the unprecedented threat by Ambassador Austin to veto any candidate but Lie, the Security Council's deliberations were at an end. And so on November 1, the General Assembly voted 46–5–8 to extend Trygve Lie's term of office for three years.

Trygve Lie accepted the General Assembly's recommendation as a vote of confidence for "my interpretation of the Secretary-General's duties." In a broader sense, however, the assembly majority had also reaffirmed the political independence of Lie, and his successors, from pressure by the member nations. The renomination fight also reflected existing attitudes about Lie's political initiatives over the years. In light of the secretary-general's stand on Korea, Communist opposition was predictable, although the vicious personal attack against the secretary-general by the communist delegates in the General Assembly was excessive even by cold war standards. The Arab bloc, still bitter over the secretary-general's position on Palestine, abstained, as did Nationalist China over Lie's more recent support of Peking. In fact, the now familiar majority vote that the United States was able to muster on virtually all cold war issues, was more of an expression of U.S. influence in the organization than of support for Lie's continuing political leadership. Immediately following the vote in the General Assembly, Vishinsky announced that the Soviet Union would not recognize Trygve Lie as secretary-general. A diplomatic and social boycott of Lie by the communist bloc nations followed and, until his retirement two and one-half years later, Lie had no political influence on matters involving the Great Powers.

Meanwhile, massive intervention by Communist Chinese forces in Korea in November 1950 led to a cease-fire the following year and finally, in 1953, to a truce that restored an approximation of the status quo antebellum. With the start of delicate negotiations that included the Communists, any continuing role on Korea proved impossible for the secretary-general. In December 1950, a delegation from Peking arrived at UN headquarters in New York to participate in the Security Council debate on Communist China's complaints against "the armed invasion of Taiwan" by the United States. Secretary-General Lie attempted to mediate a settlement of outstanding differences between Peking and the United Nations. The effort failed because Lie, who had backed away from his support of Communist Chinese representation, insisted on separating the issue of Chinese aggression in Korea from Peking's major complaints—U.S. aggression and the illegal occupation of the China seat by Taiwan. On December 19, the Chinese delegation left New York, bringing to an end Trygve Lie's final important diplomatic initiative.

The thunder of gunfire in Korea brought the United Nations to a critical juncture in its young life. Less than five years after the horrors of World War II, the organization that had been created "to save future generations from the scourge of war" had failed to prevent another war, one that would claim thousands of lives. Korea came to symbolize the determination of both sides in the Cold War to achieve their ends, if need, by military means. While the United Nations called for an end to the fighting, North Korea defied Security Council cease-fire orders, pressing its initial military advantage to near-total victory. Within hours of the attack, the United Nations had become involved, but disaster was only narrowly averted and the conflict ground slowly to its uneasy stalemate in 1953.

The Korean conflict revealed more about the basic flaws in the Great Power conception of collective security than it did about the capacity of the world body to mount a response to aggression. The unique circumstances that enabled the United States to pursue its Korean policy were unlikely to occur again. To make matters worse, Lie was faced with an impossible choice: he could vigorously support the American-led UN action in Korea and risk Soviet hostility or he could recognize the political limitations on his authority, remain aloof, and offer his services as an impartial mediator. His subsequent actions in support of U.S. policy totally alienated Lie from the Soviet Union, marking an end to whatever leadership he might have exerted on the reduction of East–West tensions.

5

The Dream Revisited

With war raging in Korea as a constant reminder of the breakdown in Great Power cooperation, it appeared that the dream of a world community relying on the combined might of the superpowers to resist aggression had been extinguished. But did this tragedy mean the end of any international role for the United Nations itself?

Conceptually, deep pessimism was understandable since the success of the United Nations depended largely on the unlikely survival of the victorious wartime alliance into the postwar era. It was also widely understood that the Allies—who had brought the organization into existence—would permanently define its role, dictate its aims and, by virtue of their relationship toward one another, ultimately control its destiny. Although the General Assembly was the most representative of the major UN bodies, it was originally intended that the assembly would meet for a few weeks each year to deal with essentially noncontroversial issues. Rarely would the assembly, as originally conceived, involve itself in matters that the Security Council considered. It would never act regarding problems over which the major powers were divided.

However, the failure of the superpowers to use the Security Council as a forum to resolve the problems of world order and justice was accompanied by a shift in the institutional focus of the United Nations away from the council and toward the General Assembly. It also meant that the focus of the organization might change. The majority of smaller nations in the General Assembly had little stake in cold war politics; their interests centered on the economic, social, and humanitarian goals envisioned in the charter. If they could successfully implement this agenda, the United Nations might yet take an active part in bringing about a better world.

The shift to the General Assembly did not reflect the capacity of the charter, like any written constitution, to adapt to new political realities. Neither did it result, as many Western analysts rushed to point out, from a sincere desire on the part of the West to reinvigorate the UN's flagging conceptual and institutional response to world problems. Rather, at least initially, it was part of the same cold war maneuvering that had already threatened to destroy the organization.

When the UN was pressed into full service in the struggle for moral superiority over the Soviet Union following the announcement of the Truman Doctrine, the United States exhibited a marked preference for the General Assembly as a means to pressure its adversary. In the assembly, condemnations of Soviet policy were not subject to the veto. Washington came to view the assembly as an ideal forum in which to clarify and enlist support for American–UN initiatives, an important substitute for more risky military and diplomatic challenges to Soviet policy behind the Iron Curtain. It was only a matter of time before the United States, faced with a steady stream of Soviet vetoes to the Security Council, would seek to formalize the shift, a step taken with the passage in November 1950 of the Uniting for Peace Resolution.

At the core of the Uniting for Peace Resolution was the United States' desire to legitimize military operations in Korea north of the thirty-eighth parallel following the Soviet delegate's return to the Security Council on August 1, 1950. The resolution was not the first attempt by the West to make the assembly permanently available for condemnations of Soviet policy. In November 1947, at the urging of then Secretary of State George Marshall, the General Assembly had created the Interim Committee on Peace and Security. The Little Assembly, as it came to be called, was a body that could meet between regular sessions of the General Assembly and was composed of all UN members. But the Little Assembly was not directly empowered to deal with security matters and, with the expansion of the assembly's regular sessions, it soon fell into disuse. The Uniting for Peace Resolution, on the other hand, authorized a simple majority of the Security Council to request an emergency session of the General Assembly in cases involving "breaches of the peace or acts of aggression" when the council was paralyzed by the veto. Other provisions created a fourteen-member Peace Observation Committee that could quickly be dispatched to trouble spots, and a Collective Measures Committee that could coordinate military actions taken by individual states. The General Assembly was authorized to recommend collective actions, including "the use of armed force," and members were invited to maintain standby military forces for use by the UN. In effect, the resolution converted the General Assembly into a reserve Security Council.

As a practical matter, the Uniting for Peace Resolution carried neither the constitutional nor the political importance that defenders assigned to it. No recommendations of the Collective Measures Committee were ever implemented and the Peace Observation Commission was used only once, in the Balkan crisis of December 1950. There was widespread opposition to making military units permanently available to the United Nations for the purposes envisioned in the resolution, particularly so in the West, which had been instrumental in securing its passage. While the resolution was used to condemn Communist Chinese aggression in February 1951, and again some months later to order an embargo of war materials to Peking, these were measures that were possible under the General Assembly's existing powers. In fact, some scholars argue that by tying the assembly's powers over peace and security to a previous Security Council veto, the Uniting for Peace Resolution actually contracted its powers. Nevertheless, in 1950 nearly every state outside the Soviet bloc could relate national advantage to the expansion of the General Assembly's powers.

The Western allies commanded large majorities on virtually all East–West issues; this provided opportunities to attack Soviet policy that were not available in the veto-plagued Security Council. Moreover, since majority rule could be equated with the objective application of charter principles, Western victories were given added moral weight. The emerging U.S. preference for the General Assembly reflected America's faith in the persistence of Western influence there, and the belief that deliberations could be confined mainly to cold war issues. Lesser powers like India, however, felt that the dominance of the Security Council exaggerated the real influence of the Great Powers within the organization. Not only had the paralysis of the council raised serious questions on the reliability of the Big Four to preserve the peace, but the United Nations had rapidly been transformed exclusively into an instrument of cold war propaganda. For many members, the shift of focus to the General Assembly represented a welcome opportunity to stimulate interest in economic development and human rights, and for attacks on racism and colonialism. As these matters came to supersede the Cold War as the dominant focus of the General Assembly, the United States and its Western allies—now on the receiving end of hostile resolutions on social, economic, and colonial issues—would, like the Soviet Union, retreat to the safety of the Security Council. The process of change took years, but its parameters were clearly evidenced early in the 1950s.

FIGHTING FOR HUMAN RIGHTS

With the Nazi horrors still fresh in their minds, the delegates at San Francisco had inserted seven references to the protection of human rights in the charter, including a provision for the creation of a Commission on Human Rights. Historically, the protection of human rights had been the exclusive concern of national states, because states were the main source of human rights violations. Citizens were in the somewhat paradoxical circumstance of relying upon the oppressor for protection, and more diabolically, on the luck of the draw. Individuals either lived in societies that constitutionally protected civil rights or they did not; they could not claim these rights under international law or look to any international agency to enforce them. Not even the Covenant of the League of Nations made any explicit reference to human rights, except for the protection of national minorities in Europe.

Yet in his closing remarks at San Francisco, Truman had declared, "Under this document [the UN Charter] we have good reason to expect the framing of an international bill of rights, acceptable to all nations." But when the UN Commission on Human Rights met for the first time in 1946, there was little agreement on the content and meaning of this concept. The United Kingdom and other delegations favored a convention, a multilateral treaty to which the standard legal duties with respect to treaties would apply. Others preferred that the bill be issued in the form of a declaration or manifesto, to be followed later by the drafting of a legally binding covenant.

By far the most serious clash, which struck at the core of the commission's aims, occurred between the Soviet Union, which insisted that the rights of individuals flowed from the state, and the West, which emphasized a Lockean doctrine of inherent rights. It was evident that a UN majority would tie the enjoyment of human rights to the absence of state power in the life of the individual. The Soviet Union also differed sharply with the West over the content of any final statement, insisting that it include social and economic rights as well as civil and political liberties. Over the opposition of the U.S. State Department, Eleanor Roosevelt, who chaired the commission, prevailed in the view that the declaration include a commitment on the part of the international community to promote higher standards of living, education, leisure time, and participation in cultural activities. But while this represented a major concession on the part of the United States, Washington continued to argue that the role of states must be restricted to promoting access to these rights and not, as the Soviet Union insisted, to guaranteeing them.

If the declaration were to command widespread respect and allegiance across a broad spectrum of cultural, ideological, and legal views, it was necessary that the language be both flexible and inclusive. Minor differences were easily resolved. On the recommendation of Mrs. Hampa Mehta of India, the original first article that read, "All men are created equal" was changed to "All human beings." Mrs. Roosevelt also agreed to delete the word "created" and substitute "born" to meet the Soviet objection that "created" suggested divine origin. The task of incorporating many divergent concepts into a series of coherent articles, however, proved more difficult.

There was general agreement within the commission that the declaration should be "clear, concise, and relatively short, and that it should be easy for all peoples, everywhere to understand." Still, it took from June 1947, when the commission first received a draft outline of a bill of rights from the Secretariat, until June 1948 for the commission to hammer out a final document. In September, this was sent by the Economical and Social Council to the third session of the General Assembly meeting in Paris. There, during eighty-one sessions of the assembly's Social, Humanitarian, and Cultural Committee, the commission's draft was subject to a meticulous, often heated, line-by-line revision. On December 10, following further amendment in the General Assembly itself, the United Declaration of Human Rights was adopted by a vote of 48—with 8 abstentions—the Soviet bloc, Saudi Arabia, and South Africa. Briefly, the declaration set forth the following civil and political rights:

> The right to life, liberty, and the security of persons; the right to freedom of thought, conscience, and religion; the right of freedom of opinion and

expression; freedom of movement within the state and from one state to another; equality before the law and freedom from arbitrary arrest; freedom from arbitrary interference within the privacy of one's family, home and correspondence; the prohibition of slavery and other forms of servitude; the prohibition of torture; and the right to asylum in another state.

Economic and social rights included:

The right to work; equal pay for equal work; the right to a decent standard of living, including food, clothing, shelter, and medical care; the right to education and participation in the cultural life of the society; and the right to rest and leisure.

Everyone, according to Article II of the declaration, is entitled to these rights without distinction "of any kind" as to race, color, sex, language, religion, political or other opinion, national or social origin, property, birth, or status. The General Assembly ordered that the declaration be given the widest possible distribution and publicity; therefore, the text was translated into forty-seven languages by the Secretariat. December 10 was officially declared by the General Assembly to be Human Rights Day.

This remarkable milestone in the history of human rights legislation—stretching back to the Magna Carta and including the *Droit de l'homme*, the Bill of Rights, and the UN Charter itself—no doubt owed its existence to the fact that the declaration was a nonbinding statement of familiar, if high-minded, norms. Although all members were expected to abide by its terms, the declaration was not subject to ratification by member governments, and thus involved no legal obligations. Putting teeth in the declaration through the adoption of binding covenants, a hard procedure given the actual practices of many states, was quite another matter, and would take another twenty years to accomplish.

Not surprisingly, the long debate over enforcement took place in a climate of insincerity. On few issues did noble impulses and sovereign rights collide so directly as they did on the issue of human rights. Most Western members were lukewarm at best, and insisted that any covenant on human rights contain a "federal clause" that would exempt federal governments from undertaking responsibility on behalf of state, provincial, or cantonal authorities. As a practical matter, this would free the United States from applying the covenant to segregated schools in Mississippi while still complying with its obligations as a signatory. No doubt tongue-in-cheek, the Western members also proclaimed an exemption for non-self-governing territories that, they claimed, were in various stages of progress toward self-government and, therefore, had to be consulted prior to the acceptance of obligations by a ruling authority on behalf of the indigenous inhabitants. Ironically, this permitted the Soviet Union, whose record on human rights could scarcely stand up to international scrutiny, to pose as a staunch advocate of vigorous enforcement. Most Latin American delegations supported this view but were unwilling to break with the West and, thus, hand the Soviet Union an important propaganda victory.

Many members in the Soviet Union favored the adoption of a single covenant that covered economic, social, and cultural rights as well as civil and political guarantees. This, it was argued, would remove the artificial distinction between the two spheres and emphasize the broad spectrum of living conditions that formed the basis of true freedom. Most Western members argued that while civil and political liberties might be protected through judicial and legislative action, the enjoyment of social, economic, and cultural rights depended on living conditions that varied from place to place. Moreover, since these rights were not capable of precise definition, their inclusion would rob the covenant of needed clarity.

The controversy was resolved in 1951 when the General Assembly instructed the Commission on Human Rights to draft two covenants, a decision resulting from much U.S. pressure. The West reluctantly agreed to the inclusion of the right of self-determination among the protected political rights, although the concession did not appear so important at the time. Taken together, the covenants that were finally presented to the General Assembly in 1953 contained little that was not already in the declaration. Fundamental positions, however, remained unchanged. Western opposition to the Covenant on Economic, Social, and Cultural Rights in general and to other specific provisions, together with the Soviet claim that the social and economic provisions did not go far enough, combined to delay passage of the two covenants until 1966.

The long struggle to obtain final adoption of the covenants attests much to the persistence of human rights advocates at the United Nations as it does to the reluctance of governments to relinquish any control over their citizens. This persistence may have contributed to important advances in the protection of human rights in the intervening years. In 1951, the Ad Hoc Committee on Slavery of the Economic and Social Council conducted a sixty-four nation survey on slavery and other forms of servitude. As a result, world attention was focused on a dimly understood but widespread problem that, five years later, led to the replacement of the 1926 League of Nations Covenant on Slavery by a new and more comprehensive agreement. The year 1951 also brought into force the Convention on the Prevention and Punishment of the Crime of Genocide. It condemned "all acts with intent to destroy in whole or in part, a national, ethnic, racial, or religious group." All who were guilty of such acts were to be punished "whether they [were] constitutionally responsible rulers, public officers or private individuals." Thus, the victims of Nazi concentration camps, of mass deportations, and of other despicable acts had left this legacy to the world: *genocide,* a term not yet coined in 1945, was condemned and made a crime punishable by international law because of the United Nations.

The UN was also hard at work on a program to ensure political, social, and economic equality for women long before the accomplishments of the modern feminist movement. Early in 1951, the Commission on the Status of Women proposed international legislation on the nationality of married women, the status of women in public and private law, equality of educational opportunities for women, the status of nurses, women in the work of the United Nations, and equal pay for equal work. An important feature of the commission's early work was condemnation of the sex-based discrimination experienced by millions of women who were the victims of cultural and legal obstacles to their rightful place in society. Subsequently, after long debate, the General Assembly in 1952 adopted the Convention on the Political Rights of Women. This was the first human rights convention concluded under the terms of the declaration and the first of many conventions to promote equality for women. The convention guaranteed the right of women to vote on equal terms with men, to be eligible for election to all elected bodies, to hold public office, and to exercise public duties without regard to sex. Disputes between states arising out of interpretations of the convention were to be decided by the International Court of Justice, in the event that direct negotiations failed to produce a settlement.

Human rights was not the only peacetime issue raised in the UN. The Western notion of a free press was foreign to the Soviet Union, where the spread of information was aimed less at an informed public than at ensuring conformity with communist doctrine. To some members from emerging nations, state control and even censorship were justified; only this could correct abuses in Western "news gathering" practices. Nevertheless, in 1951, the Economic and Social council adopted a preamble and nineteen articles of a draft convention on the freedom of information. Contact was made with more than 600 government and professional agencies to solicit their views on the form and content of international standards dealing with access to and distribution of information. By 1953, valuable work was completed on a code of ethics for journalists, and the General Assembly had approved the adoption of a Convention on the International Right of Correction. The latter was intended to encourage peaceful relations among nations by the creation of guidelines and procedures to control the dissemination of false and distorted reporting.

PROMOTING THE EMANCIPATION
OF DEPENDENT PEOPLES

In no other area has the United Nations enjoyed greater success than in promoting the emancipation of dependent peoples. Its period of greatest achievement would come in later years, particularly after 1960 when dozens of new members, all former colonies, were added to the growing anticolonial majority in the United Nations. But it was during these early years that the anticolonial movement emerged to set the terms for the breakup of the great colonial empires; self-determination became the watchword of an international effort to eliminate all forms of political dependency. To appreciate the magnitude of this achievement, we should glance at the history and nature of colonialism. Between the sixteenth and eighteenth centuries, the nations of Europe had established colonial empires that extended from the Americas to the Cape of Good Hope. For most of the nineteenth century, the European imperial powers seemed more concerned with securing the sea routes to existing colonies than with expanding their empires. The scramble for overseas empires resumed in earnest in 1870 and on the eve of World War I, the European powers had carved up all of Africa, save for Liberia and Ethiopia, and much of Asia. More than once the competition nearly led to conflict between the Great Powers, reinforcing growing liberal sentiment concerning the link between imperialist expansion and war. However, pre-World War I colonial policy was attacked on a more basic level, namely, the unfair treatment that native populations received at the hands of their mostly white colonial masters. The harsh treatment of the Congo natives by King Leopold of Belgium was but one of the more striking examples of how inhuman colonial exploitation could become if left unchecked by international controls. True, the imperialists had brought law and order, modern facilities and medicine, not to mention the "blessings" of Christianity, to the natives. Missionaries established schools and at least at the local level, the indigenous populations were encouraged to learn and practice the administrative arts of the West. However, it was not Western culture that took root in Asia and Africa, but resentment, even hatred, and a burning desire on the part of native leaders to take back their birthright.

In the twentieth century powerful voices were added to the growing chorus of opposition to colonialism. On January 6, 1918, David Lloyd George declared at the Trade Union Conference in London that Arabia, Armenia, Mesopotamia, Syria, and Palestine "in our judgment" were entitled to their separate identities. He extended this principle to the German colonies in Africa and went so far as to apply the principles of self-determination to the tribes of Africa. President Woodrow Wilson's Fourteen Points address to Congress on January 8, stressed the interests of native populations in the adjustment of all postwar colonial claims. But it was Jan Smuts, the South African statesman, who proposed that enemy colonies in Africa not be treated as spoils of war but that they be held in trust by the victors on behalf of the international community. His plan became the basis for the League mandates system.

The mandates system applied to only the former colonies of Germany and the Ottoman Empire, a fraction of the total number of dependencies in the world. Moreover, the Permanent Mandates Commission, a body of experts that was created to supervise the administration of these territories on behalf of the League, had no enforcement powers. And in the period between the wars only one mandate, Iraq, achieved independence while two others, Syria and Lebanon, were brought to the threshold of full sovereignty. But while the mandates system failed to meet the expectations of its more ardent supporters, it established the principle that the welfare of colonial peoples was not a private matter to be dealt with entirely within the framework of European parliaments. The evils of colo-

nialism were rather the proper concern of the international community, which could enforce standards of colonial administration and
actively promote the ideal of self-government.

As a result of these forces, the anticolonial mood was even stronger
at San Francisco than it had been at Versailles. There was widespread
agreement that the example of the League would form the basis for a
stronger and broader system of international supervision of territories
detached from the Axis Powers; the trusteeship system was envisioned
as an improved successor to the League mandate order. But many
smaller powers, including the Arab bloc, Australia, New Zealand, and
the nations of Latin America, insisted that the charter ought to include
a broad commitment on the part of the United Nations to the welfare
of all colonial peoples. Because of this unity and over the vigorous
opposition of the colonial powers, Chapter XI of the charter became a
Declaration Rewarding Non-Self-Government Territories.

In many respects the UN trusteeship system did not improve greatly
on its League predecessor. By 1949, trusteeship agreements had been
approved for only eleven territories—all but one, Somalia, a holdover
from League days. In fact, with the refusal of South Africa to accept an
agreement on the former mandated territory of South-West Africa and
the exclusion of Lebanon, Syria, Iraq, Palestine, and Transjordan, the
system was actually smaller. The trusteeship system depends for its
existence on the voluntary conclusion of agreements between the
United Nations and administering members. Although nations were
free to submit agreements for any of their colonial possessions, none
did. In fact, since the trusteeship system was not, strictly speaking, the
successor of the mandate systems, there was no legal obligation to submit agreements even on the former mandated territories.

Nevertheless, in two important regards, the trusteeship system
greatly advanced the principles of international accountability toward
dependent peoples. Mandated territories had been categorized according to their levels of political maturity and, in some cases, were eventually annexed by the mandatory power.

Under the trusteeship system, the United Nations is responsible for
the social, educational, and political advancement of all inhabitants and
for their development toward self-government. The charter also places
these obligations under the political authority of the General Assembly,
which administers the system through the Trusteeship Council, a public governmental body. By contrast, the Permanent Mandates Commission was a quasi-private body only indirectly responsible to the

League itself. Thus, the system envisioned self-government as the only acceptable alternative to political dependency and conferred the authority to supervise this process directly on the United Nations.

Broadly speaking, these principles had little impact on the administration of the trusteeship system. They were more important for the rationale they provided anticolonialists to establish authority similar to, if not greater than, the authority of the trusteeship system over the vast number of colonies covered under Chapter XI. Constitutionally, this authority flowed from Article 73e, which obliged member states to regularly supply the secretary-general with technical information concerning social, economic, and educational conditions in colonial areas other than trust territories. From the outset, the colonial powers maintained that Chapter XI was merely a "declaration of principle," and not a demand for international accountability for colonial policy. They ascribed no special moral significance to political independence, a concept that the British delegate reminded the General Assembly "should not be confused with liberty." Article 73e, insisted the colonial powers, merely invited the voluntary transmission of non-political information; it did not imply supervisory functions on the part of the United Nations. Since the charter established no agency to evaluate this data, it could not be used as the basis for political debate, as was information submitted to the Trusteeship Council. Neither could it be the basis for recommendations by the General Assembly regarding conditions in specific colonies.

The Western view was almost immediately challenged by the anticolonial majority in the General Assembly. In 1946, the assembly, despite the bitter opposition of the colonial powers, established an Ad Hoc Committee on Information from Non-Self-Governing Territories. In theory, this measure merely responded to a glaring omission in Article 73e—what to do with the information transmitted by colonial powers—but it quickly became the principal battleground for the anticolonial struggle within the United Nations. By the end of 1950 the committee had become a permanent UN organ, paralleling the duties of the Trusteeship Council in colonial matters not under the council's jurisdiction. Despite threats by the colonial powers to boycott the committee if the General Assembly continued to endow it with "illegal powers," the committee became the source of a stream of controversial anticolonial initiatives. Using friendly majorities in the General Assembly, the emerging international power of the Third World progressively expanded the UN's supervisory functions. In 1951 the

committee disapproved decisions by France and Britain to stop transmitting information on certain of their colonies and required the
transmission of information relating to political conditions in all
colonies. It also proclaimed its authority to determine when a territory
ceased to be "non-self-governing," an issue that the colonial powers
insisted they alone could legally decide.

Between 1951 and 1953, the work of the Committee on Information
from Non-Self-Governing Territories also took on a revolutionary
quality, when the General Assembly asked it to consider the factors to
be taken into account in determining whether a territory was or was
not a non-self-governing territory within the meaning of Chapter XI.
A crisis developed when Britain and France informed the secretary-
general that they intended to discontinue transmitting information on
a number of possessions, insisting that they alone could legally determine the status of territories in their possession. Over their bitter opposition, however, the anticolonial majority insisted that the transmission of information was a legal obligation that only the UN could
terminate. A list of factors was drawn up to further "clarify" the duties
of administering powers under the charter. Faced with the determination of the colonial powers to preserve their colonial privileges, even
at the risk of defying the United Nations, the UN, it seemed, could gain
little by clarifying obligations only to have them ignored. However,
the debate that surrounded the study added to the mounting international pressure on the colonial powers to recognize UN authority to set
the terms for the eventual transfer of power to colonial peoples. In the
General Assembly, speaker after speaker insisted that political independence was the primary route to self-government and time would
soon make it the only route. In addition, merely adopting a list of factors as "a guide in determining whether constitutional changes in the
status of a territory justified releasing an administrating member from
its obligations," served to declare the General Assembly's power to
control the destiny of millions of dependent peoples.

In a very real sense, an extraordinary doctrine had begun to
emerge. Because they possessed colonies, the colonial powers were
simply not entitled to enjoy the same rights under the charter as other
nations. In December 1950, for example, the General Assembly acted
on the initiative of Haiti, Mexico, the Philippines, and Syria, and
requested that colonial powers inform the United Nations on measures undertaken to implement the declaration on human rights.
Most administering powers were already voluntarily providing data

on human rights and loudly protested transforming this service into a legal obligation. Since no machinery yet existed to enforce the declaration, legal duties were being imposed on colonial powers that other members did not share with respect to their own citizens. But for the anticolonial majority, this double standard was justified, even at the price of bending the organization's basic operating principles. Thus, while the member states were entitled to the domestic jurisdiction guarantees of article 2, paragraph 7, they could not rely on the mantle of national sovereignty to frustrate the legitimate aspirations of colonial peoples for self-determination and independence.

It would be wrong to conclude that with these actions by the General Assembly the great colonial empires began immediately to crumble. In the period under review, only a handful of territories achieved independence: Jordan, Palestine (Israel), and Libya, former mandated territories; and Burma, Ceylon, Pakistan, Indonesia, Laos, and Mongolia. Virtually all of Africa and much of Asia remained under colonial domination, while the blood-soaked battlefields of Algeria and Indochina would later attest to the will of the colonial powers to defy the United Nations. Still the anticolonial majority had successfully used the UN to arouse world opinion against the abuses of colonialism. The imperial powers were forced to publicly defend their policies against growing sentiment that colonialism was forbidden by the charter. The Committee on Information rapidly spawned other bodies concerned with specific colonial issues such as South-West Africa, the Spanish colonies, and the treatment of Indian nationals in South Africa. In the latter case, after the victory of the conservative Nationalist Party in the elections of 1948, the South African government had extended the policy of apartheid to all segments of the society. In 1951, the General Assembly first condemned this policy, the beginning of a forty-year United Nations campaign for racial justice in South Africa.

SEEKING PEACE THROUGH ECONOMIC AND SOCIAL PROGRESS

There existed at San Francisco a widespread conviction that the roots of war thrived in ignorance, economic instability, and backwardness. As a result, national leaders such as Hitler could, through their aggressive designs, divert popular attention from domestic problems. It was hoped that the United Nations could ensure orderly change and world peace, promoting higher standards of living as well as economic and social progress. Except for the Soviet bloc, most delegates agreed that the promotion of economic prosperity and social justice should be featured among the organization's political objectives. Extensive references in the charter to the economic and social functions of the United Nations demonstrate a much broader commitment to the so-called functionalist approach to peace than had existed, for example, under the League.

Implicit in the decision to establish the Economic and Social Council (ECOSOC) as one of the principal organs of the United Nations was support for a broad initiative on the part of the organization in matters of global economic and social cooperation.

Clearly, the system envisioned by the charter suffered from significant conceptual, political, and administrative shortcomings. Not the least of these was the decision to base membership in ECOSOC on government representation rather than on expertise, thus tying the council's deliberations on hunger, sickness, literacy, and other technical matters to perceptions of national self-interest. Moreover, while the permanent members enjoyed no special privileges, the fact that the world's major industrial powers enjoyed continuous membership was certain to contribute to a conservative attitude on funding of development programs.

The system also suffered from the inherent limitations of national sovereignty. ECOSOC and the General Assembly, under whose authority it functions, are restricted to making non-binding recommendations on economic and social matters. They do not enjoy the legislative and taxing power typically associated with the welfare activities of national governments and, of course, can exercise no authority over the citizens of any member government. The United Nations is, therefore, restricted to initiating studies, setting up programs, and hoping that the members will see fit to support them.

U.S. willingness to assume a large part of the early financial burden proved to be a mixed blessing. While it placed the United States in a unique position of leadership, it also gave substance to the Soviet claim that the West was pursuing the Cold War through the social, economic, and humanitarian activities of the specialized agencies. Indeed, United Nations policy in these areas was no more free from the pervasive blight of Cold War than were the UN's more strictly political activities. Moscow, it will be recalled, opposed the inclusion of social and economic provisions in the charter. Soviet opposition reflected a broad lack of faith in the capacity of international organizations to further Soviet interests, and distrust stemming from the Soviet Union's brief but unhappy experience with the League of Nations. Stalin at times viewed the United Nations simply as a capitalist conspiracy organized to enhance Western influence in its ideological struggle with communism. When it became clear, as early as mid-1945, that the United States was unwilling to grant large-scale loans to the Soviet Union to rebuild its devastated economy, this attitude deepened. United Nations pilot programs, which could hardly begin to meet huge Soviet demands, were attacked as pretexts for capitalist penetration into Soviet domestic affairs. Moscow refused to join most specialized agencies and, throughout the Stalinist period, confined its participation in ECOSOC to systematic limiting of its operations. Its delegates to ECOSOC often attempted to manipulate its programs so as to drive a wedge between the United Nations and the emerging nations.

The United Nations condemned the attitude of the Soviet Union, yet it too remained unconvinced of the value of channeling funds for European recovery or economic development through the United Nations. This reluctance stemmed, in part, from a natural resentment experienced in the United States over the lack of appreciation on the part of many nations; criticism was often coupled with demands for even greater U.S. generosity. At a deeper level, however, the United States was reluctant to entrust the flow of its capital to any third party, least of all an uncontrollable institution in which the interests of the communist members and Third World countries might some day converge to offset Western influence. There was also a fear in U.S. business circles that the United Nations was becoming the source of alien (noncapitalist) ideas.

Actually, Washington's attitude about the relative merits of multilateral and bilateral approaches to foreign aid was grounded less on theory than on the threat posed by Soviet domination of Eastern Europe and the widespread fear that powerful Communist parties in France and Italy might exploit economic misery in those nations. Rebuilding the shattered economies of Western Europe through the Marshall Plan was perceived in the United States as a powerful incentive for the region to remain in the Western bloc. Appeals by supporters of the United Nations, like the Rockefeller Brothers Fund, that greater use of UN-sponsored programs might actually contribute to lessening tensions between the superpowers, went unheeded in Washington, which opted after 1949 for an expanded military presence in Europe. A deaf ear was turned as well to the proposition that a firm U.S. commitment to multilateral economic development aid would ensure its position in the struggle with the Soviet Union for the hearts of the emerging nations.

Nowhere was the attitude of the United States on multilateralism more vividly spelled out than in its stiff opposition to the Special United Nations Fund for Economic Development (SUNFED). In 1951, the General Assembly requested ECOSOC to develop a plan for the creation of a special fund to provide low-interest long-term loans to underdeveloped countries to help them with basic economic-development projects. The request grew out of complaints by the less-advanced nations over the conservative lending policies of the World Bank and the ensuing shortages of development capital. The plan that was finally presented to the General Assembly in March 1953 envisioned the creation of a specialized UN agency, initially capitalized at $250 million from donations by at least thirty nations; underdeveloped countries would have a special claim on these UN funds. Unlike loans from the World Bank, which had only recently begun to flow to Third World nations for sound investments in gas pipelines or electric power projects, this UN money would be earmarked for shakier but no less important investments in the infrastructure (schools, transportation, roads, and so on) of developing countries.

6

SUNFED

In 1945, the economies of Asia, Africa, Latin America, and the Middle East trapped millions in substandard living conditions, well below the levels enjoyed in the industrialized nations. The UN Charter gave consideration to this problem in its preamble and specifically in Article 55, which pledged the United Nations to "promote higher standards of living, full employment, and social progress and development." Beginning in 1946, Secretary-General Trygve Lie, pursuant to this aim, initiated a program of technical assistance through which experts, drawn mainly from the developed nations, were sent to underdeveloped countries to help improve living conditions. Under the impetus of President Truman's 1949 Point Four Program, the General Assembly on November 16, 1949, established the Expanded Programme of Technical Assistance, committing $20 million for the initial eighteen months. While these programs were modestly successful, they failed to generate the large transfers of capital required to stimulate economic prosperity in the developing world. Capital could be obtained only from the competing great powers blocs, which, for different reasons, opposed any expansion of UN aid programs. Washington was committed to European recovery but opposed multilateral aid in principle, preferring instead that economic development be financed through private investment and expansion of existing lending practices. Soviet opposition, mainly ideological, depicted all economic and social programs of the United Nations as a cover for Western imperialism.

From the standpoint of the emerging nations, such arguments were unconvincing and as early as 1948, they began to press for the creation of a new development agency. Speaking at this time before the Sub-Commission on Economic Development, a subsidiary organ of the Economic and Social Council's (ECOSOC) Economic and Employment Commission, Vijendra K.R.V. Rao, professor of economics at the University of Delhi, proposed that the United Nations create an Economic Development Administration to make grants-in-aid and long-term loans with liberal repayment terms to backward nations. The idea quickly took hold and under the vigorous leadership of Hernan Santa Cruz, Chile's permanent representative to the United Nations, it was circulated in the various economic bodies of the United Nations. Early in 1951, Santa Cruz stated the need for the new agency in the following three terms:

First, private investment had failed to meet the needs of economic development. The annual level of U.S. private investment, for example, was less than $1 billion, nearly three-quarters of which was in petroleum-related industries. Moreover, the governments of underdeveloped countries preferred that basic projects be undertaken and run by themselves, not by foreign interests.

Second, the amounts provided through such programs as Point Four and the Colombo Plan had not produced even a modest improvement in living standards in backward areas. Many nations opposed bilateral aid in principle and preferred multilateral programs that were not tied to a particular political ideology or "subject to charges of imperialism."

Third, existing financial institutions, such as the World Bank, could not generate the funds needed to spur economic growth in the underdeveloped world because loans were not permitted to finance non-self-liquidating projects such as highways, schools, and hospitals.

The Santa Cruz statement quickly became the rationale for a comprehensive study of the problem. Under the auspices of the secretary-general, a distinguished panel of experts was assembled, which in the spring of 1951 unanimously agreed on sixteen major recommendations, including a far-reaching proposal to establish an authority to help underdeveloped countries prepare, coordinate, and implement economic development programs.

In the summer of 1951, the committee report began its rocky journey through the United Nations. At the Geneva meetings of the Economic and Social Council, the advanced nations led by the United States defeated a resolution to immediately establish the new agency, an outcome made possible by the nearly equal number of developed and underdeveloped countries on the council. However, the idea was revived that autumn during the Sixth General Assembly in Paris. Following an acrimonious debate, the assembly, in a remarkable expression of independence, instructed ECOSOC to submit a detailed plan for establishing a fund for grants and low-interest loans to underdeveloped countries.

The vote was not widely reported in the United States, but in the European press it was seen as the most serious diplomatic defeat yet experienced by the West in the General Assembly. Pressure for action was certain to mount against the advanced nations, particularly the United States, which might be perceived to be retreating from promises implicit in its International Development Act of 1950. This legislation formally established the Point Four Program and was widely understood to support the efforts of backward nations to develop their resources and improve living conditions. Moreover, the hard line by the West would undoubtedly deepen the disappointment of the Third World, an area that was rapidly becoming a new battleground in the Cold War. However, the advanced nations had apparently concluded that the dangers of relinquishing control of foreign aid programs to UN majorities outweighed any possible benefits of courting the emerging nations.

Lacking U.S. support, the fund was virtually assured defeat, but the stormy Sixth General Assembly had wider implications for the emerging nations, whose people were restless and hungry. The major powers were subjected to an unprecedented outburst of criticism. Many delegates disputed Western claims that the high cost of fighting communism left little money to fund economic development. Beginning in 1951, economic development and international assistance became a constant and recurring theme in all UN organs and the specialized agencies. A new sense of urgency characterized Third World demands for the elimination of ignorance, poverty, and disease in what was termed a revolution of "rising expectations." Increasingly, these demands were merged with attacks on the colonial powers in the Commission on Human Rights and the Trusteeship Commission. The United Nations, till now caught exclusively in the diplomatic crossfire of the Cold War, came to reflect a new political division, one that cleaved along a North–South axis.

Meanwhile, in accordance with the resolution of the General Assembly, the secretary-general in the summer of 1952 appointed a panel of nine experts to prepare a detailed plan for a Special United

Nations Fund for Economic Development (SUNFED). The committee met for seven weeks beginning January 21, 1953, and over the continued opposition of the industrialized nations, made its report to the Economic and Social Council in March 1953. The report envisioned a fund with an initial capital of $250 million raised from voluntary contributions by thirty members. SUNFED would resemble in structure a specialized agency with control and management vested in a director general and a general council composed of all participating members that would approve grants or low-interest loans to contributing members. The report emphasized that close contact be maintained with the World Bank and the International Monetary Fund.

In the months that followed, the industrialized nations were determined to kill the SUNFED proposal. When the Economic and Social Council met in the summer of 1953 to consider the SUNFED report, the United States seized the offensive with a disarmament package that linked development funding to savings from reductions in military spending. The idea was not new. Some months earlier, President Eisenhower had announced the willingness of the American people to devote a portion of savings from arms reductions to help develop the underdeveloped areas of the world. In the current circumstances, the initiative was undoubtedly motivated by a desire to divert attention from the SUNFED report and to delay council action on the fund. It benefited further from the fact that it appeared to be consistent with the policy of emerging nations who in 1950 overwhelmingly backed a similar Indian resolution. However, unlike the U.S. proposal, the Indian initiative was not intended as a substitute for an independent development agency but as an addition to the assembly's Peace Through Deeds Resolution that urged the regulation of all armaments "under a United Nations system of controls." In any event, the council approved a disarmament resolution patterned on the Eisenhower proposal, temporarily postponing a showdown on SUNFED until the Eighth General Assembly later in the year.

When the General Assembly opened in November 1953, the gap that separated the industrial and nonindustrial countries could hardly have been wider. A solid bloc of twenty developing countries led by Yugoslavia, India, and Bolivia favored the immediate drafting of SUNFED statutes and the convening of a conference to establish the fund. The opposition was led by David Zellerback, the U.S. representative to the second committee, who declared that the U.S. government would not contribute to a new international development fund, and recommended against pursuing the "establishment of such a fund." Zeller-back's only concession was to resurrect the U.S. disarmament resolution of the previous summer.

Realistically, the position of the emerging nations had become impossible. Their voting strength in the General Assembly proved meaningless in the face of a resistance by a minority of governments whose cooperation was vital to the success of the fund. With the United States determined to press for passage of its disarmament plan, one that emerging nations could scarcely afford to oppose, there was a real danger that it would become a substitute for SUNFED. Typically, debates on economic matters at the United Nations—SUNFED was no exception—were vehicles for Soviet bloc propaganda against Western imperialism. This, combined with the refusal of the Soviet Union to accompany its support for the principle of economic development with even a token offer of cash, relieved any pressure on the United States to curry the favor of the emerging nations.

Against this background, the underdeveloped bloc salvaged what it could. During a series of closed door talks in early November, which often teetered on collapse, a compromise was reached. The underdeveloped bloc agreed to support an American disarmament measure in exchange for a resolution that authorized the continued study of SUNFED. On December 3, 1953, the General Assembly approved both measures.

The defeat of SUNFED confirms the harsher lessons of this period in the United Nations' history. Human needs were secondary to the political dynamics of the cold war. American opposition was doubtless influenced by the burgeoning costs of the Korean War and European rearmament, but also reflected the truth that the United Nations was useful only to the extent that it served U.S. diplomacy. Washington was unwilling to allow the UN to function as an agency of international cooperation if that meant, as SUNFED did, that U.S. influence within the organization might decrease. The Soviet Union was also unconcerned with suffering in the emerging nations, seeking principally to depict UN efforts to help as novel forms of Western imperialism. Moscow's rigid ideological stance deprived it of the flexibility needed to exploit the political advantages that might have resulted from aligning its policy with support of UN development programs. Finally, the underdeveloped countries were made painfully aware that the emerging assembly majorities would not automatically result in the achievement of political goals. Votes counted for very little when money was needed, especially when the minority controlled the purse strings.

In a broader context, the defeat of SUNFED in 1953 marked the beginning of a longer struggle, and the lessons of the "SUNFED debate" would permeate all UN organs for the remainder of the decade. Moscow moved considerably beyond its lukewarm endorsement of SUNFED to align itself more closely with the Third World: the West was thus forced to reevaluate the importance of the underdeveloped countries in world politics. As the Third World became a central focus in the "competitive coexistence" that characterized the Cold War of the 1950s, Western opposition to UN programs of economic development correspondingly diminished. By 1957, for example, the United States was willing to increase its contributions to the Expanded Programme of Technical Assistance from $30 million to $100 million and to give its qualified support to other multilateral aid programs. It seems impossible to separate U.S. willingness to expand its participation in UN economic development from the pressures generated by the issue of SUNFED.

The plan was defeated by the opposition of the United States, which claimed it could make no contributions until the Cold War ended. Economic troubles in the emerging world were blamed on Moscow, whose policies had forced the West into a costly arms race. Development needs, the United States suggested, might be financed from savings achieved through disarmament. While this argument was disingenuous, it underscored U.S. hostility to aid programs over which the United States did not exercise significant political control. In subsequent years U.S. opposition to SUNFED deepened, and all such programs came to be viewed as attempts by the General Assembly majorities to tax the West for the development needs of the Third World. Apprehensions grew when, following Stalin's death in 1953, the Soviet Union began to support an emerging liberation doctrine at the United Nations that advocated the expropriation of Western investments in developing countries.

Nevertheless, as early as 1948, the United Nations' system of functional programs was rapidly becoming integrated into the organization's shifting institutional and political focus. Naturally there were many difficulties. At first ECOSOC devoted much of its time to World War II relief and reconstruction projects, along with refugee resettlement. Only after the Korean War did it turn to long-term reconstruction and economic development planning. From 1945 to 1948, aside from emergency programs, most of its activities involved technical assistance, statistical services, publication of studies, and so on, and not the diversion of capital to the needy sectors of international society. ECOSOC seemed always swamped with projects demanding funds it simply could not raise, leading skeptics to conclude that the ideals invested in ECOSOC exceeded political realities. By 1947 ECOSOC had already sponsored twenty-two committees and agencies that essentially contributed to the elaborate documentation of problems it could not hope to solve.

Still, like the emerging anticolonial movement, ECOSOC helped to establish links between the United Nations and a host of problems that were largely unconnected to the Cold War. Under the direction of the General Assembly, it expanded the organization's field of vision beyond what Lie had warned was an excessive preoccupation with the affairs of Europe on the part of the Great Powers. In this sense ECOSOC encouraged subsequent interest in the political importance of the underdeveloped world. Debates within ECOSOC focused international attention on the problems of Latin America, Asia, and Africa, while programs under its authority became an integral part of a political agenda that emphasized decolonization and economic growth over the narrow concerns of the Cold War.

Putting this political agenda aside, it is clear that the United Nations still did much to ease economic and social suffering, and generally improved the level of international cooperation during Lie's tenure. Eleanor Roosevelt aptly described the world of the specialized agencies as the "UN nobody knows"; much of their work occurs in such arcane fields as postal administration, refugee resettlement, weather prediction, control of epidemic diseases, improvement of statistics, international exchange of printed material, and control of drug traffic. This is a world of surveys, field missions, statistics, and conferences. Highly trained individuals travel to the four corners of the globe to administer technical assistance programs and to ease human suffering, often on a one-to-one level. Rarely do these activities make headlines, as do the bitter debates in the UN's political organs, and more often than not, actual accomplishments are often difficult to measure. Still they represent the fullest expression of the philosophy that international organization can play a vital role in the furtherance of nonpolitical global cooperation.

It is impossible in a limited space to evaluate fairly the activities of these UN programs. It is hoped that a few impressions bearing on the human dimension of their work will shed some light on their valuable contribution to the alleviation of suffering in the world.

THE EARLY FIGHT AGAINST DISEASE, HUNGER, AND IGNORANCE

The Food and Agriculture Organization

The spirit and dedication of the many men and women who fight the UN's war on poverty, hunger, and disease is revealed in the work of the Food and Agriculture Organization (FAO), whose masthead reads: *Fiat Panis* (Let there be bread). In 1946, the FAO opened its doors to a world in which half the inhabitants went to bed hungry, and it was projected that by the end of the century, there would be an additional four billion mouths to feed.

Although the FAO did not operate a food program of its own, through its studies, reports, programs of technical assistance, and demonstration projects, the organization had an immediate effect on international awareness of hunger and malnutrition and on the effectiveness of government efforts to deal with these problems. In 1946, the FAO conducted the World Food Survey, the first study of its kind, which encompassed 70 countries and more than 90 percent of the globe's population. It revealed that in the following twenty-five years, food supplies would need to double in underdeveloped areas to maintain adequate levels of nutrition and allow for orderly population growth. The study included the preparation of soil maps for every region of the world. By 1949, the FAO had developed a "seed fund" of the outstanding varieties of legumes, cereals, oil seed crops, and vegetables, which member states were invited to use for experimental purposes; the FAO then would collect and distribute the data. Food-growing nurseries were developed to identify disease-free varieties among seeds provided by the Rome-based Seed Distribution Service of the organization. Successful anti-locust programs were launched in ravaged areas of Latin America, Asia, and the Middle East. Excellent studies were published on the control of rats and fungi, and on rat-infestation of food held in storage, contributing importantly to the efficient redistribution of food supplies.

By 1950, the FAO had initiated a broad assault on a variety of diseases that were depleting dairy herds in Europe and in other parts of the world. FAO veterinarians developed a successful vaccine against contagious miscarriage, found a cure for mastitis, and pioneered important advances in the practice of artificial insemination. In China, where rinderpest, a virus deadly to cattle, was killing nearly a million animals a year, FAO veterinarians cooperated with the Chinese Ministry of Agriculture to develop a vaccine, and helped the Chinese government inaugurate a program to vaccinate fifteen million animals annually. Similar programs were subsequently set up in many countries of Africa and Asia. Scientists from FAO have also contributed valuable research in the elimination of foot and mouth disease, hog cholera, poultry diseases, and tuberculosis in cattle.

Cattle and poultry are, however, not in the diet of all people. Rice is the staple in the diet of more than half the world's population. In 1949 the FAO created the International Rice Commission, the first international body concerned with the supply and use of a single food. It developed data on fertilizer application and all other phases of rice production. Valuable work has been done in the scientific cataloging of rice varieties and in the breeding of new strains. From this pioneering work, other agencies evolved to tackle similar problems in the production and use of wheat, barley, and corn.

Much of the success of FAO has resulted from the unheralded dedication and ingenuity of technicians in the field, as in China after World War II. At the time, only the richest farmers used modern techniques of pest control: however, many farmers were aware of the value of certain native plants in killing insects. One such plant, derris, grew wild in China and its roots produced an insecticide called rotenone, but methods of producing and applying it were primitive and limited. A team of FAO technicians in China discovered an abandoned war plant in Shanghai and, using old kerosene drums, pipes, and other junk, built an extractor to manufacture rotenone. With the aide of crude sprayers and dusters, the per-acre production of rice was increased by four to five bushels. Often progress was impeded by cultural resistance to even minor changes to traditional ways of doing things. A single FAO worker in Afghanistan, for example, was able to increase cotton output in the remote north by getting the government to order 30,000 hoes. These illustrations, though modest, are typical of the contributions that FAO technicians, working in close contact with local people, have made in the improvement of nutrition and food production throughout the world.

World Health Organization

Insufficient food was not the world's only problem. At the close of World War II, the scope of human suffering from infirmity and disease was almost too vast to calculate; money was in short supply and the prospects of dealing adequately with global health problems seemed remote. Yet, the World Health Organization (WHO) made its impact felt almost immediately. One of its initial projects was to control the incidence of malaria and the devastating effect this disease had upon the health and productivity of affected populations. Working closely with the Greek government in 1946, a WHO mission supervised DDT spraying of more than 90,000 acres of swamp land and more than 200,000 homes; within three years, the death rate was cut sharply. By 1949 WHO had begun a worldwide assault on the disease, with anti-malarial operations in place in twenty countries, including major campaigns in India and Lebanon. Greek authorities also credited the WHO with helping to bring about significant increases in rice and olive production, and with the near doubling of per capita income of workers in these areas.

From its inception, the WHO has led the international fight against communicable disease. Since the black plagues of the Middle Ages, the world has lived in fear of deadly epidemics. With modern air travel, the rapid spread of contagious disease is unchecked by natural and cultural barriers or even through local quarantine measures.

In the fall of 1947, Egypt faced a cholera epidemic that wiped out 10,000 people within a few weeks of its outbreak. With an incubation period of about five days, cholera could have rapidly spread undetected to other parts of the world. Within hours of the first reported case, the WHO had sprung into action. Agency officials quickly contacted the thirty-six countries that maintained land, sea, and air links with Egypt and instructed health officials on the proper quarantine steps. It assembled data on available supplies of cholera vaccine, promptly delivered the vaccine at reduced cost, and aided Egyptian health authorities in completing a countrywide inoculation program.

Not all achievements of the WHO included the dramatic elements of the Egyptian crisis; many were the result of measured responses to diseases that had afflicted huge populations for generations. Beginning in 1950, the WHO mounted campaigns against smallpox, plague, yellow fever, and typhus. In 1951 it launched the first international attack on tuberculosis. Working with the United Nations Educational, Scientific, and Cultural Organization (UNESCO), the agency undertook the most massive vaccination program in history: 130 million people in forty-one countries during the following decade. Tuberculosis centers, equipped with Bacille Calmette-Guerin (BCG) vaccine, were set up in many countries of Africa, Asia, and Latin America.

Venereal diseases and other diseases with similar symptoms like yaws, bejel, and pinta had long taken a heavy toll in underdeveloped countries, cutting dramatically into productivity levels. Single-shot penicillin drives conducted by the WHO after 1951 in areas with a high incidence of these diseases had a marked effect on their incidence and spread. Since the antibiotic not only arrested but actually cured these diseases, such campaigns had been accompanied by important economic side effects. An anti-yaws campaign in Haiti, for example, was credited with putting 100,000 people back to work. To facilitate its surveillance and control of these and all communicable diseases, the WHO staffs a 24-hour-a-day monitoring service in Geneva.

In addition to its disease-control activities, the World Health Organization quickly became involved in promoting the creation and improvement of health-care systems, especially in underdeveloped countries. By the end of 1952, about twenty-five hundred WHO fellowships had been granted to doctors, nurses, and sanitary engineers in seventy countries. Consultative services were made available to many nations on such matters as maternal and child care, school health programs, nutrition, and environmental sanitation. Special training seminars and demonstration sessions were widely conducted, and literature, lab materials, and teaching equipment provided. Because it is critical that drugs and other biomedical products be manufactured and labeled according to uniform standards, the WHO internationalized the pharmacopoeia, the standard work in the preparation of drugs, making it possible for someone to walk into any drugstore in the world, order a prescription, and obtain the correct formula.

UNITED NATIONS EDUCATIONAL, SCIENTIFIC, AND CULTURAL ORGANIZATION

The men and women of the WHO and the other organizations that lead the UN's fight on hunger, disease, and ignorance have the best of intentions; the work of UNESCO has revealed the basic tension between these good intentions and the utopian quality of these efforts.

The organization was created in the belief that enlightenment, stimulated through intellectual and cultural collaboration, would further respect for "justice and the rule of law." Idealists were naturally drawn to the prospect of overcoming the parochialism of the nation-state by sharing the world's intellectual heritage through cultural and scientific exchanges. Inevitably, the vast scope of UNESCO's mandate invited a duplication of functions performed by other agencies, such as the WHO, the FAO, and the United Nations International Children's Emergency Fund (UNICEF). This often lent an illusory quality to much of UNESCO's own work. Meanwhile, mobile museum units, traveling art exhibits, and orchestras were promoted with little thought given to the actual relationship of these activities to the reduction of world tensions. Criticism also developed over the proliferation of UNESCO seminars and conferences whose benefits did not filter down to those most in need. Finally, UNESCO suffered from controversy surrounding the concept of "global citizenship" it sought to promote. One fortunate reading of UNESCO's plea for global understanding was that it espoused a philosophy of world government, a confusion of aims that UNESCO did little to dispel and that the U.S. right-wing successfully exploited in the early 1950s. Powerful voices in the United Nations accused UNESCO of actively spreading the gospel of atheism and international communism, a factor that explained Washington's early reluctance to support the agency's programs.

Despite these problems, UNESCO embodied the spirit of international cooperation that inspires the United Nations itself. Moreover, it did achieve modest gains, particularly in the field of education, even during the years of its greatest travail. When World War II ended, more than half of the world's population was illiterate; 1.5 billion people could not read a road sign or the label on the merchandise they bought. Illiteracy mired millions of people in superstition, tied them to outmoded agricultural methods, and made them prey to disease. For the millions of people who could not read a newspaper, the blessing of democracy seemed permanently out of reach. In some African nations only a handful of the more than 500 spoken dialects existed in written form.

With a total budget of $9.3 million in mid-1953, UNESCO could scarcely hope to conquer the vast educational needs of the world. It was restricted, instead, to training, research, emergency relief, and cultural exchanges in the hope that broader governmental responses would follow. In 1952 a UNESCO study concluded that the task of bringing basic reading skills to the world's illiterate required an annual expenditure of $1.5 billion and the recruitment of 50 million teachers. It proposed to monitor the educational needs of member states through an education clearinghouse, which also facilitated the exchange of educational data and materials. Educators from various nations worked together at UNESCO seminars and created an impressive body of literature concerning the general problem of illiteracy and its local manifestations.

Basic education centers were established in Latin America and the Middle East; the one at Patzuaro, Mexico, is a notable example of the successful application of basic reading skills to the improvement of living standards. Using technical advice from the FAO and the WHO, UNESCO successfully introduced villagers to modern methods of farming, water resources, insect control, home economics, and nutrition. The villagers' ability to continue to reap benefits depended on their mastering basic skills in reading and writing. UNESCO staff members provided these skills, often by adapting experimental methods to local needs. Visits by training teams from a score of other Latin American nations soon made Patzuaro a model for raising literacy rates throughout Latin America.

In addition to improving the basic education of the world's inhabitants, UNESCO promotes the spread of knowledge through many programs aimed at a more intellectual audience. During the Lie years, UNESCO began to translate the great works of literature into many languages. An impressive collection of the world's folk music was cataloged and housed in the French National Record Library in Paris, and in Turkey, UNESCO established the Educational Film Institute. In addition to traveling museum exhibits, UNESCO sponsored meetings to encourage interaction among museum curators and educators, and lent broad support to such major cultural associations as the International Council of Philosophy and Humanistic Studies, the International Theatre Institute, the International Association of Art Critics, and the International Pen Club.

Not all of UNESCO's work is done in conjunction with private groups. In 1950 UNESCO succeeded in obtaining a lower postal rate on newspaper and periodical subscriptions from the Universal Postal Union. Two years later, an international treaty sponsored by UNESCO abolished import duties on many educational, scientific, and cultural assets in the event of war.

By providing token grants for books, periodicals, museums, laboratories, sound projectors, and so on, UNESCO hoped to stimulate greater contributions on the part of member governments. A unique system of book coupons was developed that enabled soft-currency nations to purchase reading materials in hard-currency nations. In the absence of sufficient political will and funding by the richer nations for its basic education programs, UNESCO could do little to relieve illiteracy in the Third World. It relied, therefore, on the intrinsic ability of art, music, literature, and science to promote international understanding.

There was much about UNESCO's work that could be criticized. There was an elusive quality, not to mention an elitist appeal to many of its programs. It is difficult to believe, for example, that the well-tailored audience at a piano recital came away with a deeper appreciation of the need to relieve world tensions. For that matter, what did the performance have to do with the millions who were mired in poverty and ignorance? Still, it is from sharing the world's cultural gifts at all levels that the links of global understanding are forged. Thus, while those activities could not end the dangerous competition among nations, they, in small ways, renewed faith in knowledge as a way to a better life and ultimately to social and economic justice.

CREATING AN INTERNATIONAL SOCIETY

The history of these specialized agencies demonstrates that the United Nations could contribute significantly to the creation of an international society based on justice and peace. Economic, social, and humanitarian responsibilities were areas of only marginal concern to the Great Powers at San Francisco, yet during the Lie years a reformulation of the UN dream itself was taking place. International concern for the problems of hunger, disease, and ignorance became even more important because they represented the daily reality for more than half the world's population. Colonialism and the gap between the rich nations of the West and the poor nations of Africa, Asia, and Latin America came to be seen as evils that the international community had a duty to eliminate. For an increasingly vocal majority, economic injustices and colonialism were linked less to war than to each other; existing poverty and other social problems were more and more blamed on colonial exploitation.

To a significant degree, this change in the basic focus of the United Nations was a compensatory response to its failure to deal decisively with its primary peacekeeping duties. Supporters of the United Nations welcomed the view that human misery, colonialism, and human rights, matters where the vital interests of the superpowers did not clash directly, were legitimate political concerns of the organization.

Although the United States and its Western allies provided the original impetus for this shift, much of the content and political dynamics of the UN programs were supplied by the emerging nations. Their interests were best served through nonalignment in the struggles of the Great Powers, and so they advocated and pushed a series of anticolonial resolutions and developmental proposals through the General Assembly. A main feature of this was the desire on the part of these nations to avoid cold war entanglements and to seek support from both camps.

Since the General Assembly was the most representative international body in the world—by contrast, the Security Council resembled a strife-ridden private club—its decisions could be equated with genuine world opinion. General Assembly resolutions were invested with great moral authority, even though they lacked the political backing to give life to the ideas they espoused. Paradoxically, the fact that General Assembly resolutions were unenforceable worked in a positive way, because it allowed the assembly to avoid the image of failure associated with the Security Council. The unwillingness of governments to comply with General Assembly resolutions did not lessen their moral force nor did it damage the stature of the United Nations. In the Security Council, the veto paralyzed actions, damaged public confidence, and eventually led to diminished use of the council. But the continued defiance of governments, like that of South Africa over apartheid, only strengthened public perceptions of the positive role of the United Nations in promoting international norms. The General Assembly became a powerful advocate of the world's poor, sick, and oppressed; its functional and humanitarian programs grew and became more diversified. It was, of course, impossible when Lie left office in early 1953 to foresee the political implications of these changes, but even at this early stage, it was evident that the United Nations would continue to influence international events if not in settling disputes, then at least in determining the humanitarian agenda for the future.

7

A Matter of Perspective

The architects of the United Nations were part visionary and part guardians of the past. The organization and the principles embodied in the charter linked a familiar yet dangerous past with a future full of novel political relationships and new perils. World War II had destroyed all illusions about the manageable character of modern warfare. Aerial bombardment and advancing armies laid waste to much of Europe and Asia, while Hiroshima and Nagasaki introduced the grim prospect of total annihilation.

Motivated by widespread sorrow and public revulsion to war, the victorious Allies fulfilled their wartime pledges to create a permanent international organization devoted to the maintenance of peace and security. For guidance they looked to the past: to the League of Nations for the structure and rationale of the new organization, and to the nineteenth-century Concert of Europe for the organization's basic operational principle. Nations would confirm their common devotion to the concept of collective security through the obligations they undertook as a condition of membership in the United Nations, much as they did under the League. In assigning the main responsibility to control war to the permanent members of the Security Council, the charter sought to institutionalize the concert system by which the major powers of Europe had cooperated to limit and control violence following the Napoleonic wars.

Obviously, something went wrong. An unbridgeable gap quickly developed between the agreement to uphold the principles of the charter and the applicability of those principles to specific disputes. Common membership did not produce consensus on the procedural role that the United Nations would assume in the management of international conflict. Rarely, if ever, did opposing parties to a dispute agree on the forum of the United Nations as a suitable site for negotiation. Instead, one side initiated a complaint in the Security Council or General Assembly while the other denied all allegations, justified its actions on existing treaty obligations, or retreated to the domestic jurisdiction provisions of the charter. Complaints to the United Nations were likely, therefore, to be regarded as hostile acts by the party being hauled before the world body.

One by one the pillars on which rested the United Nations system of collective security toppled. Efforts to provide the organization with military forces were a dismal failure. Members retreated to old habits, seeking safety in military alliances and arms buildups, justifying these activities on the right to "individual and collective self defense" guaranteed under Article 51. Even the concept of universality, a principle upon which the vitality of any international organization fundamentally rests, was sacrificed to the momentary passions of the Cold War.

World leaders resolved the tension between their loyalties to humanity and to their national interests by invariably choosing the latter. They might justify foreign policies by reference to the charter since a universal respect for its principles was recognized, but they refused to recognize that the charter could inhibit them in any way. The United Nations thus assumed an important but limited function in the diplomatic calculations of both sides in the Cold War. As the French philosopher Jean-Jacques Rousseau once said of international law, resort to the United Nations was simply war by other means.

Understandably, the UN's record of accomplishment under these circumstances was meager, especially in the resolution of international conflict. Some success was achieved in reducing or controlling violence in Indonesia and Palestine and in the India–Pakistan dispute over Kashmir. However, only in Indonesia were the underlying political differences also resolved. Despite the absence of a direct clash in Great Power interests, no settlement of outstanding political differences proved possible in Palestine or the Indian subcontinent. If anything, divisions became even more pronounced. It may be that the United Nations hastened the withdrawal of British and French forces from Syria and Lebanon by focusing world attention on these problems, but it should be pointed out that even broader condemnations at the UN of French policy in Tunisia and Morocco had no material effect. Some observers have speculated that the risk of war in Berlin was reduced because the United Nations provided a supplementary diplomatic channel while talks in the Council of Foreign Ministers and the Allied Control Council were stalled. But it would be a mistake to overstate the importance, for example, of the Jessup–Malik talks, which merely confirmed Stalin's decision to lift the blockade in the face of the successful airlift. Finally, while the Korean War is widely viewed as the high point in the practical application of the theory of collective security, its true historical importance is that it ended any effective operation of the system envisioned under the charter.

Much early frustration over the failure of the United Nations to fulfill its peacekeeping functions centered on the veto and particularly on its frequent use by the Soviet Union. Not only was the veto power widely considered a major defect in the design of the United Nations, but also Moscow was perceived as placing its selfish interests above the needs of the international community. Conversely, the absence of Western vetoes was equated with support for the principles of the charter. Strengthening the United Nations became associated, therefore, with charter reforms, like the Uniting for Peace Resolution that sought to modify the veto, or eliminate it altogether. But the frequency of Soviet vetoes was a symptom, rather than a cause, of the breakdown in Great Power unity that paralyzed the Security Council. It was also a natural result of using the council for the accomplishment of divergent political ends. As a consequence, the council became burdened with issues such as Greece, Iran, Czechoslovakia, Trieste, and Berlin that it could not hope to settle. Soviet vetoes, therefore, equally reflected the United States and its Western allies' disregard of the underlying conditions that would allow the Security Council to function smoothly. In the absence of prior agreement among the permanent members on the suitability of the Security Council as a forum to resolve a dispute, deadlock was inevitable.

True, the Western members of the Security Council had yet to cast a veto when Lie left office early in 1953. However, this was less a reflection of self-discipline than of the fact that the West could protect its vital interests without resort to the veto. On all cold war issues the West could count on at least seven Security Council votes or a "hidden veto" to block passage of hostile communist initiatives. As observed earlier, only the move to seek an extension of Lie's term of office in the General Assembly had prevented the United States from casting its first veto in 1950. And it is interesting to note that when the United States eventually broke its pledge on the veto in 1970 on the Rhodesian question, it was not to protect vital interests, but as a gesture of support for the United Kingdom.

On the other hand, the Soviet Union used the veto less irresponsibly than is commonly believed. Only twice, in the Syria-Lebanon case in 1946 and on the Indonesian question in 1949, did Soviet vetoes reflect cold-war posturing and in neither case did the vetoes impede the outcome sought by the United Nations. Mostly, the Soviet Union relied on the veto to protect its vital interests, support client governments, or generally to overcome its isolation in the organization. Of the fifty-nine Soviet vetoes cast during the Lie years, thirty-six were used to block approval of Western-supported membership applications, a block that the West was able to achieve through its "hidden veto" of Russian favorites.

8

The Case of Indonesia

The Indonesian dispute arose out of the clash between Indonesian desires for independence and Dutch resolve to restore colonial ties with its island empire, ties that had been temporarily suspended by the war. On August 17, 1945, just two days after the Japanese surrender in the Pacific, Indonesian nationalist leaders declared their independence from the Netherlands and announced the formation of the Republic of Indonesia. In the following weeks the republic adopted a constitution and extended its control over much of Indonesia. An Allied liberation force under the command of Adm. Lord Louis Mountbatten arrived in Indonesia on September 29, and found itself caught between the fires of Indonesian nationalism and demands for a restoration of Dutch authority. Almost immediately, fighting broke out between Mountbatten's British and Indian empire troops and Indonesian rebel units. An influx of Dutch troops led to a rise in violent incidents and protests from republican leaders that Britain was easing the return of Dutch colonialism. Burdened by the costs of keeping the peace, London pressured Dutch and republican leaders into negotiations. But in the existing climate of extremism, talks begun under the guidance of Sir Archibald Clark Kerr, a top British diplomat, collapsed and by the end of 1945, the crisis in Indonesia had become acute.

On January 21, 1946, the representative of the Ukrainian Socialist Republic (SSR) charged in the Security Council that Dutch and Indian troops were violating the Indonesian people's right of self-determination and that the situation in Indonesia posed a threat to international peace and security. Clearly, the complaint was prompted by more than devotion to charter principles. Lodged simultaneously with a Soviet complaint regarding the presence of British troops in Greece, the Ukrainian charges were probably in retaliation for the Iranian complaint against the Soviet Union only weeks earlier. Realistically, Soviet bloc support short of military intervention could do little for the Republic, but the Soviet Union might use the issue to embarrass the West and possibly to enhance Russian influence in Southeast Asia.

Against this background, the effect of the Ukrainian complaint was to submerge the Indonesian cause within broader East–West tensions and to direct the focus of the Western members of the council to the political demands of that conflict. The United States seemed most concerned with minimizing adverse public reaction in the Third World and in preventing Soviet participation in any committee of investigation. France and the United Kingdom supported Dutch claims that under article 2, paragraph 7 of the charter, the Security Council lacked jurisdiction over the dispute. Under these circumstances, no action on the substance of the Ukrainian complaint was possible, and on February 13, the council declared the matter closed.

With the Security Council debate at an end, the dispute resumed its original shape. Indonesian leaders persisted in their demands for independence and the Dutch were equally determined to reassert sovereignty over the archipelago, although they were unable to deliver a decisive blow against the poorly equipped rebel forces. Meanwhile, under a direct British threat to remove all troops from Indonesia, the Dutch finally agreed to meet republican officials at Hoge Velewe to discuss a federated plan patterned on the recently concluded French–Indochina agreement. On November 15, 1946, an agreement, marked by important concessions on both sides, was apparently reached at Lingadjati. However, differences of interpretation quickly arose, assuring a renewal of hostilities. Charging that the presence of Dutch troops in Indonesia amounted to aggression, the republic disputed the authority of The Hague to set the terms for a transfer of power. On July 22, 1947, the Netherlands responded with a broad military offensive.

In separate letters dated July 30, 1947, India and Australia brought the situation in Indonesia to the attention of the Security Council once again. Although Australia stressed that it was "condemning no one," India, more concerned with its image in the Third World, charged that Dutch actions constituted a "breach of the peace" under Chapter VII of the charter. In contrast to the inaction that followed the Ukrainian complaint eighteen months earlier, the council quickly approved a number of pro-Indonesian measures. An immediate cease-fire was ordered that momentarily relieved Dutch military pressure on rebel forces, and Indonesian representatives were invited to participate in future Security Council deliberations. The council also established a consular commission to observe the cease-fire and a three-member Good Offices Committee to "assist in the pacific settlement" of the dispute.

However, Dutch interests were also importantly reflected in the Security Council's actions. The council failed to provide a mechanism to enforce the cease-fire or to order a withdrawal of troops, an omission that allowed Dutch forces to continue occupying areas formerly under republican control. There was no reason to believe that the Dutch would not augment these gains by violating the cease-fire, and it was widely expected that the Consular Commission, because of its procolonial bias, would reflect Dutch interests in reporting violations. Moreover, since the survival of the republic depended on a quick settlement, the likelihood that the Good Offices Committee would be mired in protracted negotiations, combined with the Netherlands's war of attrition threatened to further erode the republic's position.

Thus, although the United Nations was now directly involved, the fate of the republic was still greatly in doubt. Nearly two years of Dutch military pressure had weakened its authority in many parts of the islands and another full-scale offensive threatened complete collapse. As anticipated, the Dutch did violate the cease-fire and in September 1947, the Consular Commission reported that the war might resume at any moment.

A Dutch victory now appeared assured and when the Good Offices Committee arrived in Batavia on October 27, The Hague's attitude had markedly stiffened. Nevertheless, prolonged and difficult negotiations were begun aboard the USS *Renville,* which produced a truce agreement on January 17, 1948. A second accord, consisting of eighteen points, provided the basis for further talks on the shape of a future Dutch–Indonesian federation. The accord reflected the weakened position of the republic, for while the Netherlands agreed that the federation would emerge from free elections, it insisted on the full restoration of Dutch sovereignty in the interim period. For practical purposes, this meant that during this period, the republic would cease to exist. Despite the inequitable terms of the Renville Accords, the Security Council approved the agreement on February 17, 1948.

In the aftermath of the Renville Accords, Dutch negotiators showed little inclination to cooperate with the Good Offices Committee to implement a political settlement. During June 1948, the Security Council met at the request of Australia to discuss the matter, but the failure of the council to strengthen the role of the Good Offices Committee only added to Dutch intransigence; in July, negotiations completely collapsed and fighting resumed. By the end of the year, Dutch forces had imposed a virtual blockade of Indonesia and had set up friendly governments through the archipelago. On December 18, the Dutch arrested rebel leaders, including President Achmed Sukarno and Prime Minister Mohammed Hatta, and mounted a broad offensive to totally crush the rebellion.

The following day the United States called for an emergency meeting of the Security Council. This startling shift in American policy was undoubtedly influenced by Sukarno's suppression of a communist uprising the previous September. The debate was barely under way when a U.S. State Department bulletin expressed confidence in the Indonesian leaders, the Republican government of President Sukarno and Prime Minister Hatta. On December 22, the United States withdrew $15 million in aid from the Netherlands East Indies.

Not surprisingly, the Security Council passed a sweeping resolution that ordered another cease-fire and the release of all political prisoners. On January 7, 1949, the Security Council met again at Lake Success, following a brief holiday recess, to learn from the Good Offices Committee that the Dutch were violating the resolution on December 24. After a heated three-week debate, the council decided to intervene directly in the peace process. On January 29, it reconstituted the Good Offices Committee into the UN Commission for Indonesia and instructed it to supervise negotiations leading to the establishment of "an independent and sovereign" United States of Indonesia no later than July 1, 1950.

The Netherlands could hardly fail to grasp the meaning of the situation that was unfolding. U.S. economic and military aid were vital to the success of Dutch policy in Indonesia. In April 1949, the U.S. Congress threatened a further withdrawal of funds through an amendment to the Economic Assistance Act that tied Marshall Plan aid to compliance with "prevention or enforcement actions by the United Nations." The move meant that the policy of the United States was virtually synonymous with that of the Security Council. Meanwhile, international support for the republic grew. In New Delhi, a conference of Asian nations led by Prime Minister Jawaharlal Nehru called for the transfer of power to the republic. India, joined by Australia, brought the dispute to the General Assembly, which passed a resolution urging the parties to reach an accord consistent with the wishes of the Security Council.

Against this background the Netherlands asked for talks. In April and May, preliminary agreements in Batavia ended the fighting and established the framework for a Round Table Conference at The Hague. On November 2, 1949, The Hague conferees, with the prodding of the UN Commission for Indonesia, agreed to the complete transfer of sovereignty over the Dutch East Indies from the Netherlands to the Republic of Indonesia. The agreement brought almost four years of intermittent fighting to an end. On December 29, 1949, the final transfer of sovereignty took place in Amsterdam and nine months later, the United States of Indonesia was admitted to the UN.

Indonesia represents the major exception in an otherwise dismal early United Nations record of response to rising Third World demands. The Netherlands, like other members of the victorious Western alliance in World War II, was determined to reestablish colonial ties in areas that had been occupied by Axis powers. Without external assistance, the poorly equipped Indonesian rebels were almost certain to be crushed. For more than three years the UN had been the principal link between the struggling republic and the outside world, and it was apparently pressure from the Security Council that eventually forced the Netherlands to capitulate to Indonesian demands.

Undoubtedly, this satisfactory outcome was the result of the unusual measure of agreement among the Big Four. This agreement enabled the Security Council to maintain a positive role in the dispute at junctures critical to the republic. Divergent interests in the Cold War were present throughout the council's prolonged consideration of the case but were not allowed to decisively impede progress. In a bitter footnote to the successful outcome, the Soviet Union did veto a resolution that sought to congratulate the parties, but throughout the lengthy and torturous negotiations, Soviet actions appeared to have been motivated mainly by a desire to embarrass the West and by the fear of jeopardizing its own standing in the Third World. Although the Netherlands attempted to capitalize on American anti-communism, aroused by the Ukrainian complaint in 1946, the United States remained an active participant in the work of the Consular Commission and the Good Offices Committee.

Outwardly, the Security Council had compelled the Dutch to abandon Indonesia, but by the end of 1948, after almost three years of UN
intervention, the military balance greatly favored the Dutch, and
Indonesia was about to capitulate. It was not until the United States
determined that Western interests would best be served through the
creation of an independent and non-aligned Indonesia, that the survival of the rebels was assured. The American decision was made
against the certainty of Dutch resentments and uneasiness on the
part of Britain and France who opposed any expansion of the role of
the United Nations in colonial disputes. It also occurred as the Cold
War was taking shape and Western Europe was being mobilized
behind U.S. leadership against the background of the Czech coup
and the Berlin blockade. It is difficult to know the exact calculations
that convinced the United States to choose support for the Indonesian nationalists over its European allies, but once the decision was
made, the Dutch were forced to abandon their island empire. It might
be argued that the UN was irrelevant to this outcome, but it is impossible to fully separate U.S. actions from the public exposure that the
dispute received in the United Nations, which induced Washington
to favor a result consistent with Charter principles.

Conflicting East–West attitudes on the veto, therefore, had little to
do with relative devotion to the charter; rather, they underscored the
fact that the United Nations was not a world government but a league
of sovereign states. In the absence of a political consensus on the content of resolutions, the United Nations would, in any event, be powerless to give effect to its decisions. From this perspective, divergent
interpretations of the charter were an expression of political realism.
Soviet policy benefited from a strict construction of its veto provisions
while Western interests were served by a more generous view.

More important, the early years established a vital precedent for the
future when cold war issues would cease to dominate the organization. In 1965 the membership of the Security Council would be
expanded to fifteen, reflecting the growing influence of the emerging
nations, but also depriving the West of its council majority on colonial
and development issues. It was predicted that, as Moscow came to
align its interests with those of the Third World, a dramatic decline in
the frequency of Soviet vetoes would also occur. Correspondingly, the
number of vetoes by Western members would greatly increase as they
became the target of hostile initiatives on colonial and other issues.

From a more realistic standpoint, Soviet vetoes merely exposed the limits that existed on international cooperation for the maintenance of peace and the promotion of solutions to social, economic, and humanitarian problems. In fact, in the face of Western determination to transform the organization into an instrument of its cold war policy, the veto may have avoided a deeper retreat into isolation on the part of the Soviet Union. It seems fair to say that by setting the limits of permissible intrusion into the sovereign affairs of the major powers, the veto also established the boundaries of potential consensus within which solutions to international political problems were possible.

Actually, the paralyzing weight of the veto was the most overt sign of a deeper problem: the discrepancy that existed between the "world of the charter" envisioned by the framers at San Francisco and the global arena in which the United Nations was forced to function. World leaders were expected to set high standards of international behavior and to choose the rule of law over power politics in their dealings with one another.

Membership in the UN implied acceptance of the organization as the supreme spokesman for the international justice and morality members were pledged to uphold. It followed that they would bring their problems to the United Nations with some confidence in the wisdom of the outcome. These assumptions, however, rested on an image of the world that was largely fictitious. The conduct of world affairs continued to be based on calculations of national self-interest and not on the existence of a global community organized around the central vision of the charter. Not only would the members deny the authority of the United Nations to settle disputes among themselves, but the organization would also come to mirror the tension and discord in its external environment.

Even under conditions of moderate, localized unrest, a discrepancy of this magnitude would impose immense strains on the capacity of the UN to preserve its functional independence. But as we have seen, the Cold War that descended on the world in the wake of World War II was neither moderate nor local in character. The choice that the Cold War offered was between absolute good and absolute evil. The battlefield became the entire globe. World politics became dominated by a bipolar pattern of hostility anchored in the mutual fear and suspicion of the United States and the Soviet Union. To make matters worse, in Western controlled areas, conditions more than resembled the ideals of democracy and the rule of law expressed in the charter. This encouraged the leadership in Washington to equate

the containment of communist expansion with support for the charter and to downgrade the value of the United Nations as a vehicle for
bridging East–West hostility.

The bipolarity of the external world was quickly reflected in the
pattern of political influence developed within the United Nations
itself. In the General Assembly the smaller nations, operating under
the one-nation, one-vote rule, attempted to exert some influence over
world affairs through the mechanism of General Assembly majorities. But even there the Cold War quickly inflicted itself on assembly
deliberations. Under the leadership of the United States, a majority
of forty to forty-five votes was forged to register disapproval of
Soviet violations of the charter. The pattern was no different in the
Security Council. Although, like the United States and the USSR,
China, France, and the United Kingdom were permanent members
of the Security Council, their political influence was not commensu-
rate with their legal status. Save for rare occasions, such as Indonesia
and Palestine, Security Council deliberations were dominated by the
relationship between the two superpowers. Even when the common
interests of the Western Big Three were at stake, as they were during
the Berlin crisis and Iran, decisions about the use of the Security
Council were made essentially by the United States.

While it is not surprising that external political realities would be
mirrored in the work of the United Nations, the pervasive effect of the
Cold War shocked even hard-bitten realists. No organ was immune.
Cold War positions were reflected in the debates of the Economic and
Social Council and in those of the Trusteeship Council. They penetrated into discussions about economic development, colonialism,
and disarmament. Even the admission of new members to the United
Nations, a matter linked intrinsically to the basic purposes of the organization, became mired in cold war hostility. The agendas of the various organs became cluttered with issues that the organization could
not hope to settle. Accusations by Moscow of U.S. warmongering—
such as American support for the Baruch plan and "open skies"—
scored propaganda points but did little to test the UN's actual capacity to reduce world tensions.

In fact, the ease with which the United States legitimized its containment policy in the United Nations revealed an even deeper irony:
relationships between the superpowers may actually have become
worse because of the United Nations. As we have seen, the organization was always available to register condemnations of communist

policy and to confirm that the "opinion of mankind" supported the West. Winning votes in the United Nations was far easier than nego- tiating with the difficult and suspicious Joseph Stalin. Whenever negotiations stalled, whether on disarmament, Berlin, or Korea, the United States could press its case in the UN and win. Naturally, the Soviet Union was unlikely to accept majority support for the Baruch plan or the General Assembly's program for the unification of Korea as substitutes for lengthy and complex negotiations. Condemnations by the United Nations could not alter the fate of Czechoslovakia or dispose Soviet leaders to a less brutal suppression of human rights behind the Iron Curtain. Their sole effect was to deepen the crusade atmosphere that already was attached to cold war differences.

It is, of course, impossible to know precisely how much more diffi- cult the normalization of relations between the United States and the Soviet Union became because of public confrontations that occurred at the United Nations. What we do know is that nations sincerely inter- ested in reducing tensions rarely expose adversaries' weaknesses to public humiliation but, instead, emphasize positive aspects of their relationships. We know also that later thaws in the Cold War were invariably accompanied by diminished resort to public forums like the United Nations unless agendas were agreed on beforehand. Indeed, the United Nations would prove to be of little use in the future resolu- tion of outstanding differences between the superpowers.

SECRETARIAT BECOMES
HOSTAGE TO COLD WAR

Nowhere was the effect of the Cold War more devastating than on the office of secretary-general. While it was impossible to foresee the per- manent impact that the Cold War's strains on Trygve Lie would have on the future of his office, the short-term implications became imme- diately clear. Lie assumed office in 1946 as the ideal compromise can- didate; his uncynical devotion to internationalist ideals and his many years in public life had earned him the respect of both Washington and Moscow. Yet, when he left office seven years later, few mourned his departure. Moscow, infuriated with Lie's stance on Korea, forced him to live his final years in office in lonely isolation. Furthermore, Lie's early stands on Iran and Berlin, together with his strong support for seating Peking in the Security Council, had alienated the U.S. State

Department. For good measure, the Arabs were outraged over his support of the Palestine partition plan and, because of his timid response to State Department loyalty investigations of Secretariat personnel, Lie had also lost the confidence of much of his staff.

Although Washington vigorously backed Lie's bid for reappointment, this was more a test of American prestige and influence within the organization than it was genuine approval of the secretary-general's conduct of his office. When Lie had outlived his usefulness on Korea, Washington's ardor also diminished. By the time Lie left office in early 1953, his main claim to impartiality seemed to rest on the fact that he had incurred the wrath of both sides in the Cold War. And while much of the animosity directed toward Lie resulted from the courageous stands he had taken on more than one occasion, the net effect was to ensure that the office of the secretary-general would for a time remain a hostage to the Cold War.

In fairness, Trygve Lie was probably saddled with an impossible job. The expectation at San Francisco was that the secretary-general would assume a more active diplomatic role than had his predecessors under the League. The authority of the secretary-general to bring breaches of the peace before the council under Article 99 not only conferred unprecedented legal authority on the chief administrative officer of an international organization, but also implied a wide range of political initiatives that he might independently undertake. The problem, of course, was that the secretary-general's legal powers were severely limited by the political understanding on which they rested. First of all, the appointment of the secretary-general was subject to the veto, which meant that his political effectiveness rested on the continued influence of the permanent members. It was also understood by the Big Five that the secretary-general's powers under Article 99 would be invoked only rarely—actually, when one of them for political reasons saw fit not to bring a breach of peace to the Security Council—and never in a dispute in which one of them was involved.

The disintegration of Great Power unity meant that, on most issues, Lie lacked consensus for his political initiatives. Only if the major powers could be persuaded to dissociate their vital interests from issues that came before the United Nations would Lie have enjoyed any room to maneuver. Conceivably, Lie might have adopted the Drummond model of quiet efficiency, concentrating on his broad administrative duties and offering his good offices only when his neutrality remained assured. It is doubtful, however, that he could have avoided becoming embroiled in East–West problems or, for that matter, that the major powers would have tolerated a posture of total neutrality. This was particularly true under the conditions that applied, for example, to an issue like Korea, where the United Nations had become fully integrated into Washington's diplomatic calculations. When Lie chose a bolder course, he abandoned all hope that he could remain free of criticism by one or the other side in the Cold War. He justified his actions by claiming that the charter made the secretary-general the chief spokesman for international morality and asserting that the UN was expected to play an independent role in world affairs. But Lie was forced by circumstances to implement this approach against the background of a political struggle between mutually exclusive views of justice. Neither the Soviet Union nor the West recognized the UN as "representing a third way," but instead strove to align the charter with their respective political interests. Thus, when Lie's defense of the charter coincided with Soviet interests, as it did on Iran or Chinese representation, he was applauded for his independence; when it did not, as with Korea, Lie was ostracized politically and socially. In fact, the secretary-general's vulnerability to criticism was uniquely personal. Although he spoke officially as the representative of the Secretariat, much as any delegate to the UN spoke for his nation, the positions he took were likely to be attributed to him directly.

In retrospect, Lie brought many of his problems on himself. He seemed not to fully appreciate the need to subordinate his private feelings to his role. Although he occasionally took positions that conflicted with Western interests, Lie's basic loyalties lay with the West. Broadly speaking, Lie believed that Western policy expressed the values of the charter more fully than the Soviet Union's. His stand on Korea, no doubt, reflected his belief that Soviet designs were basically aggressive and, although it may have been morally correct to publicly criticize the North Korean attack, his total identification with U.S. interests destroyed his credibility as a diplomatic channel in the Cold War.

The secretary-general also demonstrated naiveté in judging national attitudes about the place the UN occupied in world affairs. For example, he appeared genuinely shaken by Moscow's extreme reaction to the part he had played in Korea. From his perspective, the Soviet Union should have been able to separate its unhappiness over UN policy from any ill will toward those who, like himself, were only discharging their duties under the charter. Palestine provides a further illustration of Lie's tendency to misread national reactions. For reasons that remain unclear, Lie lobbied intensely for General Assembly approval of the partition plan for Palestine, despite Arab pledges to oppose the plan with force if necessary. He was deeply dismayed when the Arab states went to war, apparently believing that, since thirty-three members of the General Assembly had voted for partition, the Arabs would adjust their policies accordingly. When the permanent members of the Security Council refused to back the plan with force, Lie concluded that the credibility of the United Nations itself had been damaged. The secretary-general seemed oblivious to the huge gap that often existed between the political factors that influenced a government's vote on a UN resolution (the United States and USSR voted for partition) and those that determined a government's willingness to back a resolution politically or militarily.

More importantly, Trygve Lie appeared incapable of tying his actions to a coherent doctrine of the office he occupied. Many supporters of the United Nations stressed its value as an instrument of public diplomacy, a view that stemmed from the widely cherished belief that wars were, in some measure, the result of secret agreements. Although this view did not deny the fact of private negotiations, it asserted that suspicions engendered by secrecy might be reduced by appeals to world opinion, recorded agreements, the setting of deadlines, and even the opportunities to publicly blow off steam. The secretary-general was at the center of these activities; he was the most visible UN spokesman for world opinion and, through the staff of the Secretariat, provided governments with legal advice, conference facilities, and other services. His successful advocacy of public diplomacy, however, depended on the ability to present himself as a valued intermediary in private and often delicate negotiations, and demanded that he retain the trust and confidence of all parties to a dispute.

While Lie understood the dynamics of this process, he failed to apply them consistently. He began by boldly asserting his powers in Iran, Trieste, and Palestine, apparently believing that if he tied his actions to the charter, the office itself would remain immune from criticism. After the Berlin crisis, Lie pulled back from political controversy, showed bitterness against both protagonists in the Cold War, and stressed the needs of the emerging world. However, with the unveiling of his Twenty-Year Peace Plan, Lie seemed to undertake a mission to save the United Nations single-handedly. But this led not to statesmanlike aloofness from the trials of the Cold War but rather to Lie's calamitous identification with U.S. interests in Korea. The net effect of all this was to deny to future holders of the office a developed conceptual or institutional framework to build on. Dag Hammarskjöld, Lie's successor, had to rebuild the shattered relationship with the Great Powers and to fashion a concept of the office that was uniquely his own.

The effectiveness of the secretary-general was not the only cold war casualty in the UN. One of the more striking features of the failure of the Security Council to discharge its peacekeeping responsibilities was a growing preference of many members for the General Assembly, a shift in the organization's political center of gravity. The ability of the superpowers to control the content and direction of political debate diminished as an increasing volume of non-cold war issues came before the world body. As the General Assembly's activities expanded, the image of the United Nations as the "town meeting of the world," to borrow Sen. Arthur Vandenberg's phrase, also grew. General Assembly resolutions came to represent for many the aspirations of mankind for a saner and more prosperous world. But this shift implied both serious limitations and dangerous tendencies.

Clearly, the "town meeting" analogy was misleading. Decisions of the General Assembly were not law. The powers of the General Assembly, unlike those of the Security Council, were strictly recommendatory. While assembly resolutions carried some moral weight, which in the long run might prove more valuable than statutes, their practical application remained nominal. For assembly resolutions to be more than symbolic, there would have to be a reasonable likelihood that they could influence a change in the behavior of states with whose vital interests they clashed. This required delicate political calculations about complex and often unknown relationships, which, at a minimum, demanded restraint in pursuing unenforceable resolutions simply because a majority existed for their passage.

Unfortunately, the sober restraint required to give assembly resolutions their maximum political impact was too often missing. For the West in the early years, the temptation to align foreign policy with majority rule in the General Assembly was too great to resist. Inevitably, the emerging nations came to realize that the burdens of actions were infinitely heavier than the responsibilities of decision.

Additionally, the idea that nations could be persuaded by the weight of world opinion to adopt moral positions that conflicted with national self-interest was illusory. A vivid reminder of the limitations involved is contained in the following exchange that took place at the Paris Peace Conference in 1919. Woodrow Wilson, who wished to apply the mandates principle to islands that Australia occupied, challenged William Hughes, the Australian Prime Minister: "Mr. Hughes, am I to understand that if the whole civilized world asks Australia to agree to a mandate in respect to these islands, Australia is prepared to defy the appeal of the whole civilized world?" Hughes replied, "That's about the size of it, President Wilson." The attitude of the Australian leader is neither an isolated nor an extreme expression of sovereignty that nations have consistently adopted. It is not surprising, therefore, that the Soviet Union defied world opinion in Czechoslovakia; that Australia would implement its "White Australia Policy" despite adverse world opinion; that human rights violations around the world would mount in the face of broad international opposition; or that South Africa would continue to inflict apartheid on its black majority in defiance of hundreds of UN resolutions. States accused in the UN of violating human rights inevitably defended policy on claims of domestic jurisdiction, a favorite defense of the colonial powers, or, like the Soviet Union, insisted that all such attacks were politically motivated.

The credibility of United Nations' moral pronouncements was further weakened by the emergence of bloc politics in the General Assembly. Majorities tended to reflect the political influence of powerful members like the United States or the political dynamics of regional unity that existed, for example, in the Middle East or within the emerging Afro-Asian bloc. This resulted in the uneven, often hypocritical, character of many General Assembly resolutions. The United States, for example, supported the right to self-determination for peoples living behind the Iron Curtain, but refused to apply this principle to those living under the political domination of its principal NATO allies. Early U.S. control of a solid anticommunist bloc on virtually all Cold War issues resulted in a steady stream of Soviet condemnations and, at the same time, contributed to the impression that human rights violations did not occur in the West.

A double standard quickly became evident. Members of dominant blocs within the General Assembly were largely immune to attacks on their moral shortcomings. The forums of the United Nations, for example, were simply not available for human rights initiatives by outsiders like the Soviet Union. Unfortunately, this pattern persisted, even after the Cold War ceased in the 1960s, to control the agendas of the various organs. As the General Assembly came to reflect the interests of the Afro-Asian anticolonial majority, denunciations would be largely reserved for the Western colonial powers, South Africa, and later Israel, while the iniquities of Afro-Asian members would remain largely ignored. Under these circumstances, agreement on the charter as a source of moral guidance was severely shaken.

PURSUING POLITICAL OBJECTIVES AT THE PRICE OF INCREASED TENSION

An even greater danger lay in the possibility that the General Assembly majority's continued recourse to confirm the righteousness of foreign policy might actually intensify hostilities. Reducing international tensions requires the promotion of habitual attitudes designed to allay suspicions, create positive feelings, and build goodwill. Such attitudes are reinforced through the development of diplomatic rules and of institutions that contribute to the success of difficult negotiations. As we have seen, these factors were largely missing in the broadening of the General Assembly's powers. For example, from Moscow's perspective, the West's decision to move into the General Assembly those issues that the Soviet Union had vetoed reflected an unwillingness to live by the rules. Consideration of these issues by the General Assembly was unlikely, therefore, to alter the outcome or strengthen the organization's constitutional authority; it would merely confirm the West's determination to overcome the inevitability of the veto on further action. Trygve Lie observed, for example, that the United States' move to seek Assembly action on the Balkans following Soviet vetoes in the Council indicated that "the issue had passed beyond the stage of possible negotiations between the West and the Soviet Union." In moving non-negotiable issues to a friendlier forum, therefore, the West signaled its willingness to pursue its political objectives even at the price of exacerbating tensions with a difficult opponent.

The wider implications of this pattern were ominous. The constitutional responsibilities of the Security Council and the General Assembly became increasingly blurred following the breakdown of the council's primary responsibilities; the choice of one organ over the other became, therefore, largely a tactic related to broader, often hostile, political strategies. The constitutional meaning of unenforceable resolutions became less important than the spotlighting of political grievances. For example, Third World complaints to the Security Council in the early 1950s regarding French colonial policy in Tunisia and Morocco were unrelated to the council's authority over matters of peace and security, but were brought there to show the seriousness of French violations. When the Western-dominated council refused to deliver the desired condemnations, recourse was sought in the friendlier confines of the General Assembly. On these and other issues, therefore, the tendency to seek political victories in whatever forum became available.

Much as the Western powers had introduced various cold war items onto the assembly's agenda with no thought given to their effect on East–West relations, the emerging nations would seek similar opportunities to denounce imperialism and racism with a similar disregard for actual results. The anticipation of majority support for hostile resolutions encouraged repeated recourse to the General Assembly. It also tended to invite more extreme language in assembly debates and in resolutions, particularly in the face of continuing noncompliance, which the majority was inclined to view not as protection of vital interests, but as defiance of world opinion.

As the Trygve Lie years drew to a close, it became evident that a huge discrepancy existed between the international system envisioned in the charter and the revolutionary forces that the UN was expected to manage and control. The former relied on a successful merger of traditional democratic concepts with the emergent needs of a war-weary world. It presupposed the existence of a consensus on the value of a global organization to control conflict and on the purposes—basically revealed in the Atlantic Charter—for which World War II had been fought. In short, the UN hoped it could reestablish and make more secure the status quo antebellum. But the major postwar challenges to world order came from the fierce ideological competition that developed between the Soviet Union and the West, and from the bitter struggle waged by colonial peoples to break free of foreign domination. Under these circumstances, an updated and strengthened version of the Concert of Europe would not work. Not only did the Soviet Union fail to share the West's vision of political stability in Europe, but it also supported destabilizing political movements in Asia, Africa, and the Middle East. Violent struggle, through revolution and wars of national liberation, was quickly incorporated into the doctrines of the anticolonial movement, which also denied the value of charter-based—mostly Western—concepts of democracy and economic development. In a real sense, therefore, the United Nations was a relic before it went into operation, an organization predicated on a concept of world order that was irrelevant to the struggles that were taking shape.

Still, the United Nations in 1953 remained the most powerful symbol of mankind's highest aspirations for peace and justice. It had survived—if not terminated—the awful strains of the Cold War that threatened to strangle it. The Soviet Union retained its membership despite near-total isolation within most UN organs and the bitter defeat it endured over Korea. With the passing of the Stalin era, Moscow would increasingly link its own self-interest with majority decisions of the General Assembly. By 1955, the deadlock over admissions would be broken, and the organization would move toward the ideal of universality. Eventually, the United Nations would represent virtually every human being on earth. The Lie tenure, sadly, also demonstrated that the dream of a functioning system of collective security was still an illusion. But this expectation had rested on the unrealistic belief that the UN could be insulated from the political conflicts that surrounded it; it presupposed politicians so devoted to peace that they would hardly have need of the United Nations. As the UN prepared for its first change of leadership, only the symbol remained vital. It remained to be seen if statesmen could ever move the organization beyond the symbolic stage and allow the principles of the charter to influence the choices they made.

Chronology

1939

July 12   League of Nations Secretary-General Joseph Avenol accepts an American offer to move the technical sections of the League Secretariat to Princeton, New Jersey.

August 23   Prime ministers Vyacheslav Molotov and Joachim von Ribbentrop sign Nazi–Soviet Treaty of Non-Aggression; a secret protocol provides for future territorial arrangements in Poland, Finland, and the Baltics.

August 31   Under a cloud of suspicion for his rightist sympathies, Avenol resigns his League post.

September 1   Germany invades Poland and war in Europe begins.

September 3   Britain and France declare war on Germany and Belgium declares its neutrality. President Franklin D. Roosevelt's "fireside chat" announces American neutrality but encourages moral support for the Allies.

September 28   Meeting in Moscow, Molotov and Ribbentrop agree on the division of Poland.

September 29–October 5   Moscow forces the Baltic states to sign treaties of mutual assistance.

October 2   Under the leadership of publisher William Allen White, the Non-Partisan Committee for Peace through revision of the Neutrality Act is formed to lobby for changes in American neutrality.

October 11   President Roosevelt is informed by Albert Einstein and fellow scientists that an atomic bomb is a possibility.

November 4   Congress modifies the Neutrality Act of 1939 to allow "cash-and-carry" delivery of arms to belligerent nations; the arming of U.S. merchant ships is approved.

November 29   Russia severs diplomatic relations with Finland and, without a declaration of war, invades its territory.

November 30   Russia invades Finland.

1940

March 12   Treaty of Moscow ends Russo–Finnish War.

April 9   Germany invades Denmark and Norway.

May 10   German forces invade the Low Countries.

May 15   British Prime Minister Winston Churchill asks Roosevelt for the loan of over-age destroyers.

May 29   In a nationwide broadcast, James B. Conant, president of Harvard University, warns of the dangers of Nazi victory and urges release of air and naval equipment to France and England.

June 4   With the evacuation of Dunkirk virtually completed, Churchill rallies the British people to defend their homeland.

June 5   Germany invades France. General Charles de Gaulle vows continued French resistance.

June 10   "Stop Hitler Now" advertisements prepared by historian Robert E. Sherwood appear in newspapers around the country.

June 22   Vichy France signs an armistice with Germany.

June 26   Berlin accedes to Russian territorial demands in the Romanian provinces of Bukovina and Bessarabia; the territory is later formed into the Maldavian SSR, bringing the total number of union republics to sixteen.

July 20   President Roosevelt signs a bill authorizing a two-ocean navy to defend the Western Hemisphere.

September 3   Roosevelt authorizes the transfer of fifty over-age destroyers to the British naval command.

September 27   The Italo-German-Japanese "axis" military alliance is formed.

November 12   Moscow refuses an offer by Berlin to join the Axis coalition.

December 17   During a press conference in Washington, Roosevelt defends actions to support Britain in the war as vital to U.S. security.

December 30   During one of his fireside chats, Roosevelt declares that the United States must become the "arsenal of democracy."

1941

January 6   During his annual State of the Union message to Congress, Roosevelt recommends a "lend-lease" program; he proposes the "Four Freedoms" as basic to the Allied war effort.

January 10   Historic lend-lease bill is introduced in Congress.

January 27   Secret United States–British strategic talks begin in Washington and agreement is reached on a defeat "Germany first" policy.

March 11   Roosevelt approves the Lend-Lease Act allowing the Allies to receive arms and equipment from the United States by sale, transfer, or lease.

April 24   Greek army surrenders to Hitler's forces.

May 3   In a telegram to Roosevelt, Churchill suggests that the United States enter the war on the side of the Allies.

May 10   Rudolf Hess, Hitler's chief deputy, flees to Scotland.

May 27   In a Pan American Day speech, President Roosevelt proclaims a state of national emergency and orders German and Italian consulates in the United States to close by July 10.

June 22   German, Finnish, and Romanian troops invade Russia in Operation Barbarossa; Italy and Romania declare war on the Soviet Union.

June 24   Roosevelt approves lend-lease aid to Russia.

July 12   Anglo–Soviet agreement is signed pledging each power to cooperate in the war against Germany.

August 14   Roosevelt and Churchill meet at sea and issue a joint statement of principles known as the Atlantic Charter. The two leaders pledge support for the creation of a "permanent structure for peace" following the war.

October 2   Battle of Moscow begins; successful Russian resistance results in the first major setback to Germany in land fighting since 1939.

October 11   Roosevelt privately proposes Anglo-American merger of resources to develop an atomic bomb.

October 17   Japanese Prime Minister Prince Fuminaro Konoye resigns and is replaced by the more militant General Hideki Tojo.

November 17   U.S. Ambassador Joseph Grew cables from Tokyo that the Japanese are planning a surprise attack somewhere in the Pacific.

December 7   Japanese bomb the U.S. fleet at Pearl Harbor.

December 8   The United States declares war.

December 22   Churchill arrives in Washington to discuss plans for the conduct of the war.

1942

January 1   UN Declaration, signed in Washington, pledges twenty-six nations to a joint effort against the Axis based on the principles of the Atlantic Charter.

January 6   In his annual State of the Union Address to Congress, Roosevelt commits U.S. support to postwar collective security arrangements.

February 15   Singapore falls to Japanese forces.

February 28   U.S. Gen. Dwight D. Eisenhower proposes a cross-channel invasion of Europe.

March 9–July 15 Committee of the U.S. State Department meets secretly to begin work on a charter for a postwar international organization.

May 26 England and Russia sign treaty of alliance against Germany; each agrees not to join any coalition against the other for twenty years.

May 30 Roosevelt promises Soviet Premier Joseph Stalin to open a second front in Europe by the end of the year.

July 2 Major Nazi attack is launched on the Soviet Union, which leads to the heroic Russian defense of Stalingrad.

July 16 Churchill persuades U.S. officials to put off a cross-channel invasion in favor of the liberation of French North Africa.

July 23 Secretary of State Cordell Hull publicly announces U.S. support for a collective security system backed by force.

August 7 U.S. Marines land on Guadalcanal, beginning the long process of seizing Japanese-held strategic points in the Pacific.

October 23 Hull initiates State Department study on a charter for an international organization.

November 8 Eisenhower leads the Allied invasion of French North Africa.

November 19 Red Army begins long-planned counteroffensive at Leningrad, forcing the defeat of the German Sixth Army and the eventual collapse of Germany's Russian campaign.

1943

January 14–24 Roosevelt and Churchill meet at Casablanca and announce a policy of "unconditional surrender" as the basis for ending the war.

February 24 Allies begin around-the-clock bombing of Germany.

March 16 Bipartisan support for a postwar security organization is expressed by U.S. Sens. Joseph Ball (Minnesota), Harold Burton (Ohio), Carl Hatch (New Mexico), and Lester Hill (Alabama).

March 26   U.S. State Department produces a rough plan for a world organization.

May 12–25   Anglo-American Conference takes place in Washington to discuss global military strategy; Britain tentatively agrees to the creation of a postwar international organization.

May 18   Conference on Food and Agriculture takes place in Hot Springs, Virginia. The Food and Agriculture Organization (FAO) is established.

May 22   As a concession to its Western allies, Moscow announces the dissolution of the Third Communist International (Comintern), the association of world communist parties.

July 10   Allied armies led by Gens. George Patton and Bernard Montgomery begin the invasion of Italy.

July 25   Benito Mussolini, Italian dictator, is deposed.

August 14   Meeting in Quebec, Churchill and Roosevelt confirm plans for Operation Overlord, the cross-channel invasion of France.

September 21   Fulbright Resolution, adopted by the House of Representatives, favors U.S. participation in the creation of a lasting security system.

October 19–30   Allied foreign ministers meet in Moscow. Britain, China, United States, and the USSR declare their intention to create, "at the earliest practicable date," an organization to maintain "international peace and security."

November 5   Connally Amendment expresses Senate approval for U.S. participation in permanent security system. Amendment reserves Senate prerogative of approving all treaties by two-thirds vote.

November 9   Forty-four nations meet in Washington to form the United Nations Relief and Rehabilitation Administration (UNRRA), a means to channel aid to war-devastated areas.

November 28   Big Three meet at Tehran and agree on opening a second front in France.

December 24   Roosevelt appoints Eisenhower Supreme Commander of the Anglo-American invasion forces.

1944

January 4   Soviet dispatches report that the Red Army has crossed the 1939 border into Poland.

January 10   Moscow announces its readiness to guarantee a strong and independent Poland, provided the Polish government accepts the Curzon Line as the border between Poland and Russia.

January 17   *Pravda* charges that Nazi Foreign Minister von Ribbentrop and British officials have secretly met to arrange peace.

May 12   International Labor Organization (ILO) issues a "last warning" to Nazis that they will "pay with their lives" in the event of further destruction in occupied territories.

May 20   Communist Party of the United States is dissolved by the Party convention in New York.

June 4   Rome is occupied by Allied forces.

June 6   D-Day. Allied invasion of continental Europe is launched along a 100-mile front in northeastern France.

July 1–22   Forty-four nations attend the UN Monetary and Financial Conference at Bretton Woods, New Hampshire. The conference establishes the International Monetary Fund and the World Bank.

August 21   Dumbarton Oaks Conference opens in Washington, D.C. Agreement is reached on many details relating to the creation of a permanent international organization, but the United States and Soviet Union fail to agree on the scope of the veto.

August 25   U.S. and French forces liberate Paris.

September 2   U.S. forces enter Belgium.

October 23   United States, Great Britain, and Russia recognize the regime of Charles de Gaulle as the provisional government of France.

November 1   Fifty-four nations gather in Chicago to draw up the Convention on International Civil Aviation. The Provisional International Civil Aviation Organization (PICAO) is established.

November 21   Secretary of State Hull, the driving force behind a

U.S. commitment to a postwar international organization, resigns because of ill health.

1945

January 3   In outlining America's war aims before Congress, Roosevelt stresses unconditional surrender; self-determination for Greece, Poland, and all liberated areas; and peace based on the principles of the Atlantic Charter.

January 5   Conventions on maritime and aerial travel are signed in Washington.

January 17   Soviet forces take Warsaw, after permitting German armies to destroy its ghetto.

January 20   In Moscow an armistice is signed between the Provisional National Government of Hungary and the Allies.

February 4–11   Big Three meet at Yalta. Agreement is attained on a veto formula and the United Nations formative conference is scheduled for April 25 in San Francisco.

February 13   Soviet forces capture Budapest after a fifty-day siege.

March 8   U.S. Army troops enter Germany across the bridge at Remagen.

April 12   Roosevelt dies suddenly at Warm Springs, Georgia. Harry S. Truman becomes thirty-second president of the United States; he immediately decides to open the San Francisco conference on schedule.

April 17   President Truman signs an extension of the Lend-Lease Act.

April 22   Soviet forces enter Berlin.

April 25   First contact of Soviet and U.S. troops is made at Torgau on the Elbe.

April 25–June 26   Fifty nations attend the United Nations Conference in San Francisco and the Charter of the United Nations is drafted.

April 28   Benito Mussolini is shot to death by partisans near Lake Como.

April 29 At Allied headquarters in Italy, Germany signs an unconditional surrender covering Italy and Austria.

April 30 In Berlin, Soviet forces seize the shattered Reichstag building and hoist the Soviet flag.

May 1 Adm. Karl Doenitz succeeds Adolf Hitler, who committed suicide at German operational headquarters beneath the Reich Chancellery.

May 4 German forces in the Netherlands, northeast Germany, and Denmark surrender to Sir Bernard Montgomery.

May 6 In a little red schoolhouse at Reims, France, German military forces surrender unconditionally to the Allied Command.

May 23 In London, the coalition government of Prime Minister Churchill, formed in 1940, resigns.

June 5 European Advisory Commission establishes German occupation zones. Berlin is divided among the occupying powers but is situated wholly within the Soviet zone.

June 6 Interim agreement on International Civil Aviation comes into force.

June 8 Acting U.S. Secretary of State Joseph Grew denies report of a secret understanding at Yalta by which the Soviet Union would receive Korea in exchange for entering the war against Japan.

July 17–August 2 Truman, Churchill (later, Clement Attlee), and Stalin meet at Potsdam to set terms for the Japanese surrender. A Council of Foreign Ministers is created to negotiate outstanding territorial differences in Europe and to prepare peace treaties with Austria, Hungary, Bulgaria, Romania, and Finland.

July 18 State Department denies that Stalin brought a Japanese surrender offer to the Potsdam Conference.

July 21 Senate approves U.S. membership in the United Nations Food and Agriculture Organization.

July 28 Senate ratifies UN Charter by a vote of 89–2.

August 3 Allied forces institute a complete blockade of shipping to and from the Japanese home islands.

August 6   Atomic bomb is dropped on Hiroshima, a city of 343,000 people, on Truman's order.

August 8   In accordance with arrangements made at Yalta, the Soviet Union declares war on Japan. Truman denies that any secret deals were made at Potsdam.

August 9   A second atomic bomb destroys Nagasaki.

August 10   Japan offers to surrender providing that the emperor retains his throne. Washington agrees, but on condition that the emperor submit to the authority of the Allied Supreme Commander Gen. Douglas MacArthur.

August 14   Sino–Soviet treaty is signed, incorporating concessions made to the Soviet Union at Yalta. Japan surrenders unconditionally.

August 16   Dean Acheson becomes undersecretary of state, succeeding Grew.

August 23   Stalin announces that Soviet forces have conquered Manchuria and the southern portion of Sakhalin Island.

August 27   U.S. troops begin the first occupation of Japan in 1,000 years.

September 6   Truman submits a twenty-one point program to Congress designed to ease the transition from war to a peacetime economy.

September 8   In London, during the Big Five foreign ministers' meeting, Foreign Minister Molotov proposes that the Soviet Union assume responsibility for administering a UN trusteeship over the former Italian colony of Tripoli.

September 9   MacArthur announces a complete takeover of the Japanese government, including the emperor. Self-government would be restored only under Allied direction.

September 11   Council of Foreign Ministers fails to reach agreement on peace treaties for Italy, Bulgaria, Hungary, and Romania.

October 2   In London, following twenty-two days of talks, the first postwar peace conference fails to reach agreement on European peace terms.

October 8   Speaking in Union City, Tennessee, Truman announces that the United States will not share technical information about the atomic bomb with any nations but the United Kingdom and Canada.

October 9 Gen. George Marshall warns against a precipitous U.S. demobilization and urges retention of universal military training.

October 23 Occupation authorities decree a new bill of rights for Germany, providing equality before the law for all Germans and revoking all Nazi penalties.

October 24 UN Charter goes into effect; the organization formally came into being when the Soviet Union deposited the twenty-ninth ratification in London.

October 27 Speaking in New York City, Truman announces that the United States will not recognize any governments imposed by force; he urges international cooperation on atomic energy.

November 6 Speaking at Moscow's celebration of the 1917 Revolution, Molotov promises the Russian people that they, too, will have an atomic bomb.

November 10 Prime Minister Clement Attlee of Great Britain and Prime Minister W. L. Mackenzie King of Canada arrive in Washington to discuss a plan for international control of atomic energy under the UN.

November 15 Truman, Attlee, and King issue a joint declaration calling for the creation of an international atomic energy commission.

November 16 Constitution for the United Nations Educational, Scientific, and Cultural Organization (UNESCO) is adopted in London.

November 20 Nazi war crime trials begin in Nuremberg, Germany.

December 27 Moscow Foreign Ministers Meeting endorses the creation of the Atomic Energy Commission (AEC).

1946

January 10 General Assembly has its first meeting at Central Hall, Westminster, London. Representatives of all fifty-one charter members are present. Paul-Henri Spaak, foreign minister of Belgium, is elected first president of the assembly.

January 12   General Assembly elects the first Economic and Social Council. Elected for one-year terms are Colombia, Greece, Lebanon, Ukrainian SSR, the United States, and Yugoslavia; two-year terms go to Cuba, Czechoslovakia, India, Norway, USSR, and United Kingdom; those with three-year terms are Belgium, Canada, Chile, China, France, and Peru. The General Assembly selects Brazil, Egypt, Mexico, New Zealand, Norway, and Poland as nonpermanent members of the Security Council, and elects the fifteen members of the International Court of Justice.

January 16   Before the first General Assembly in London, Norwegian Foreign Minister Lie, recently defeated for the presidency of the assembly, proposes a role for the small nations in the maintenance of peace.

January 19   Allies create an International Military Tribunal for the Far East (IMTFE) to try Japanese war criminals. Iran complains to the Security Council that the presence of Soviet troops in its northern provinces constitutes interference in its internal affairs and a threat to international peace.

January 21   Soviet Union protests before the Security Council the continued presence of British troops in Greece, citing their presence as a violation of Greek sovereignty and a threat to the maintenance of peace. The Ukraine lodges a complaint with the Security Council that accuses the British government of using troops to suppress a movement of national liberation in Indonesia.

January 23   First session of the Economic and Social Council (ECOSOC) is held in London.

January 24   By unanimous vote, the General Assembly creates the Atomic Energy Commission (AEC).

January 25   Albania applies for admission to the UN.

February 1   Lie, foreign minister of Norway, becomes the first secretary-general of the United Nations by a vote of 46–3.

February 2   General Assembly instructs the Economic and Social Council to emphasize rehabilitation of areas devastated by the war.

February 4   Syria and Lebanon ask the Security Council to order the immediate and unconditional withdrawal of British and French troops from their respective territories. The Security Council establishes the Military Staff Committee and instructs it to study the creation of a UN "police force." (Article 43)

February 5   Britain and the United States recognize the reconstituted government of Romania.

February 6   Following an inconclusive discussion of the Greek situation, the Security Council removes the issue from its agenda.

February 9   General Assembly bars Franco's Spain from membership in the United Nations or its specialized agencies. The General Assembly asks that Secretary-General Lie's annual report include information on non-self-governing territories under Article 73e. The war on colonialism at the United Nations begins.

February 12   General Assembly approves creation of an International Refugee Organization (IRO) to examine the problems of displaced persons. General Assembly assumes all League of Nations responsibilities in the field of narcotics control. Shortly, all remaining League assets are transferred to the United Nations.

February 13   Following a short debate on the Ukrainian complaint on Indonesia, the Security Council closes the matter with no action taken.

February 14   General Assembly resolution urges all members to help ease the international shortage of grains and rice.

February 15   Security Council refuses to hear a Soviet complaint that the presence of a Polish émigré "army" in Italy threatens "calm and order" on the Italian–Yugoslav border.

February 16   Soviet Union vetoes Security Council resolutions calling for British and French troop withdrawal from Syria and Lebanon; it claims neither resolution goes far enough in condemning the presence of troops.

March 5   Churchill delivers his famous "Iron Curtain" speech in Fulton, Missouri; he denounces "police governments" in East Europe and calls for an "alliance of English-speaking peoples" to resist Soviet expansionism.

March 21   United Nations moves into temporary headquarters at Hunter College in the Bronx, New York.

March 25   Soviet troops begin to leave Iran, a UN triumph.

March 28 U.S. State Department makes public the Acheson-Lilienthal proposals for international control of atomic energy.

March 31 Western powers supervise elections in Greece after the Soviet Union refuses to participate.

April 2–3 Separate letters to the secretary-general from the Soviet Union and Iran report the successful negotiation of Soviet troop withdrawals.

April 3 International Court of Justice officially opens at The Hague.

April 8 UN Committee on Refugees and Displaced Persons meets in London and concentrates on the chaotic situation in Europe. Poland asks that the Security Council advise all members to sever diplomatic relations with Franco's Spain.

April 14 Iran withdraws its Security Council complaint against the Soviet Union.

April 16 Lie's legal memorandum opposes retaining the Iranian complaint on the future Security Council agenda. Over strong Western objections, Lie argues that Soviet–Iranian negotiations end any role for the Council.

April 18 Mandates system comes to an end: twelve of the League's mandated territories remain in existence.

April 21 The Socialist Unity Party (SED) is established in the Soviet zone of Germany; two days later it merges with the Communist Party.

April 25 Acting on an Australian proposal, the Security Council creates a committee to determine if the Franco regime in Spain is a threat to peace and security.

April 30 Following negotiations with the governments of Syria and Lebanon, Britain and France agree to withdraw their troops.

May 3 Gen. Lucius Clay, the U.S. representative on the Allied Control Council, announces the end of reparations to the Soviet Union from the United States in Germany.

May 22 Security Council completes its discussion of the Iranian complaint but decides over strenuous Soviet objections to retain the item on its agenda.

May 25 In his opening speech to the Economic and Social Council in New York, Lie reflects the hope that the UN's social and economic functions will contribute to world peace despite East–West tensions.

May 31 Security Council refuses to hear Siam's complaint of provocative acts by French troops on its border with Indochina.

June 6 A subcommittee finds no basis for Security Council action against Spain under chapter VII of the Charter; it recommends the diplomatic isolation of the Franco regime.

June 16 Presidential adviser Bernard Baruch presents the United States' plan for international control of atomic energy but the Soviet Union rejects the plan.

June 21 Economic and Social Council creates the temporary Subcommission on Economic Reconstruction of Devastated Areas and creates working agreements with the International Labor Organization (ILO), UNESCO, and the Food and Agriculture Organization (FAO).

June 24 Mongolian People's Republic applies for UN membership.

June 26 Lie uses the introduction to his first annual report to assert an independent political role for the secretary-general as spokesman for the United Nations.

July 2 Afghanistan applies for UN membership.

July 5 FAO is asked by the General Assembly to make a country-by-country study of food supplies, the first survey of its kind.

July 8 Jordan applies for UN membership.

July 11 Britain and the United States agree to merge Western occupation zones in Germany.

July 29 Paris Peace Conference opens; delegates from twenty-one states meet in Luxembourg Palace to discuss draft treaties with enemy powers.

August 2 Ireland, Iceland, and Portugal apply for UN membership.

August 5 Siam (Thailand) applies for UN membership.

August 9 Sweden applies for UN membership.

August 24 Ukraine requests a Security Council investigation of

Greek actions on the Albanian border as a threat to Balkan political stability.

August 28   With eight membership applications pending before the Security Council, Lie publicly supports the principle of universal membership and *en bloc* admission of applicants.

August 29   Security Council unanimously recommends the admission of Afghanistan, Iceland, and Sweden. Albania and Mongolia fail to receive seven affirmative votes in the Security Council, and the Soviet Union vetoes the applications of Jordan, Ireland, and Portugal.

September 6   Secretary of State James Byrnes pledges U.S. support for the social and economic unification of Germany.

September 19   Churchill proposes the creation of a Council of Europe, a first step toward a "United States of Europe."

September 20   Western and Communist members of the Security Council remain hopelessly divided over the situation on the Greco–Albanian border. The council defeats Soviet and Polish resolutions and drops the matter from its agenda. Lie, under Article 99, publicly claims broad discretionary powers to perform diplomatic functions in matters threatening international peace.

October 3   UNESCO assumes responsibility of the International Institute for Intellectual Cooperation created by the League of Nations.

October 5   Britain and the United States declare that recent Bulgarian elections, which returned a majority for the Communist Party, violated Yalta's pledge of free elections.

October 11   The Economic and Social Council instructs the secretary-general to study the financial implications of reconstruction efforts in war-torn areas.

October 24   In his supplementary oral report to the General Assembly, Lie seeks authorization for the construction of additional office space to relieve cramped conditions at Lake Success, N.Y.

October 27   Moscow signs peace treaties with Italy, Bulgaria, Hungary, Romania, and Finland and urges the United Nations to admit Bulgaria, Hungary, and Romania as members.

October 30   After months of inconclusive debate, the Security Council is unable to adopt any measure regarding Franco's Spain that is acceptable to all permanent members. The Spanish question is dropped from its agenda.

November 12   United States and Britain denounce "rigged" elections in Romania; communists and social democrats join to control the government.

November 18   Soviet troops briefly occupy the Iranian province of Azerbaijan.

November 23   Haiphong is bombed by France, and the Indochina War begins.

December 1   Secretary-general estimates reconstruction costs for Europe at almost $11 billion. Iran reoccupies Azerbaijan without opposition.

December 3   Greece complains to the Security Council that Albania, Bulgaria, and Yugoslavia are interfering in its civil war and requests an immediate investigation.

December 4–12   Council of Foreign Ministers meets at Waldorf Hotel in New York to put five treaties with the enemy in final form.

December 10   American millionaire John D. Rockefeller offers $8.5 million to purchase an East River site for the United Nations.

December 11   General Assembly establishes the Economic Commission for Europe to plan the economic reconstruction of Europe. UN recommends that all members adopt measures to ensure the equality of men and women. A General Assembly resolution declares genocide a crime under international law. Appealing for funds to meet relief needs for 1947, the assembly asks members to give the equivalent of one day's pay from each of their workers.

December 12   General Assembly calls on all members to sever diplomatic relations with Spain.

December 13   Trusteeship agreements for New Guinea, Ruanda-Urundi, French Togoland, French Cameroons, Western Samoa, Tanganyika, British Togoland, and the British Cameroons are approved.

December 14   General Assembly asks the Security Council to consider the general regulation and reduction of armaments. UNESCO is authorized by the assembly to translate the world's classics into the languages of the members of the UN. The Trusteeship Council is officially established as a principal organ of the United Nations.

General Assembly creates an International Refugee organization as a temporary specialized agency; it assumes the refugee responsibilities of the United Nations Relief and Rehabilitation Administration (UNRRA) and, like that agency, is financed by private contributions. By unanimous vote, the assembly instructs the secretary-general in cooperation with the specialized agencies to assume the social functions of UNRRA; the action is the first program of technical assistance undertaken by the UN. The United Nations rejects a petition by South Africa to annex the former mandated territory of South-West Africa. World Health Organization (WHO) is created.

December 18   Security Council establishes a Commission of Investigation to study foreign interference in the Greek civil war.

December 30   Atomic Energy Commission (AEC) approves the "Baruch plan" for international control of atomic weapons.

December 31   Council of Foreign Ministers asks the Security Council to approve draft treaties regarding the Free Territory of Trieste. Afghanistan, Iceland, and Sweden are admitted to the UN. The first report of the AEC advocates placing atomic energy and its uses under United Nations' control by international agreement. UNRRA ceases operations.

1947

January 1   U.S. and British occupation zones in Germany are merged.

January 10   Security Council unanimously approves the statute for the Free Territory of Trieste and the instrument for the Free Port of Trieste. In an unsolicited legal opinion, Lie supports the Security Council's authority to enforce the provisions that deal with Trieste in the Italian peace treaty.

January 13   Acting on a United Kingdom request, the Security Council agrees to consider the appointment of a governor-general for Trieste. The Soviet Union opposes the move, pending the signing of a peace treaty with Italy.

January 19 Communist-controlled elections in Poland result in the defeat of the Peasant Party. Western governments again accuse the Soviet Union of violating its Yalta pledge of free elections.

January 20 Security Council takes up the Corfu Channel dispute between Britain and Albania. Britain claims damage to ships and loss of life due to the presence of mines laid by Albania.

January 23 Economic and Social Council establishes the Commission on Narcotic Drugs.

January 27 Eleanor Roosevelt, widow of President Roosevelt, becomes the first to chair the Commission on Human Rights, a body created by ECOSOC on January 23.

February 10 Allies sign peace treaties with Italy, Bulgaria, Hungary, Romania, and Finland.

February 13 Security Council instructs the Military Staff Committee to develop the principles that should govern the organization of the UN armed forces.

February 14 Economic and Social Council creates an Economic Commission for Asia and the Far East.

February 17 United States submits a draft trusteeship agreement for the Marshall, Mariana, and Caroline islands in the Pacific.

February 25 Economic and Social Council creates an Economic Commission for Latin America.

March 4 Britain and France sign the Treaty of Dunkirk, which pledges mutual support against a future German attack. This is the first step toward a new alliance system in Western Europe.

March 10 Moscow Foreign Ministers Conference opens but fails to reach agreement on the future of Germany or further reparations.

March 12 Truman requests congressional aid for Greece and Turkey and announces U.S. intentions to aid all victims of tyranny. The Truman Doctrine recognizes the global competition between the West and the Soviet Union, which comes to be known as the "Cold War."

March 24 Commission for Conventional Armaments has its first meeting at Lake Success, N.Y.

March 26   In his first address to the Trusteeship Council, Lie calls its work vital to the Third World's peaceful and orderly transition from dependency to self-government.

March 28   Economic and Social Council creates the Economic Commission for Europe.

March 29   Lie undertakes a study of the methods of social welfare administration in use in different countries.

April 2   Security Council approves United States trusteeship over the Trust Territory of the Pacific Islands. The United Kingdom requests a special session of the General Assembly to consider the question of Palestine.

April 9   Security Council agrees to a British request that the Corfu Channel dispute be submitted to the International Court of Justice.

April 28   Siam (Thailand) is admitted to the UN.

April 30   Military Staff Committee submits its first report to the Security Council, but reaches no agreement on the nature or size of UN forces. Security Council rejects the membership application of Hungary, submitted April 22.

May 9   World Bank grants France a reconstruction loan of $250 million.

May 15   General Assembly establishes the United Nations' Special Committee on Palestine (UNSCOP).

June 5   Marshall Plan is launched in a Harvard commencement speech as Secretary of State George Marshall proposes U.S. participation in the economic rehabilitation of war-torn Europe.

June 22   Soviet Union vetoes the Baruch plan.

June 25   Commission on Human Rights begins to draft the Universal Declaration of Human Rights. The Commission of Investigation for Greece issues a three-volume report on border unrest; Albania, Bulgaria, and Yugoslavia are blamed for aiding Greek rebels in the civil war.

June 26   General Assembly approves the Headquarters Agreement with the United States.

June 27   Good Offices Commission to investigate and settle frontier disputes between Greece and its neighbors is approved by the Security Council.

July 1   Former Counsellor of Embassy in Moscow George F. Kennan signing his article as X outlines the U.S. policy of "containment" in the July issue of *Foreign Affairs*. International Refugee Organization (IRO) begins to function; more than 700,000 people become dependent on it for food and shelter.

July 2   Soviet Union rejects the Marshall Plan and forces its East European satellites to refuse to participate.

July 4   In the introduction to his second annual report, Lie expresses disappointment over the world political situation, which has prevented progress on signing of peace treaties, war relief, and atomic energy. He urges the superpowers to cooperate in strengthening the United Nations.

July 8   Egypt complains to the Security Council about the presence of British troops in Egypt and the Sudan.

July 18   Argentina requests that the General Assembly call a general conference to "abolish the veto."

July 21   The Economic and Social Council defeats a Norwegian proposal for the universal adoption of the metric system.

July 30   Australia and India bring the issue of Dutch military activities in Indonesia to the attention of the Security Council.

August 1   Security Council calls for a cease-fire in Indonesia.

August 7   World Bank grants the Netherlands a reconstruction loan of $195 million. Security Council establishes the Consular Commission and the Good Offices Commission to investigate the situation in Indonesia.

August 15   India and Pakistan achieve independence; the latter immediately applies for UN membership.

August 18   Security Council approves the membership applications of Yemen and Pakistan. However, six requests—Transjordan, Italy, Austria, Bulgaria, Hungary, and Romania—are not approved because of Western opposition or Soviet vetoes. Millions of people continue to be unrepresented in the UN as the membership issue is submerged within East–West tensions.

August 20   Following a Soviet veto in the Security Council, the United States requests that the General Assembly include the Greek civil war on its agenda.

August 22   World Bank grants Denmark a reconstruction loan of $40 million.

August 27   Luxembourg receives a $12 million reconstruction loan from the World Bank.

August 31   United Nations Special Committee on Palestine (UNSCOP) proposes the partition of Palestine. A minority plan favors a single federated state.

September 10   Security Council fails to act on the Egyptian complaint regarding the presence of British troops in Egypt and calls for direct negotiations between the parties.

September 11   After months of inconclusive debate, the issue of the Greek civil war is dropped from the agenda of the Security Council.

September 15   General Assembly takes up the issue of the Greek civil war.

September 16   General Assembly approves the agreement of association between the World Bank and the United Nations.

September 17   United States proposes the creation of the Interim Committee on Peace and Security of the General Assembly. Known as the "Little Assembly," it is a device to keep the General Assembly in permanent session in the event that a Soviet veto paralyzes the Security Council. The United States requests that the General Assembly place on its agenda "The Problem of the Independence of Korea."

September 18   Soviet Union requests that the General Assembly address the "war psychosis" being encouraged in the United States and other Western nations.

September 23   In a statement to the General Assembly, Lie urges universal membership, despite the opposition of the United States. He asserts that, despite East–West tensions, the United Nations will survive and lauds advances made in the social and economic fields.

September 24 According to the interim report of the Consular Commission in Indonesia, fighting continues in violation of the Security Council cease-fire order.

September 30 Pakistan and Yemen are admitted to the United Nations.

October 1 Soviet Union once again vetoes the applications of Italy and Finland for membership in the United Nations.

October 20 United Nations assumes the responsibilities of the League of Nations Convention on Traffic in Women and Children. The blue and white UN flag is adopted as the official emblem of the United Nations.

October 21 Special Committee on the Balkans is created to investigate threats to Greek independence resulting from interference in the civil war by Albania, Bulgaria, and Yugoslavia.

October 29 U.S. Ambassador Warren Austin notifies Lie that Truman has asked Congress to approve a $65 million interest-free loan to finance construction of a permanent UN headquarters.

October 31 General Assembly proclaims October 24 to be United Nations Day. The Economic and Social Council creates the Economic Commission for the Middle East.

November 1 After approving a trusteeship agreement submitted by Australia, New Zealand, and the United Kingdom for the territory of Nauru, the General Assembly urges South Africa to submit a similar agreement for South-West Africa. South Africa refuses.

November 3 The General Assembly, increasingly dominated by former colonies, creates the Special Committee on Information from Non-Self-Governing Territories despite the opposition of the imperial powers.

November 8 General Assembly condemns all "propaganda" designed to encourage threats to international peace.

November 10 General Assembly requests the International Court of Justice to rule whether admission to the United Nations by one state can be conditioned by admission of another.

November 13 General Assembly approves the creation of the Interim Committee.

November 14   General Assembly creates the UN Temporary Commission on Korea to supervise elections to take place no later than March 31, 1948.

November 15   United Nations enters into agreements of association with the International Monetary Fund, the World Health Organization (WHO), the Universal Postal Union, the International Telecommunication Union, and the World Bank.

November 17   WHO assumes all health activities of the League of Nations. The General Assembly declares Ireland, Portugal, Jordan, Italy, Finland, and Austria to be "peace-loving states" and urges the Security Council to approve their admission to the UN. General Assembly recommends that all members teach the UN Charter and the principles and activities of the United Nations in schools and institutions of higher learning.

November 21   Opposition parties in Poland and Hungary are dissolved by the ruling Communist Party. General Assembly establishes the International Law Commission and orders it to formulate a list of offenses based on the charter of the Nuremberg Tribunal.

November 29   General Assembly approves a plan of partition for Palestine, and establishes a Palestine commission to supervise the transfer from Britain to the proposed Arab and Jewish states.

December 2   United States informs the Security Council that Eniwetok atoll in its Trust Territory of the Pacific will be closed for "security reasons."

December 19   Security Council urges Italy and Yugoslavia to consult directly on the choice of a governor general for the Free Territory of Trieste.

1948

January 1   In a complaint to the Security Council, India accuses Pakistan of inciting opposition to the independent government of Kashmir.

January 9   Lie assures the UN Commission for Palestine of the "fullest" Security Council support to enforce partition.

January 12   United Nations Special Committee on Korea arrives in Seoul, Korea.

January 17 The Netherlands and the Republic of Indonesia sign a truce agreement aboard the USS *Renville*.

January 20 Security Council establishes the United Nations Commission on India and Pakistan (UNCIP).

February 3 Legal memorandum by Lie asserts the authority of the Security Council to implement the General Assembly's partition plan, including the use of international armed force.

February 16 The Korean People's Republic (North Korea) is proclaimed.

February 24 ECOSOC proposes that the UN establish a program to train public servants.

February 25 Soviet-backed coup in Prague results in a communist takeover of the government of Czechoslovakia.

March 4 French Foreign Minister Georges Bidault agrees to collaborate in opposing Soviet expansionism; France also accepts coordination of Allied policy regarding Germany.

March 6 Soviet communiqué denounces the "six-power" agreement on Germany reached at the London Conference. East and West move toward a showdown over Berlin.

March 10 Marshal Vasili Sokolovsky walks out of the Four Power Control Council meeting after claiming Soviet authority to inspect all rail transportation between West Germany and Berlin.

March 12 Chile presents the Soviet-backed coup in Czechoslovakia to the Security Council.

March 17 Britain, France, and the Benelux countries sign the Brussels Pact, pledging mutual assistance under Article 51 of the UN Charter against any "armed attack in Europe."

March 20 After a fierce Soviet attack on Western policy regarding Germany, the Four Power Control Council adjourns, never to meet again. Britain and the United States call for the revision of the peace treaty with Italy and the return of Trieste to Italian control.

March 23 The Conference on Freedom of Information opens in Geneva and considers journalists' rights to report political events.

April 1 Security Council asks the General Assembly to convene in special session to discuss Palestine; it is the first such request in UN history.

April 10   Security Council approves Burma's application for UN membership, and on April 19 it becomes the fifty-sixth member of the United Nations.

April 12   Lie's memorial address at Hyde Park warns of the increasing dangers to world peace from the tensions of the Cold War; he appeals to East and West to rely on the United Nations to secure world peace and prosperity.

April 23   Security Council establishes the Palestine Truce commission.

May 10   UN Special Committee on Korea supervises South Korean elections, which make Syngman Rhee president. The committee reports that the result is not recognized by the regime in the North.

May 15   British leave their Palestine mandate; the territory is invaded by Arab armies from Libya, Lebanon, Jordan, and Egypt.

May 16   In confidential letters to the Big Five Lie appeals in vain for direct intervention by the Security Council to restore order in Palestine.

May 17   Security Council orders a cease-fire in Palestine and instructs the Palestine Truce Commission to determine compliance. President David Ben Gurion proclaims the creation of the state of Israel and wins immediate recognition by France, the United States, and the Soviet Union.

May 21   Security Council appoints Count Folke Bernadotte, head of the Swedish Red Cross, as mediator for Palestine.

May 24   Soviet Union vetoes a Security Council resolution establishing a Committee of Inquiry to investigate the Czech coup.

May 26   In South Africa, the Nationalists, with the support of the small Afrikaner Party, come to power. Daniel François Malan becomes prime minister on a platform of apartheid (racial apartness).

May 28   Advisory opinion of the International Court of Justice opposes "package deals" on the admission of new members to the United Nations.

June 2   All parties in Palestine agree to a temporary cease-fire to take effect June 10.

June 5   United States adopts the Vandenberg Amendment, clearing the way for U.S. participation in the Atlantic Alliance (NATO).

June 7   Allied powers in London announce a joint policy for western Germany, which includes currency reform and the creation of a constituent assembly to draft a federal constitution.

June 10   At the Harvard commencement exercises, Lie unveils his proposal for a UN guard; it is later described as a force of 1,000 to 5,000 men, permanently available to enforce decisions of various UN organs.

June 16   United Nations Special Committee on the Balkans (UNSCOB) reports that support by Albania, Bulgaria, and Yugoslavia to guerrillas in northern Greece threatens the territorial integrity of Greece.

June 20   Over Soviet objections, Lie places fifty armed guards, mostly U.S. citizens, at the disposal of the UN mediator for Palestine; Lie later justifies the action as falling within his authority to staff UN activities.

June 23   Soviet Union ends rail traffic between Berlin and the Western zones and so begins the Berlin blockade. Conference of Soviet and East European foreign ministers declares London conference to be a violation of Potsdam Agreement and demands four-power action to create single German government.

July 2   Military Staff Committee fails to agree on a plan to provide the Security Council with troops.

July 4   General Assembly approves a Universal Postal convention bringing the Universal Postal Union into association with the United Nations.

July 5   In his introduction to the third annual report Lie offers his most comprehensive and independent analysis of world affairs; he chides the superpowers for lack of progress on atomic energy, reaffirms his stand on universality, and warns that Berlin should only be brought to the UN in a "genuine" attempt to reach a settlement.

July 9   Bernadotte's temporary truce in Palestine is shattered and fighting resumes.

July 12   India charges that abusive treatment of Asians in South Africa remains unchanged and requests that the General Assembly consider the matter. South Africa claims that the issue involves only domestic jurisdiction.

July 13 Trusteeship Council appoints a United Nations mission to East Africa, the first on-site inspection of conditions in trust territories.

July 15 Security Council declares that the situation in Palestine constitutes a threat to international peace and security under Article 39 of the charter.

July 23 South Africa refuses to submit a trusteeship agreement for the former mandated territory of South-West Africa.

July 28 Yugoslavia accuses the United States and Britain of violating the terms of the Italian peace treaty since monetary and postal reforms threaten the independence of the Free Territory of Trieste. The Security Council refuses to act on the complaint.

August 3 On recommendation of the Commission on Narcotic Drugs, ECOSOC proposes a single convention to replace existing multilateral treaties on narcotics control.

August 11 After months of delay, the U.S. Congress approves a loan for the construction of UN headquarters, and on November 20, the General Assembly unanimously approves Lie's plans for construction.

August 13 UN Commission for Kashmir reports that fighting continues there between Indian and Pakistani troops.

August 15 Republic of Korea (South Korea) is proclaimed.

August 18 Soviet Union vetoes Ceylon's application for membership in the United Nations.

August 21 Princely State of Hyderabad accuses India of threatening its independence.

August 24 Economic and Social Council releases the first volume of the *Yearbook on Human Rights.*

September 11 Indian troops invade Hyderabad.

September 15 The Big Four refer their dispute over the disposition of former Italian colonies to the General Assembly.

September 16 Security Council receives report of UN mediator for

Palestine; it recommends resettlement of refugees and territorial adjustments on partition. The following day, Bernadotte is murdered in Jerusalem by Jewish extremists.

September 20 Nizam (ruler) of Hyderabad capitulates to India, and withdraws a complaint to the Security Council.

September 21 Fifty-six nations agree to submit to the compulsory jurisdiction of the International Court of Justice.

September 24 General Assembly takes up the question of the former Italian colonies in Africa. The Soviet Union declares that it considers the UN Temporary Commission on Korea to be an illegal body and the May elections there to be null and void.

September 28 Secretary-General Lie proposes the creation of a United Nations guard, a force of about 300 men to protect UN field missions.

September 29 France, the United Kingdom, and the United States bring the Soviet blockade of Berlin to the attention of the Security Council.

October 3 Russia disputes UN competence on Berlin and insists that the Council of Foreign Ministers is the proper forum for dealing with the dispute.

October 4 Security Council includes the Berlin dispute on its agenda.

October 8 General Assembly unanimously approves an international protocol on the manufacture and regulation of narcotic drugs.

October 22 Smaller powers on the Security Council propose a resolution calling for the lifting of all restrictions on Berlin and for the negotiation of outstanding differences between the Soviet Union and the West. In Mexico City, the International High Frequency Broadcasting Conference begins five-month effort to end anarchy existing in high frequency broadcasting. Fifty of sixty-nine nations reach agreement on frequency allocations; the United States and Russia are among those that refuse.

October 23 In the wake of Bernadotte's murder, Lie asserts the legal right of the UN to sue a member state for reparations.

October 25 Soviet Union vetoes small powers resolution on Berlin.

A report of the United Nations Special Committee on the Balkans (UNSCOB) blames the governments of Albania, Bulgaria, and Yugoslavia for aiding guerrilla forces against Greece.

November 3   General Assembly requests administering powers to integrate their colonial policies with ECOSOC and inform the United Nations of constitutional changes in all non-self-governing territories. The colonial powers condemn this interference in their "domestic" affairs.

November 4   Over the opposition of the Soviet Union, the General Assembly approves the Baruch plan to establish a system of international control over atomic energy.

November 13   President of the General Assembly and the secretary-general jointly appeal to the superpowers to resolve the Berlin issue.

November 16   Security Council orders an armistice agreement for Palestine.

November 19   General Assembly identifies aid to Palestine refugees as the minimum condition for peace; it appoints a director of the UN Relief and Works Agency for Palestine Refugees and requests $32 million in member contributions to fund the agency from December 1, 1948, to August 31, 1949.

November 26   South Africa refuses to transmit information on South-West Africa to the General Assembly.

November 27   General Assembly accuses Albania, Bulgaria, and Yugoslavia of threatening peace and security in the Balkans; it urges the repatriation of kidnapped Greek children. Poland and the USSR withdraw from UNSCOB, which continues to function in the face of Soviet objections.

November 29   Israel applies for admission to the UN.

November 30   General Assembly unanimously appeals to the Great Powers to settle their differences.

December 1   General Assembly establishes the United Nations Relief for Palestine Refugees Organization (UNRPR).

December 3   General Assembly authorizes Lie to seek the advice of the International Court of Justice on the matter of reparations for the death of Folke Bernadotte.

December 4   General Assembly approves a Declaration on the Rights of the Aged.

December 8   General Assembly requests the Security Council to reconsider the membership applications of Portugal, Jordan, Italy, Finland, Ireland, Austria, and Ceylon, all vetoed by the Soviet Union. General Assembly approves the UN Appeal for Children, a voluntary nongovernmental aid program to benefit needy children, and lauds the efforts of the United Nations International Children's Emergency Fund (UNICEF) to meet the nutritional needs of 5 million children in war-torn areas.

December 9   General Assembly adopts the Convention on the Prevention and Punishment of the Crime of Genocide.

December 10   General Assembly passes the Universal Declaration of Human Rights by a vote of 48–0. Abstaining are the Belorussian SSR, Czechoslovakia, Poland, Saudi Arabia, Ukrainian SSR, Union of South Africa, USSR, and Yugoslavia.

December 11   General Assembly creates a UN Conciliation Commission for Palestine composed of France, Turkey, and the United States.

December 12   General Assembly ratifies the May elections in Korea, proclaims the government of the Republic of Korea, and orders occupying powers to remove their troops. The United Nations Commission on Korea consisting of Australia, China, El Salvador, France, India, the Philippines, and Syria is created. Costa Rica complains to the Security Council of military aggression by Nicaragua.

December 15   Pakistan requests that the question of Hyderabad be placed on the agenda of the Security Council since India and the government of Hyderabad are persecuting Hyderabad's Moslem minority. India claims that the situation falls within its domestic jurisdiction.

December 18   After Dutch troops renew military operations against the Republic of Indonesia, the United States requests an emergency meeting of the Security Council to deal with Dutch truce violations.

December 24   Security Council calls for a cease-fire in Indonesia.

December 28   Acting Mediator for Palestine Ralph Bunche reports that large-scale fighting has resumed in the Negev Desert and the Security Council orders an immediate cease-fire.

1949

January 1   India and Pakistan agree to a cease-fire and to a UN supervised plebiscite in Kashmir.

January 6   Egypt and Israel agree to a cease-fire and direct negotiations leading to an armistice.

January 12   Negotiations between Egypt and Israel begin on the island of Rhodes under the direction of Ralph Bunche.

January 20   Truman announces his Point Four Program on economic aid to underdeveloped areas in the world.

January 21   Communist Army enters Peking as rebel leader Mao Tse-tung's forces gain control in China.

January 27   Stalin interview with J. Kingsbury Smith of the International News Service signals the end of the Berlin Blockade.

January 28   Trusteeship council appoints the UN mission to West Africa. The Security Council orders the timely transfer of sovereignty from the Netherlands to the Republic of Indonesia and creates the United Nations Commission for Indonesia to supervise negotiations.

February 9   Democratic Republic of Korea (North Korea) applies for membership in the UN, but the application is rejected on February 16.

February 22   Costa Rica and Nicaragua sign a "pact of friendship," ending their dispute.

February 24   Egypt and Israel sign an armistice agreement.

March 1   Israel and Lebanon sign an armistice agreement.

March 4   Commission on the Status of Women meets in Beirut to consider the legal and social rights of women.

March 16   Britain refuses to transmit information to the UN on Malta and the Pitcairn Islands. Bolivia requests that the General Assembly conduct an inquiry into the charges brought against Catholic prelate Cardinal Jozsef Mindszenty by the government of Hungary.

March 19   Australia requests that the General Assembly investigate violations of human rights in Bulgaria and Hungary.

March 22   Israel and the Hashemite Kingdom of Jordan sign an armistice.

April 4 North Atlantic Treaty, a mutual defense agreement, is signed by Belgium, Canada, Denmark, France, Iceland, Italy, Luxembourg, the Netherlands, Norway, Portugal, the United Kingdom, and the United States.

April 8 Soviet Union vetoes the membership application of the Republic of Korea.

April 11 International Court of Justice (ICJ) declares the UN to be an international person capable of bringing suits against member states for damages caused to the organization, paving the way for Israel's payment of reparations for the death of Folke Bernadotte.

April 12 General Assembly urges the immediate transfer of sovereignty by the Netherlands to the Republic of Indonesia.

April 21 Security Council establishes a commission to supervise a cease-fire and plebiscite in Kashmir. India and Pakistan pledge they will observe the cease-fire.

April 28 The Council for Mutual Economic Assistance is established to promote economic integration between the Soviet Union and East European satellites.

April 29 Insisting that the United Nations has no legal jurisdiction over non-self-governing territories, France discontinues the transmission of information on its non-self-governing territories.

May 4 Soviet Union and Western Powers agree to end the Berlin blockade, and it is lifted on May 11. The German Federal Republic (West Germany) is proclaimed; the postwar occupation zones harden into two permanent political entities. The Statute of the Council of Europe is signed by the ministers of eleven West European governments.

May 10 Security Council again rejects a Soviet demand that a governor general be appointed for Trieste. General Assembly approves a program for the protection of aboriginal populations in the Americas.

May 11 Israel is admitted to the United Nations.

May 12 Western military governors approve the basic law establishing a federal constitution for Germany.

May 13 General Assembly approves the Draft Convention on the International Transmission of News.

May 14   General Assembly urges India, Pakistan, and South Africa to convene a roundtable conference to discuss the treatment of Indians in South Africa.

May 16   General Assembly urges the free repatriation of all refugees. A Latin-sponsored resolution calling for the restoration of diplomatic ties with Franco's Spain is defeated by the General Assembly as is a Polish motion calling for economic sanctions.

May 18   In his concluding statement before the third session of the General Assembly, Lie congratulates the superpowers for resolving the Berlin crisis, but warns that the UN cannot contribute to peace until a final settlement on Germany is reached.

May 27   During a press conference at Lake Success, Lie proposes to open and close each session of the General Assembly with one minute of silent prayer or meditation; in October the Assembly accepts the proposal.

June 6   Lie's commencement address at the University of Chattanooga in Tennessee stresses multilateral aid programs to close the gap between the advanced nations and backward countries, and he suggests projects similar to the Tennessee Valley Authority (TVA) for the Nile, Jordan, and other rivers in the Middle East.

June 14   In a speech before Rotary International, Lie stresses the possible role of the General Assembly in international cooperation and world peace; "No war of importance," he says, "will ever be started while the General Assembly is in session."

June 16   Faced with Soviet opposition, Lie abandons his UN guard plan; he substitutes a proposal for a United Nations field service, a small team of uniformed but unarmed men to provide transport and maintenance services to the Secretariat.

June 24   Lie uses his press conference to assert the same diplomatic privileges and immunities for UN officials as those enjoyed by other diplomatic personnel.

June 29   United States completes the withdrawal of its forces from Korea.

July 11   South Africa declares its intention to establish a closer association with South-West Africa, and refuses to transmit further information on the former mandate to the secretary-general.

July 14   Soviet Union detonates its first atomic bomb. ECOSOC recommends making pesticides available to underdeveloped countries but instructs WHO to study the proper labeling of such pesticides.

July 20   Israel and Syria sign an armistice agreement.

July 27   ECOSOC invites member states to coordinate national cartographic services, thus increasing the world's self-awareness.

August 11   Security Council instructs the UN Conciliation Commission for Palestine to supervise armistice agreements between Israel and the Arab States.

August 18   United States discontinues the transmission of information on the Panama Canal Zone to the United Nations.

August 23   Roundtable conference on Indonesia opens at The Hague.

August 24   United Nations initiates work on a Declaration of Death and Missing Persons.

September 13   Membership crisis deepens as the Soviet Union once more vetoes the membership applications of Jordan, Portugal, Italy, Finland, Ireland, Austria, and Ceylon.

September 15   The West prevents the admission of Albania, Mongolia, Bulgaria, Hungary, and Romania.

September 18–21   International Monetary Fund approves changes in the par value of currencies of thirteen member nations; it also approves exchange votes of several other currencies with no agreed par value.

September 22   General Assembly extends the term of the Interim Committee on Peace and Security indefinitely, although it is a failure.

September 23   Soviet Union appeals to the General Assembly to condemn "preparations for a new war" by the United States and the United Kingdom; the Truman Doctrine, Marshall Plan, and Atlantic Charter are cited as examples of such aggressive actions.

September 26   In a complaint to the General Assembly, the Republic of China charges the Soviet Union with violations of China's territorial integrity.

September 29   At a dinner in his honor, Lie defends his right to speak publicly in defense of the UN.

October 1   People's Republic of China (Communist China) is established.

October 7   German Democratic Republic (East Germany) is proclaimed.

October 11   Security Council orders the demilitarization of Jerusalem.

October 12   Permanent International Rice Commission is created to promote a program of rice production, distribution, and consumption: it is the first study of a single food source undertaken by an international organization.

October 15   Colombia charges in the International Court of Justice that Peru violates existing treaty obligations by refusing to grant safe passage to a dissident granted asylum in the Colombian Embassy in Lima.

October 21   General Assembly instructs the UN Commission on Korea to facilitate the social, economic, and political integration of Korea but the Soviet Union condemns the commission as a tool of United States imperialism.

October 22   General Assembly expresses concern over human rights violations in Bulgaria, Hungary, and Romania.

November 15   General Assembly recommends flying the UN flag in all trust territories.

November 16   General Assembly approves measures to prevent discrimination against immigrant laborers. Under the impetus of Truman's Point Four Program, the General Assembly approves the Expanded Programme of Technical Assistance; it commits $20 million for the initial eighteen months.

November 18   General Assembly expresses alarm over the continued interference of Albania, Bulgaria, and Yugoslavia in the domestic affairs of Greece.

November 21   General Assembly recommends that the former Italian colonies of Cyrenaica, Tripolitania, and the Fezzan be reconstituted as the sovereign state of Libya by January 1, 1952. The General Assembly recommends that Somaliland be placed in the trusteeship system with Italy as the administering power, and establishes a commission of inquiry to ascertain the political aspirations of the population of Eritrea in Ethiopia.

November 22   General Assembly creates the United Nations panel of field observers, a severely reduced version of Lie's UN guard.

November 25   All UN members are urged to promote full employment and to institute programs to ease the hardships of unemployment.

December 1   General Assembly requests the permanent members to strengthen the Security Council by refraining from using the veto. Protocol on Narcotic Drugs comes into force.

December 2   General Assembly approves an international convention on the suppression of prostitution. Over the opposition of the colonial powers, the General Assembly creates a Special Committee on Non-Self-Governing Territories; the assembly asserts its exclusive right to determine the status of colonial possessions and criticizes the administering powers' refusal to transmit information to the United Nations. UNESCO is instructed to promote literacy in non-self-governing territories.

December 5   General Assembly urges the Security Council to study measures for the control of conventional armaments.

December 6   After South Africa again refuses to transmit information on South-West Africa, the General Assembly requests an advisory opinion from the ICJ regarding the legal status of South-West Africa.

December 8   Without specifically mentioning the Soviet Union, the General Assembly urges all members to respect the political independence of China. General Assembly creates the United Nations Relief and Works Agency (UNRWA) to carry out projects in conjunction with Middle Eastern governments; it will fail to achieve the reintegration of Palestine refugees.

December 15   ICJ, by a vote of 12–2, finds for the United Kingdom in the Corfu Channel case and orders Albania to pay $43 million in damages.

December 16   After press speculation about his plans, Lie declares publicly that he is not a candidate for reappointment.

December 27   The Netherlands recognizes the independence of Indonesia.

December 31   Military Staff Committee reports no progress on the subject of UN forces.

1950

January 1 Lie in *Scientific American* urges negotiations among Big Five to control weapons of "mass destruction."

January 5 Truman announces the United States' intention to stay out of the civil conflict in China.

January 8 Communist China calls on the Security Council to expel the "Kuomintang" delegation from the United Nations.

January 10 Soviet Union proposes that the Security Council refuse to accept the credentials of the Nationalist Chinese delegation.

January 12 Secretary of State Acheson's National Press Club speech fails to include Korea in the U.S. defense perimeter in Asia, an error that critics charge invited the North Korean attack in June 1950.

January 13 Security Council votes down the Soviet proposal to strip Nationalist China of its membership in the UN and its seat in the Council. Russia then withdraws from the Council, stating that it will not return until the "Kuomintang Group" has been removed.

January 19 Russia withdraws from the Atomic Energy Commission and the group holds no meetings for the remainder of the year. Soviet Union withdraws from the Military Staff Committee in protest over seating of Nationalist China's delegate.

January 30 General Assembly establishes Contact Committee to implement terms of the roundtable conference on Indonesian independence.

February 3 Kashmir Mediator General Andrew George Latta McNaughton of Canada reports no progress toward the removal of Indian and Pakistani forces since India insists its troops are required to maintain order.

February 12 Mixed Armistice Commission for Palestine reports progress in alleviating local problems but warns that the commission is the "only forum" where contact between Israel and the Arab states takes place.

February 14 Thirty-year Sino–Soviet Treaty of Friendship is signed.

February 28–March 2 Economic and Social Council considers methods of financing economic development in Third World countries, an increasing UN concern over the decades. An Indian resolution requiring a special section on Africa in all economic studies conducted by the council is approved on March 2.

March 3 International Court of Justice upholds Security Council veto over membership applications; the ruling supports Soviet claims regarding unanimity.

March 8 Lie publicly supports the admission of Communist China to the UN even though Washington remains opposed to the removal of the Nationalist delegation from the Security Council.

March 10 In a statement to the press, Lie responds to criticism of his support for seating Red China. He maintains that until the issue is settled, the work of the organization is jeopardized.

March 13 Nationalist China formally protests Lie's memorandum on the seating of Communist China.

March 14 Security Council orders for the demilitarization of Kashmir are ignored by India.

March 21 Lie unveils his Twenty-Year Peace Plan at Triennial Dinner of B'nai B'rith in Washington, D.C. Lie's speech is hailed as a positive step in the service of peace.

March 27–May 19 Commission on Human Rights meets in Geneva to discuss additions to economic, social, and cultural rights already included in the Covenant on Human Rights.

March 28 Trusteeship Council urges the end of corporal punishment in trust territories.

March 30 International Court of Justice holds Bulgaria, Hungary, and Romania responsible for the fulfillment of peace treaty obligations regarding the protection of human rights. Trusteeship Council defeats joint Chinese–Philippine resolution to display the UN flag in trust territories as colonial powers charge illegal intrusion into their domestic affairs.

April 1 Italy assumes responsibility for the trust territory of Somaliland as British rule ends.

April 4 Security Council approves a draft statute of international administration of Jerusalem.

April 14   Lie departs for Europe to present his Twenty-Year Peace Plan to Prime Minister Atlee and Georges Bidault.

April 21   UN assesses Israel reparations amounting to $54,628 for the death of Bernadotte; Israel pays them on June 14.

April 27   Soviet Union withdraws from the Commission for Conventional Armaments in protest over seating of the Nationalist Chinese delegate.

May 3   While in Geneva, Lie announces he will go to Moscow to present his peace plan to Stalin.

May 4   Executive heads of the specialized agencies support principle of universality, and so implicitly endorse further negotiations on the admission of Red China.

May 8–19   Commission on the Status of Women meets at Lake Success and decides to draft a convention on the political rights of women.

May 21   Greece and Yugoslavia reestablish diplomatic relations.

May 25   Three thousand cheering Secretariat staff members welcome Lie back to UN headquarters from his peace mission to Europe.

May 26   At press conference in New York upon return from Europe, Lie pessimistically assesses his peace plan. He cites the issue of Chinese representation as a major obstacle to resolving the Cold War and continues to urge seating of Peking in the UN.

June 6   East Germany recognizes the Oder–Niesse line with Poland. Secretary-General Lie presents Twenty-Year Peace Plan to the General Assembly.

June 12   Secretary-general convenes UN Technical Assistance Conference at Lake Success. Governments attending pledge more than $20 million in aid for the period ending December 31, 1951.

June 25   North Korean forces invade the Republic of Korea. On receiving confirmation of the attack from the United Nations commission on Korea, Lie brings the matter to the Security Council and urges collective measures to aid South Korea, but does not officially invoke Article 99. The Security Council approves a United States resolution ordering a cease-fire in Korea and requests members to refrain from "giving assistance" to North Korea. The Soviet Union, boycotting the council, is not present to veto the U.S.-sponsored resolution. The council invites the government of the Republic of Korea to participate in its debate, but a Yugoslav suggestion to invite the North Koreans is rejected.

June 26 Lie publicly supports forceful action in Korea, and stakes the reputation of the UN on the success of the operation. UN Commission on Korea reports that North Korea fails to observe cease-fire order. South Korean forces retreat to southern tip of the Korean peninsula as United States forces are mobilized to assist them.

June 27 Security Council adopts United States resolution calling on members to render assistance to South Korea. The vote is 7–1 (Yugoslavia), with the Soviet Union absent and Egypt and India not participating. The Korean conflict is the first UN collective security operation.

June 28 United States informs the Security Council of its decision to assist South Korea militarily, an action in conformity with the council's resolution of June 27. Gromyko denounces the United States action as an effort to stampede the Security Council.

June 29 Lie's call for member states to give military assistance to South Korea draws fire for Lie's failure to consult with delegations in advance. The Netherlands suspends, under Article 73, the transmission of information for the West Indies and Surinam. The battle over Decolonization in the UN begins to take shape.

July 7 Security Council resolution authorizes unified military command in Korea under U.S. direction.

July 10 Negotiations between India and South Africa on the treatment of Indian nationals collapse, and India requests the General Assembly to again take up the issue.

July 11 Advisory opinion of the International Court of Justice declares the mandate for South-West Africa is still in force, but South Africa is not required to submit a trusteeship agreement for South-West Africa as anticolonialists had insisted.

July 12 Lie presents his fifth annual report to the General Assembly; he supports collective security in Korea but warns that the failure to sign peace treaties with Germany and Japan and the general pattern of East–West tensions impede progress toward world peace.

July 13   Russia, in a letter to the secretary-general, charges that all UN activities in Korea are illegal since they were authorized in the absence of two permanent members of the Security Council—the USSR and the "legal" government of China.

July 14   Gen. Douglas MacArthur is officially designated commander in chief of UN forces in Korea and is authorized to fly the UN flag.

July 17   Trusteeship Council advises administering powers to respect the separate status of trust territories, thus limiting their authority to unilaterally modify trust agreements.

July 25   MacArthur assumes command of South Korean forces.

July 27   USSR announces it will return to the Security Council to assume the presidency of the Council for the month of August.

July 31   UN Special Committee on the Balkans again reports no progress in repatriation of Greek children.

August 1   Soviet boycott of the Security Council ends; council direction of UN actions in Korea is no longer possible since Russia's delegate questions the legality of all previous decisions. Security Council defeats Soviet proposal to exclude Nationalist China from the council's deliberations.

August 7   With the Inchon landing still a month away, Lie states that entry into North Korea by UN troops should be authorized by the Security Council, not by the unified command.

August 9   General Assembly appoints committee to draft the Convention on Freedom of Information.

August 10–12   Economic and Social Council unanimously approves measures to combat malaria through use of insecticides and recommends increases in private and governmental capital investments for developing areas.

August 15   President Achmed Sukarno proclaims the Republic of Indonesia as a "unitary state." Economic and Social Council unanimously agrees to annually study the problem of full employment.

August 24   Peking complains to the Security Council that the presence of the United States Seventh Fleet in the Strait of Taiwan constitutes American aggression against China.

August 28   China charges the United States with bombing Chinese territory. Jordan charges before the Security Council that Israeli forces are occupying its territory. An Israeli countercharge accuses Egypt of blockading Israeli ports.

August 31   Security Council refuses to place on its agenda a Soviet complaint regarding atrocities committed by the government of Greece.

September 2   USSR asks the Security Council to condemn United States' acts of aggression against Taiwan.

September 5   Soviet Union vetoes U.S. resolution condemning North Korea for continued defiance of cease-fire orders from the Security Council. Security Council rejects Soviet demand that Communist China and North Korea be invited to participate in the debate on Korea.

September 7   Security Council rejects Soviet charges of war atrocities committed by United States troops in Korea.

September 15   MacArthur's successful landing at Inchon begins the liberation of South Korea. The UN representative for India and Pakistan again reports to the Security Council that there is no progress toward demilitarization of Kashmir.

September 19   General Assembly establishes special committee to consider the question of Chinese representation, and over communist bloc opposition, refuses to strip Nationalist China of its Assembly seat.

September 22   MacArthur liberates Seoul.

September 26   General Assembly takes up Nationalist Chinese complaint that USSR is interfering in the domestic affairs of China in violation of the Sino–Soviet Treaty of Friendship.

September 28   In the Security Council, the representative of the People's Republic of China accuses United States of aggression. The council votes down a Soviet-sponsored resolution supporting China's charges. Indonesia becomes the sixtieth member of the United Nations.

September 30   Allied troops reach the thirty-eighth parallel. Lie proposes terms of surrender for North Korea as the war expands northward.

October 1   China warns it will not "stand idly by" if UN troops cross the thirty-eighth parallel, but Truman authorizes MacArthur's advance.

October 7 General Assembly authorizes General MacArthur to cross the thirty-eighth parallel to hasten the reunification of Korea.

October 8 United Nations troops cross the thirty-eighth parallel in force.

October 9 United States Uniting for Peace Resolution authorizes the General Assembly to consider matters of international peace and security in the event that the Security Council is paralyzed by the veto.

October 15 Truman and MacArthur meet at Wake Island. MacArthur arrogantly assures Truman that China will not invade North Korea if UN forces drive further north toward the Yalu river.

October 20 Egypt complains to the Security Council about the expulsion of more than 4,000 Arabs from Israel.

October 21 Soviet Union argues against modification of the principle of Great Power unity and blames West for weakening the Security Council by introducing provocative items to the agenda.

October 23 In the General Assembly, the Soviet Union proposes a resolution condemning war propaganda; its text calls for outlawing atomic bombs and reducing Western armaments.

October 25 Lie's completed study of social welfare systems in thirty countries concludes that each country should develop methods of administration consistent with its own traditions and needs.

October 26 USSR returns to the Military Staff Committee.

October 30 General Assembly defeats Soviet "war propaganda" proposal.

November 1 UN Relief and Works Agency for Palestine Refugees reports that 800,000 Arab refugees are living in "desperate" conditions and that the refugee problem threatens peace and security in the Near East. Following a Soviet veto of Lie's reappointment in the Security Council, the General Assembly approves a three-year extension of Lie's term by a vote of 45–5 (the Soviet bloc) with eight abstentions (the Arab bloc, Nationalist China, and Australia).

November 3 Over bitter Soviet objections, the General Assembly adopts a Uniting for Peace Resolution that empowers it to deal with peace and security matters within twenty-four hours of a deadlock in the Security Council.

November 4   General Assembly ends diplomatic isolation of Franco's Spain and authorizes Spanish participation in the work of the specialized agencies.

November 6   MacArthur confirms the presence of Chinese Communist military units in Korea as the tide of the war shifts.

November 8   Security Council "summons" Peking to explain the presence of communist Chinese units in Korea but Peking declines to appear.

November 10   Security Council warns China against intervening in Korea.

November 14   Peking admits to the presence of Chinese "volunteers" in Korea and claims they are there to protest United States imperialism. Truman publicly denies hostile United States intentions towards China.

November 14–20   General Assembly debates Indian complaint against South Africa, which rejects the complaint as interference in its domestic affairs.

November 16   General Assembly approves a Convention on the Declaration of Death and Missing Persons; it establishes procedures to conduct inquiries and creates an international bureau to process legal claims.

November 17   General Assembly resolution condemns all forms of war propaganda, but refuses to single out the West. A provisional government for the trust territory of Libya is accepted by the UN in preparation for the eventual independence of the territory. Security council resolution urges Israel, Egypt, and Jordan to settle their differences within the terms of the 1949 armistice agreements. Secretary-General Lie defends his peace plan before the General Assembly as an effort to restore the world's confidence in the United Nations. USSR calls it a "one-sided and politically biased document." General Assembly passes Western-sponsored Peace Through Deeds Resolution; it condemns military intervention in the affairs of member states and urges the control of armaments by the United Nations.

November 20   International Court of Justice finds for Peru in an asylum case. General Assembly approves appropriations out of its regular budget to finance technical assistance programs, and recommends that ECOSOC undertake a study on agrarian restructuring in developing areas. General Assembly resolution commends Lie for his "peace initiative," but the Twenty-Year Peace Plan is dead.

November 24   MacArthur begins his "home-by-Christmas" offensive in North Korea.

November 25   General Assembly encourages member states to implement measures to ensure full employment.

December 1   General Assembly orders an inquiry of Soviet intervention in China and requests the repatriation of all Greek nations from Albania, Bulgaria, and Yugoslavia. In a major defeat for United States policy, the Assembly extends the life of UNICEF for three years; the agency's focus is shifted from short-term relief in Europe to long-term child health and welfare in backward areas, and UNICEF becomes permanent in late 1953. By a vote of 51–0 the Assembly creates the United Nations Korean Reconstruction Agency (UNKRA); its purpose is to implement war relief, estimated at $250 million, in a unified Korea. After prolonged negotiations, the International Penal and Penitentiary Commission is absorbed into the UN; its purpose is to devise international policy in the prevention of crime and the treatment of offenders.

December 2   General Assembly recommends merging the former Italian colony of Eritrea with Ethiopia and urges that long-range development and educational programs in trust territories be integrated into the UN program of technical assistance. General Assembly again condemns policy of apartheid in South Africa and urges negotiations between India and South Africa over treatment of Indian nationals. General Assembly approves the integration of the former Italian colony of Eritrea into Ethiopia.

December 4   General Assembly extends the provisions of the Universal Declaration of Human Rights to trust territories and other colonial areas. December 10 is designated Human Rights Day.

December 12   General Assembly requests that administering powers submit information regarding human rights in non-self-governing territories under their authority. Special committee of the General Assembly meets to consider the matter of Chinese representation.

December 13   General Assembly establishes committee to coordinate the activities of the Atomic Energy Commission and the Commission for Conventional Armaments. Over bitter objections by the government of South Africa, General Assembly establishes a special committee to enforce South Africa's League mandate duties toward South-West Africa. General Assembly establishes the "Committee of Twelve" (members of the Security Council as of January 1, 1951, and Canada) to coordinate the activities of the Atomic Energy Commission and the Commission on Conventional Armaments. General Assembly resolution provides for international protection by the UN of spiritual interests in the Holy Land.

December 14   General Assembly urges members to facilitate repatriation of Arab refugees. General Assembly creates the Office of the UN High Commissioner for Refugees in anticipation of closing the IRO. Pakistan complains to the Security Council that India is impeding UN-ordered plebiscite in Kashmir.

December 22   After one week, three-member Cease-Fire Committee (Lester Pearson, Canada; Benagal Rau, India; and Nasrolla Entezam, Iran), admits failure to halt fighting in Korea. General Assembly recommends repatriation of all war prisoners in Korea. General Assembly condemns all restrictions on freedom of information.

December 31   Secretary-general reports the initiation of 145 projects under the UN Expanded Programme of Technical Assistance during the year.

1951

January 1   In a radio address to the nation, Truman declares a national emergency requiring a buildup of armed forces. He pledges to defend the principles of the United Nations with "arms if necessary."

January 2   General Assembly's three-member Cease-Fire Committee reports failure to initiate talks with Communist China on the terms of a cease-fire. USSR denounces the effort as a pretext for continued Anglo-American aggression.

January 3   Israel proposes a seven-point peace plan for Korea.

January 4 Communist Chinese launch a massive counteroffensive that forces UN armies back into the south. Lie enlists the good offices of the International Red Cross and the League of Red Cross Societies in his effort to gain release for Korean POW's.

January 5 U.S. Sen. Robert Taft (Ohio) accuses the Truman administration of bringing the United States to the "brink of disaster" through its policy of "executive secrecy"; he questions the legality of U.S. policy in Korea.

January 8 Truman's State of the Union message defends U.S. policy in Korea and asks Americans to oppose the "new Soviet imperialism."

January 12 President of the International Red Cross informs the UN that opposition by member states makes it impossible for his agency to participate in the ad hoc committee on war prisoners. General Assembly condemns apartheid in South Africa and creates a three-member commission to facilitate negotiations between South Africa and India on the treatment of Indian nationals. Abstentions by Western nations reflect opposition to UN interference in colonial affairs.

January 17 Peking publicly accepts the "principle" of a negotiated settlement in Korea.

January 18 In a letter to Lie, the president of the International Court of Justice endorses the secretary-general's peace memorandum appealing for greater use of international law in the settlement of disputes. In an address to the General Assembly, U.S. Ambassador Warren Austin accuses Peking of aggression against the UN and urges a collective response. General Assembly approves joint council for Togoland, moving that territory closer to national independence, and again urges the rapid achievement of self-government in all trust territories.

January 28 In a public address, Illinois Gov. Adlai Stevenson warns that reliance on military power alone cannot advance the moral leadership of the United States in the world. UN forces halt Communist Chinese advance north of the capital city of Seoul.

January 30 UNESCO approves the human rights provisions of Lie's ten-point peace memorandum.

January 30–March 16 Trusteeship Council meets to examine annual reports from all administering authorities. Nonadministering members criticize the slow pace toward self-government.

February 1   General Assembly condemns Chinese aggression in Korea. Another resolution accuses the Soviet Union of violating its treaty of friendship and alliance with Nationalist China and of masterminding Mao's communist takeover.

February 2   General Assembly authorizes the UN high commissioner to broaden his appeal for funds to ease the vast refugee problem in Europe.

February 6   In a complaint to the Security Council, USSR accuses the United States of violating Communist Chinese air space.

February 9   In a public address, former President Herbert Hoover proposes a large buildup in U.S. naval and air forces and a shift away from land-based forces for the defense of Europe.

February 9–13   Executive board of UNICEF holds its first session.

February 13   General Assembly defeats a Soviet resolution accusing the United States of aggression against the People's Republic of China.

February 14   Lie urges the new Disarmament Commission Committee of Twelve to renew its efforts to bring atomic weapons under international control. Lie has little faith in the willingness of the Great Powers to disarm.

February 16   During a press conference at Lake Success, Lie acknowledges total U.S. control over military policy in Korea; he refuses to be drawn into the controversy swirling about Truman's relationship with MacArthur.

February 19   General Assembly designates its president and two others of his choice as a Good Offices Committee to achieve UN objectives in Korea by peaceful means.

February 20–March 21   In its annual review of world economic conditions, ECOSOC cites the unequal economic growth in developed and underdeveloped nations. Rearmament is seen as an obstacle to consumer growth in the West.

February 21   Sir Owen Dixon, UN mediator for India and Pakistan, resigns following a year of failure to achieve agreement on either a cease-fire or a plebiscite in Kashmir. He is replaced by Frank Graham of the United States.

February 26   Paul-Henri Spaak, first president of the General Assembly, publicly opposes the rearmament of Germany. Technical Assistance Board reports broad participation by all specialized agencies in the Expanded Programme of Technical Assistance.

February 27   ECOSOC calls on member governments to limit the production of opium to medical and scientific needs.

February 28   Japan is granted associate membership in the Economic Commission for Asia and the Far East. Commission announces the first comprehensive study of coal and iron resources in Asia and the Far East. Resolutions of the Economic and Social Council allege restrictions of trade union freedoms by the governments of Spain, Romania, and the USSR and request the secretary-general to begin fact finding. While receiving an honorary degree from the University of Quito in Ecuador, Lie praises the work of the United Nations in raising standards of living in the world's underdeveloped areas.

February 28–March 7   Economic Commission for Asia and the Far East meets at Lahore, Pakistan.

March 2   International Monetary Fund warns that worsening balance of payments situation in nondollar nations is a serious threat to economic stability and growth.

March 6   An ad hoc committee on South-West Africa has its first meeting in New York.

March 7   USSR opposes calling an international convention to develop standards on commercial advertising.

March 7–10   World Bank's annual report shows loans of more than $1 billion, with greater emphasis on loans to underdeveloped countries in 1950.

March 12   Truce Supervision organization reports difficulties in meeting terms of the armistice agreements between Israel and the Arab states.

March 19   ECOSOC creates a committee on forced labor to study the question of "corrective" labor as punishment for political dissidence.

March 20   U.S. Joint Chiefs of Staff inform MacArthur of Truman's planned peace offer. Security Council orders the demilitarization of Kashmir despite the presence of Indian troops. ECOSOC recommends that all nations take special measures to ensure the equitable distribution of capital goods, essential consumer goods, and raw materials, especially with regard to underdeveloped areas.

March 21   Nongovernmental organizations with ties to Franco's Spain are again allowed to participate in the work of the Economic and Social Council. ECOSOC endorses the technical assistance and economic development aspects of Lie's ten-point memorandum.

March 24   MacArthur publicly announces his willingness to meet with enemy commanders to discuss an end to hostilities, a direct violation of White House directives prohibiting field statements on policy.

March 27   For the fifth time in six years, India asks the General Assembly to consider the mistreatment of 300,000 Indian nationals living in South Africa. The resulting debate subjects South Africa to harsh criticism of its racial policies.

March 31   John Foster Dulles, U.S. assistant secretary of state, announces tentative peace terms for Japan.

April 2–27   ECOSOC, considering sixty-four nations' responses on servitude, concludes that slavery "even in its crudest form" is still present and constitutes a proper concern of the international community.

April 4   World Meteorological Organization formally becomes an international body and joins the UN family of specialized agencies.

April 5   U.S. Rep. Joseph W. Martin (Massachusetts) makes public a letter from MacArthur urging the use of Nationalist Chinese troops in Korea; MacArthur had earlier advocated widening the war beyond the confines of Korea.

April 6   Despite MacArthur's provocative statements on military policy, Lie uses his press conference to emphasize efforts to achieve a negotiated settlement in Korea.

April 8   Communist Chinese forces are driven back across the thirty-eighth parallel.

April 10 Truman fires MacArthur and Gen. Matthew B. Ridgway becomes commander of UN forces in Korea.

April 11 Truman tells the nation that MacArthur was dismissed as UN commander in Korea because he refused to accept U.S. war aims.

April 12 Senator Taft criticizes Truman's decision to relieve Mac-Arthur and supports the general's strategy to widen the war.

April 14 In his Jefferson-Jackson Day speech, Truman defends against charges of appeasement his policy to limit U.S. war aims in Korea. In Belgrade, Lie welcomes Yugoslavia into the UN community and encourages economic and social ties between Yugoslavia and the West.

April 16 M. A. Gurmane, Pakistani minister for Kashmir affairs, warns that continued defiance of Security Council resolutions by India may lead to war.

April 16–30 Communist Chinese assault fails to break through UN defense perimeter.

April 16–May 10 Commission on Human Rights completes drafting the articles for a covenant on human rights regarding economic, social, and cultural rights.

April 19 In a farewell address to Congress, MacArthur warns against appeasing Communist China, a direct threat to U.S. strategic interests in the Pacific.

April 26 MacArthur announces his decision to withdraw from public life.

April 30–May 14 Commission on the Status of Women has its fifth session and urges the secretary-general to appoint women to policy-making positions in the Secretariat.

May 1 UN Economic survey for Latin America expresses concern over recent shifts in the balance of payments position of Latin nations, reducing their capacity to purchase needed capital goods. Iran nationalizes the Anglo-Iranian Oil Company under the terms of the Oil Nationalization Act.

May 4 Pakistan accuses India of pursuing a policy of annexation in Kashmir and subverting Security Council resolutions for UN-supervised elections.

May 8 Security Council urges Syria and Israel to make peace and live up to the armistice agreement of July 1949.

May 18 Led by the United States, the General Assembly votes an embargo against Communist China under the Uniting for Peace Resolution; it asks member states to report their compliance. Assistant Secretary of State Rusk announces that the United States continues to recognize the Taiwan regime as the sole legitimate government of China.

May 21 South Africa agrees to confer with the Ad Hoc Committee on South-West Africa.

May 26 United Kingdom starts proceedings against Iran in the International Court of Justice over the nationalization of the Anglo-Iranian Oil Company.

May 28–June 16 Economic Commission for Latin America meets in Mexico City; it concludes that policies of advanced nations cause balance of payments problems leading to lower standards of living for Latin Americans.

May 29–June 13 Meeting in Geneva, Economic Commission for Europe blames shortages in consumer goods on rearmament.

June 1 In Ottawa, Lie proclaims that a cease-fire along the thirty-eighth parallel fulfills the objectives of the June 25–27 and July 7 Security Council resolutions.

June 7 Jordan complains to the UN that Israel is diverting the natural flow of the River Jordan.

June 12 Israel charges before the Security Council that Egypt is restricting free passage of ships through the Suez Canal.

June 18 Lie addresses the UNESCO General Conference in Paris and praises the specialized agencies' contributions to the cause of peace.

June 23–24 Soviet Ambassador Jacob Malik's radio address suggests that discussions begin as a prelude to a cease-fire in Korea. The peace process begins as Lie endorses the Malik statement.

June 30 UN relief agency reports that nearly 900,000 Palestine refugees scattered throughout Lebanon, Syria, Jordan, and Gaza have received more than $44 million in relief aid provided by the UN.

July 1 Economic survey for Asia and the Far East (1950) indicates that much area economic progress is due to the impact of the Korean War and is unlikely to last.

July 2–25 Geneva conference drafts a Convention Relating to the Status of Refugees and a protocol relating to the status of stateless persons.

July 8 Negotiations to end the Korean War open at Kaesong, near the thirty-eighth parallel.

July 9 Iran rejects the International Court of Justice's compulsory jurisdiction in its dispute with Britain.

July 12 Chinese and North Korean armed guards deny journalists access to Kaesong conference site. Talks are suspended for three days.

July 15 Conferees at Kaesong agree on the establishment of a "neutral zone" to guarantee freedom of movement to the delegates from North and South Korea. Armistice talks are resumed.

July 24 Trusteeship Council approves a joint Anglo-French administrative council for Togoland, leading to the eventual merger of former French and British colonies.

July 30–September 21 Basic split develops in ECOSOC debate on human rights; Soviet and Arab blocs favor a single covenant on human rights; the West and most Latin delegations want to separate civil and political rights from economic, social, and cultural guarantees. Secretary-general reports the failure of Spain, Romania, and the USSR to respond to charges regarding trade union restrictions.

August 2–3 ECOSOC adopts a resolution dealing with all aspects of international road transport.

August 7 Western opposition kills proposal by the Commission on the Status of Women to appoint women to high-level Secretariat positions. United States claims the proposal restricts the secretary-general's discretion to choose the best qualified persons.

August 9 Chinese Communists charge UN forces with violation of the Korean truce terms, the first of many claims that will impede progress toward a final armistice agreement. Economic and Social Council undertakes for the first time to formulate guidelines for training of welfare personnel; it establishes that social work is a professional function to be performed by trained people.

August 10   UN Conciliation Commission for Palestine invites Israel and the Arab states to attend a Paris conference to discuss outstanding differences.

August 12   ECOSOC documents the extremely low standards of living in Africa and the Middle East.

August 13   ECOSOC adopts a Philippine resolution linking the world shortage of consumer goods to inflationary pressures caused by the Korean War.

August 15–28   In its annual review of national employment policy, ECOSOC focuses on the Third World. Emerging countries are encouraged to undertake basic reforms to attract foreign capital. Debate reveals basic split between the Eastern bloc and the West, which insists free enterprise is the only path to economic growth.

August 16   Secretary-general reports that $23.8 million in contributions to the UN war effort in Korea has been received from member states.

August 29   International Refugee organization reports the resettlement of nearly 120,000 persons during 1950.

August 30   ECOSOC requests the General Assembly to establish a special reserve fund of $3 million to assure completion of existing projects under the technical assistance program.

August 31   Food and Agriculture Organization recommends continuous surveillance of world's food supplies with special emphasis on areas susceptible to severe shortages or famine.

September 1   Egypt is ordered by the Security Council to maintain free passage of shipping through the Suez Canal. ECOSOC appeals to member governments to safeguard the right of correspondents to gather and transmit news.

September 5–8   General conference to sign peace treaty with Japan meets in San Francisco. USSR, Czechoslovakia, and Poland refuse to accept accord reached on September 8. World Health Organization expresses concern the worldwide shortage of pesticides will hinder anti-malaria campaigns around the globe.

September 5   The United Nations Commission for the Unification and Rehabilitation of Korea (UNCURK) reports no progress toward the reunification of Korea.

September 6   MacArthur criticizes the Truman administration for allowing the world to drift toward totalitarianism: he calls the UN an inherently weak agency for enforcing peace.

September 7   ECOSOC recommends that all nations institute land reforms and assure security of tenure to cultivators of land.

September 8   Soviet Ambassador to the UN Andrei Gromyko denounces as a violation of wartime agreements the United States and Great Britain's signing of a separate peace treaty with Japan. Gromyko also attacks U.S. opposition to Peking entering the UN.

September 11–13   Thirteenth session of ECOSOC establishes the Ad Hoc Committee on Restrictive Business Practices. Soviet bloc attacks the measure as camouflage for the domination of foreign markets by U.S. monopolies.

September 13   UNESCO recommends an increase in the supply and distribution of newsprint and printing paper to improve the free spread of information. Arab–Israeli conference in Paris receives a UN conciliation plan to resolve territorial and other outstanding disputes. ECOSOC postpones the creation of an Economic Commission for the Middle East since Arab states oppose any cooperation with Israel.

September 15   UN requests the Federal Republic of Germany (West Germany) to respond to claims from survivors of the Nazi death camps.

September 18   German Chancellor Konrad Adenauer calls for Germany's integration into Europe with full rights for Germany.

September 20   Lie's sixth annual report to the General Assembly renews his appeal for periodic meetings of the Security Council, the creation of a permanent UN force, the reduction of armaments, and the end to reliance on military blocs for security. Talks between South Africa and the Ad Hoc Committee on South-West Africa break down when South Africa refuses to accept UN supervision of the former mandate.

September 27   Federal Republic of Germany (West Germany) proposes German unification.

September 28   United Kingdom brings complaint before the Security Council concerning the expulsion of Anglo-Iranian Oil Company personnel. Iran claims that the matter falls within its domestic jurisdiction.

October 2   U.S. Congress passes the Mutual Security Act; it combines economic and military assistance programs into a coordinated whole, becoming a major instrument of U.S. policy to defend the free world.

October 3   Reporting to the General Assembly on his Twenty-Year Peace Plan, Lie expresses encouragement over its reception by the specialized agencies, but concedes a lack of interest on the part of the Big Four.

October 4   Egypt accuses France of human rights violations in Morocco, but the General Assembly refuses to act on the complaint.

October 6–11   Latin American delegations propose that all "peace-loving" states be admitted to the UN. Communist bloc claims that the impasse on admissions is due to the Anglo-American policy of discrimination.

October 7   Under the auspices of the Trusteeship Council, the Libyan National Assembly adopts a constitution.

October 10   U.S. Congressman John T. Woods (Idaho) attacks the UN as an instrument of Communist "duplicity and intrigue." Extreme right-wing critics accuse the UN of promoting godlessness, world government, and attacks on the American way of life.

October 15   Truman's speech at Wake Forest University in North Carolina defends the negotiated settlement in Korea as the beginning of broader contacts with the Soviets to solve outstanding cold war problems. Security Council upholds the jurisdiction of the International Court of Justice over the Anglo-Iranian dispute.

October 16   Committee on Chinese representation rejects a Polish proposal to oust the Nationalist delegation from the UN and to seat the representatives of Peking.

October 17   MacArthur warns that only military preparedness can contain Soviet expansionism.

October 23   Committee of Twelve recommends the creation of a Commission for the Control of Armaments and recommends that the commission on Conventional Armaments be dissolved.

November 3 Collective Measures Committee under the Uniting for Peace Resolution reports no progress in achieving a cessation of hostilities in Korea.

November 5 Western Big Three ask General Assembly to consider the question of reunification of Germany.

November 6 Soviet Union proposes that the question of Chinese representation be included on the agenda of the General Assembly.

November 7 International Red Cross reports no progress in the repatriation of Greek children from Bulgaria, Albania, and Romania.

November 8 USSR calls for Korean armistice and asks the General Assembly to support a pact of peace-loving nations to avoid a new world war. The West denounces the proposal as propaganda.

November 9 Before the Security Council, Yugoslavia accuses the USSR and other Eastern bloc nations of threatening its territorial integrity and national independence.

November 13 General Assembly refuses to consider the matter of Chinese representation, and Taiwan retains its right to represent Chinese people at the United Nations.

November 19 Israel and Arab states reject settlement proposed by the UN Conciliation Commission for Palestine.

November 22 In the General Assembly, Russia accuses the United States of financing a network of subversive groups in Eastern Europe under the recent Mutual Security Act.

December 3 Rome conference of FAO declares the existence of widespread hunger in various regions of the world. USSR proposes that the Collective Measures Committee be abolished since the Uniting for Peace Resolution, under which the committee was created, is illegal.

December 5 South Africa withdraws from Fourth Committee deliberations on South-West Africa to protest the committee's decision to invite spokesmen from the territory to testify at the UN.

December 7 General Assembly approves the participation of Italy in the work of the Trusteeship Council. General Assembly discontinues the work of the UN Special Committee on the Balkans.

December 8 UN hears testimony for the first time from a representative of the indigenous population of South-West Africa.

December 11 Britain, France, and the United States propose a new disarmament commission but retain the Baruch plan as the cornerstone of their attitude on atomic weapons.

December 14 Over bitter Soviet opposition, the General Assembly approves a Yugoslav resolution calling for the peaceful resolution of differences between Yugoslavia and its Eastern European neighbors.

December 17 Vietnam applies for membership in the United Nations.

December 18 India and Pakistan reject new UN terms for removal of forces from Kashmir: India opposes any plebiscite until order is restored. Chinese–North Korean command agrees to provide the UN with a list of prisoners of war available for exchange.

December 20 Over the opposition of the Soviet bloc and Israel, the General Assembly approves an Anglo-French-American proposal to examine the conditions for German reunification.

December 21 UN appropriates $300,000 to finance staffing requirements for the Expanded Programme of Technical Assistance and an additional $500,000 for the regular technical assistance program.

December 24 United Kingdom of Libya declares its independence and applies for membership in the United Nations.

December 26 In his Christmas message to the Scandinavian people, Lie is hopeful that ongoing armistice negotiations can lead to lasting peace in Korea.

December 30 Lie reports that 799 treaties were registered with the Secretariat during 1951.

1952

January 11 General Assembly dissolves the Atomic Energy Commission and creates a Disarmament Commission to draft a convention regulating all armed forces. This Western measure is strongly opposed by the USSR, which continues to insist on prior elimination of all atomic weapons.

January 11–19   During the General Assembly debates on the ECOSOC report, the Soviet bloc accuses the West of lowering living standards through costly rearmament. The West blames Soviet expansionism for its military buildup.

January 12   Over the opposition of the Soviet bloc, the General Assembly extends the life of the Collective Measures Committee for one year. General Assembly recommends that ECOSOC and the specialized agencies foster industrialization and productivity in underdeveloped countries by spreading technological knowledge; it also approves more long-term, low-interest loans. The assembly creates a three-member Conciliation Commission to resolve the Indian–South African dispute over the latter's treatment of Indian nationals. General Assembly recommends that member states contribute armed forces to the UN in accordance with a request of the Collective Measures Committee.

January 12–17   Western powers say Atlantic Alliance is purely defensive and, in assembly debate, reject Soviet charges that secret air fields encircle the Soviet Union.

January 13   After years of pressure by the emerging nations, the General Assembly approves study for a Special United Nations Fund for Economic Development (SUNFED); the advanced nations are strongly opposed and SUNFED begins its stormy history.

January 14   Following a Polish complaint, the General Assembly defers consideration of allegations of human rights violations in Spain.

January 15   The UN 1950 *Yearbook on Human Rights* contains all constitutional provisions and legislative texts on human rights enacted throughout the world.

January 16–31   Chinese and Korean insistence that all prisoners of war be repatriated after an armistice regardless of personal desires to remain in the West brings peace talks to an impasse.

January 17   Winston Churchill, in a speech to the U.S. Congress, advocates further military buildup in Europe. Yugoslavia, bowing to UN pressure, agrees to repatriate fifty-seven Greek children.

January 17–31   During a Security Council debate on Kashmir, the Soviet Union terms UN policy part of a Western plot to deny self-determination to the people of Kashmir.

January 18   General Assembly urges administering powers to bring non-self-governing territories into closer association with the work of the specialized agencies.

January 19   General Assembly declares all South African unilateral actions in the territory of South-West Africa to be invalid; South Africa rejects any United Nations authority over the mandate.

January 21   A Russian "package deal" to admit all states awaiting admission to the United Nations is rejected by the Western-dominated Assembly.

January 22   Before the Security Council, Jordan accuses Israel of violating the 1949 armistice agreement; the reality of "no peace; no war" continues in the Middle East.

January 23   General Assembly creates the Balkan Sub-Commission of the Peace Observation Commission, the only use ever made of this provision in the Uniting for Peace Resolution.

January 26   Chile–United States resolution urges governmental co-operation to eradicate hunger and famine. USSR charges that the Western military buildup is the main cause of food shortages. With FAO's August 31, 1949, report on food shortages as background, the assembly for the first time addresses the problem of future famine resulting from natural causes, but no action is possible on establishing a famine reserve. General Assembly expresses regret over the failure of Israel and the Arab states to respond to UN efforts to achieve peace.

January 28   Western Big Three announce they will seek UN action in the event of renewed communist aggression in southeast Asia.

January 29–February 8   Economic Commission for Asia and the Far East meets in Rangoon, Burma, and admits Japan as an associate member. A proposal by the USSR to exclude Nationalist China is defeated.

January 29   Israel accuses Jordan of fifty-nine violations of the 1949 armistice agreement, complaining also of threatening statements made by Syria's representative to the UN. Israel reserves its right to "consider and pass judgment" on all threats to its territory.

January 31   When the General Assembly refers Lie's peace plan to the "appropriate organs of the United Nations," the initiative is fundamentally dead. International Refugee Organization is closed after repatriating millions of Europe's war refugees. At its height, IRO maintained a fleet of thirty-nine ships and chartered forty-five trains a month. Its budget exceeded that of the entire UN.

February 1   Economic survey of Europe (1951) reports small increases in agricultural output but a 40 percent expansion of industrial capacity due to military contracts. A similar overview of Latin America cites a growing balance of payments problem in the region. General Assembly encourages the permanent members of the Security Council to reconsider all rejected applicants for membership with a view toward achieving universality.

February 2   When member states fail to agree on practical measures to implement the conventions on refugees and stateless persons, the General Assembly defers action. General Assembly again urges the return of kidnapped Greek children from Romania, Albania, and Czechoslovakia.

February 4   Disarmament Commission has its first meeting in Paris and is quickly mired in procedural details and Soviet charges of Western atrocities in Korea. A major procedural victory of the Western bloc is attained when General Assembly instructs the Commission on Human Rights to draft two covenants, one on civil and political rights, the other on economic, social, and cultural rights.

February 5   The right of "self-determination" is incorporated within the human rights covenants despite Western objections.

February 6   USSR vetoes admission of Italy to the United Nations.

February 9   USSR refuses to provide the UN with information on World War II prisoners held in the Soviet Union.

February 17   Britain announces that it will test an atomic weapon sometime in 1952; it becomes the third member of the nuclear club on October 3.

February 19 An agenda for the Korean peace talks is approved but the UN delegation rejects Chinese and North Korean proposals for a Far Eastern conference following the armistice.

February 22 South Africa refuses to cooperate with the conciliation commission on the treatment of Indian nationals, maintaining that the UN has no jurisdiction over the matter.

February 29 Dean Acheson calls for strengthening NATO as the only means of preserving Western civilization in Europe. Lie reports progress in negotiations with West Germany on the indemnification of death-camp survivors.

March 18 Subcommittee of ECOSOC on freedom of information condemns Argentine closing of opposition newspaper *La Prenza*, but the UN takes no further action in this freedom-of-information dispute. Lie is the guest at the UN Correspondents' Association program "United or Not," the first telecast from the new permanent headquarters in New York. Lie denies that regional security arrangements end any role for the UN in keeping the peace; he cites Iran, Kashmir, Indonesia, and the Balkans as proof of UN effectiveness and observes that disillusionment with the UN is confined largely to U.S. opinion.

March 23 Truman allocates $4.3 million to aid Iron Curtain refugees.

March 24–April 5 Annual meeting of the Commission on the Status of Women drafts a Convention on the Political Rights of Women.

March 25 The Korean peace talks go into secret sessions as the West continues to oppose forced repatriation of Chinese–Korean prisoners of war.

March 29 Truman announces he is not a candidate for renomination.

March 31 France is accused before the Security Council of violating the political autonomy of Tunisia and of ignoring the human rights of its citizens. France rejects UN jurisdiction over the "domestic" dispute. Reflecting high levels of underemployment in backward areas, the UN conducts the first world survey of income maintenance.

April 1 Negotiations begin between the International Red Cross and the government of Czechoslovakia to return 138 Greek children.

April 4   UN command initiates a screening process to ascertain the wishes of Chinese–Korean prisoners on repatriation; it finds 90,000 are willing to go home.

April 6   White South Africans celebrate the 300th anniversary of Jan van Riebeeck's arrival at the Cape. Africans boycott the celebrations.

April 14   Western colonial powers block inclusion of Tunisian complaints against France on the Security Council's agenda; Security Council remains unavailable as a forum for anticolonial initiatives.

April 14–June 14   Commission on Human Rights begins to draft covenants on human rights.

April 21   Human rights commission approves two controversial measures; one guarantees to all people the right to control their own natural resources, the second acknowledges their right to plan their own futures.

April 23   West Germany acknowledges receipt of only 531 applications asking for death-camp reparations.

May 2   Conciliation Commission for Palestine fails to effect the release of bank accounts in Israel that belong to Palestinian refugees.

May 4   As violations of the 1949 armistice increase, the UN Truce Supervision Organization reinstates mixed patrols along the Egyptian–Israeli demarcation line.

May 5   Office of the United Nations High Commissioner for Refugees reports a shortfall in member contributions. U.S. Secretary of State John Foster Dulles proposes that a mutual defense arrangement comparable to NATO be created in the Far East to contain the "Communist menace" in Asia.

May 6   ECOSOC requests the Committee on Information from Non-Self-Governing Territories to consider including in its annual survey information regarding violations of women's rights.

May 12   Gen. Mark Clark succeeds Gen. Matthew Ridgway as commander of UN forces in Korea.

May 13   Food and Agriculture Organization reports that international action to combat a plague of desert locusts threatening the food supply of Africa, Asia Minor, and Asia has begun. Although not a member of FAO, the Soviet Union joins the United States, Britain, and Turkey in rushing aid to blighted areas.

May 26   UNESCO reports that many nations provide inequitable educational opportunities for women. The Economic and Social Council recommends that all governments adopt a policy of equal pay for equal work.

May 27   ECOSOC proposes a draft convention on the limitation of opium production and traffic.

May 28   Bernard Baruch tells the U.S. Senate that America is losing the arms race because of its hesitancy to produce weapons. He urges modernization of weapons systems and distribution of obsolete weapons to other nations.

May 29   Annual report of the International Monetary Fund cites massive worldwide rearmament as seriously harming national economies everywhere. India and Pakistan agree to renew negotiations on Kashmir.

May 29–June 2   Economic and Social Council considers the secretary-general's World Economic Report; the council authorizes a study of water resource development in emerging nations.

June 6   Lie denies charges by U.S. right-wingers that the UN is a "Communist nest"; he maintains the UN has no policy to dismiss United States employees for their political affiliations.

June 9   General Assembly urges all members to ensure the widest possible dissemination of all UN resolutions and decisions.

June 12   Despite continued military clashes between UN and Chinese–Korean units, there have been no significant changes in forward battle positions in Korea for months.

June 14   Commission on Human Rights includes in the draft covenant on human rights an article proclaiming the right of peoples and nations to self-determination.

June 16   European Coal and Steel Community (Schuman Plan) is ratified following Italy's final approval; it will make effective progress toward integrating and revitalizing Europe's energy and steel sectors. World Bank proposes creation of the International Finance corporation to stimulate national financing of private enterprises in underdeveloped countries.

June 18   Soviet Union requests that the Security Council appeal to all members to ratify the Geneva protocol prohibiting bacteriological warfare. Denouncing the move as Soviet propaganda, the Western-dominated council defeats the Soviet draft.

June 20   Israeli military police seize offices of the Jordan–Israeli mixed armistice commission. Until the offices are reopened three months later, the meetings take place in the open air. Thirteen Asian and Arab nations request an emergency meeting of the General Assembly to consider a complaint that France continually violates civil liberties and imposes foreign rule on the people of Tunisia. Although the Communist bloc supports the request, it is defeated by the opposition of twenty-seven Western and Latin American members. This controversy indicates how anticolonial issues will shortly dominate UN debates.

June 24   Based on studies conducted by WHO, FAO, and UNICEF, the Economic and Social Council concludes there is no world shortage of insecticides.

June 26   UNESCO undertakes a study of education as a means of combating discrimination. Black South Africans declare a defiance campaign to protest varying restrictions on marriage, employment, movement, and residency. By the end of the year, more than 100,000 join the African National Congress as the nucleus of a mass movement to protest white supremacy in South Africa.

June 28–July 18   Economic and Social Council studies the development of a unified worldwide system of road signs and signals.

July 8   Final report of the International Refugee Organization indicates that during the period 1945–1951, 90 percent of all refugee cases resulted in repatriation or resettlement.

July 10   Under UN auspices, the Eritrean constitution is adopted. Eritrea becomes an autonomous unit federated with and under the sovereignty of Ethiopia, an arrangement causing bitterness, resentment, and war to the present day. ECOSOC recommends that all industrial nations consider the effect of their economic policies on underdeveloped countries. After a clash between the West and communist blocs over the impact of military buildups on the economies of the Third World, ECOSOC orders a study of the inflationary effect of militarization.

July 13   At the Panmunjom armistice talks, a plan to allow the Red Cross to ascertain individual prisoners' wishes regarding repatriation is rejected by the Communists. ECOSOC proposes a $25 million budget for the Expanded Programme of Technical Assistance.

July 23   ECOSOC suggests that the purposes and practices of the United Nations be included in the school curricula of member states.

July 25   ECOSOC reissues appeal to member governments to set equitable immigration policies through bilateral and multilateral agreements, and recommends that governments undertake long-term housing programs for people of low income.

July 30   Regular session of the General Assembly is asked to consider the Tunisian complaint.

July 31   UN commission on the reunification of Germany adjourns after the Soviet Union refuses to participate. Secretary-general sets up the Technical Assistance Board.

August 8   Thirteen Asian and Middle Eastern nations request the General Assembly to consider French violations of human and sovereign rights in Morocco. France warns the assembly that it will permit no interference in its domestic affairs.

August 25   Indian and Pakistani ministers meet in Geneva to discuss Kashmir, but reach no agreement.

August 29   A revised draft of the armistice agreement for Korea is made public.

September 1   Lie presses West Germany for a progress report on compensation of death-camp survivors who were victims of forced medical experiments.

September 2   UN Rep. Frank Graham of the United States submits to India and Pakistan new peace terms, which call for mutual force reductions in Kashmir.

September 3   India rejects plan for troop reductions in Kashmir, citing need to preserve local order.

September 8   Security Council defeats Soviet "package deal" to admit fourteen new members. UN publishes a preliminary report on the world social situation, the first worldwide survey on living conditions in both the developed and underdeveloped countries.

September 9   Jordan–Israeli mixed armistice commission reports 509 truce violations by both sides.

September 12   South Africa's policy of racial discrimination (apartheid) appears on the General Assembly agenda for the first time; it remains there to the present day [to the writing of this book].

September 14   Israel accuses Arab states of violating their charter obligations and asks for new General Assembly efforts to achieve a negotiated Middle East settlement; the request is deferred on October 16.

September 15   The federation of Eritrea and Ethiopia is announced. Twenty-seven nations pledge a total of $270 million for relief and reconstruction in Korea. With 115 truce violations pending, the Israeli–Syrian mixed armistice commission suspends operations.

September 18   Soviet Union vetoes Japan's membership application.

September 30   International Red Cross reports that a total of 469 Greek children have been repatriated from Yugoslavia.

October 1   ECOSOC Technical Assistance Board reports that 1,600 experts in various fields have been sent to sixty-five countries, and that it has awarded 2,700 fellowships around the world.

October 2   Truce Supervision Organization reports 429 violations of the Egyptian–Israeli truce agreement, nearly all occurring in the Gaza Strip.

October 10   UNICEF reports widespread success in disease control, public health education, and long-range feeding assistance throughout the underdeveloped world. In 1952, thirty-eight governments contributed almost $11 million to UNICEF programs.

October 15   Rejecting UN jurisdiction over a domestic dispute, France refuses to participate in the General Assembly debate on Tunisia. Premier Mohammed Mossadegh announces that Iran has broken diplomatic relations with Britain because of failure to achieve settlement of the dispute over the nationalization of oil interests.

Korean peace talks, deadlocked on the prisoner-exchange issue, recess till year's end.

October 17   North Korea asks to participate in General Assembly debates since measures adopted regarding Korea in the absence of its representatives are illegal.

October 18   The United Nations command denies any use of bacteriological and chemical weapons in Korea; it also denies that air strikes have occurred outside Korean territory.

October 24   In Detroit, General Eisenhower pledges that, if elected president, he will personally go to Korea to seek "an early and honorable" peace.

November 4   Eisenhower is elected president by the largest popular vote in history; Republicans control both houses of Congress. Within six months, fighting in Korea will end.

November 5   Britain and the United States propose a Security Council resolution urging India and Pakistan to undertake direct negotiations in New York under the guidance of Graham, the Security Council representative.

November 6   General Assembly increases budget relief of Palestinian refugees.

November 7   General Assembly dissolves the Sub-Committee on Freedom of Information and the Press.

November 10   Lie announces his resignation as secretary-general of the United Nations.

November 11   General Assembly requests the colonial powers permit indigenous representatives to participate in the work of the UN Committee on Information from Non-Self-Governing Territories; colonial powers ignore the suggestion.

November 14   Abraham H. Feller, general counsel to the Secretariat and close friend of Lie, commits suicide. Lie blames Feller's death on the stress of defending U.S. employees at the UN against a Communist "smear" campaign. Bowing to United States pressure, Lie appoints a commission of jurists to advise him on the rights of the permanent Secretariat personnel who refuse to cooperate with loyalty investigations. Based on the commission's findings, Lie fires nine employees.

November 16   Atomic Energy Commission announces that a hydrogen (fusion) device has been detonated at Eniwetok atoll.

November 18   All negotiations between the Ad Hoc Committee on South-West Africa and the Union of South Africa are suspended since South Africa refuses to admit any UN supervisory powers over the former mandate.

November 21–24   Majority of General Assembly members criticize Albania, Bulgaria, and Romania for their refusal to return Greek children.

November 25   During a General Assembly debate on Palestine, Arab states accuse Israel of barring the return of refugees while Israel counters that it is the unwillingness of Arab states to negotiate directly that prevents a resolution.

November 29   Eisenhower begins a three-day tour of Korea, fulfilling his election pledge.

December 2   Over the solid opposition of the Soviet bloc, the General Assembly calls for the immediate exchange of Korean prisoners of war in accordance with the Geneva Accords of 1949.

December 4   General Assembly creates a seventeen-member committee to study the possibility of creating an international court of criminal justice. Syria asks the International Court of Justice to determine the rights of Palestinian refugees. Both France and Russia oppose the request because it implies the right of assembly majorities to interfere in the sovereign rights of member states.

December 5   Despite South Africa's vow of noncooperation, the General Assembly establishes a three-member Good Offices Committee to mediate India's complaint against the Union. General Assembly recognizes the sacrifices of those who have "died for the United Nations"; it lists fourteen UN operations, including Korea, to which the honor applies. General Assembly instructs ECOSOC to study the feasibility of financing programs of agrarian reform. General Assembly declares that racial discrimination is contrary to the declaration on human rights and creates a commission to study apartheid in South Africa. Despite the moderate tone of the resolution, thirty-four nations, including most of the Western powers, abstain, and South Africa calls the commission illegal.

December 9 United Nations air force units continue to bombard Communist targets up to the Manchurian border while the armistice talks are suspended.

December 10 The anticolonial majority in the General Assembly, over the vigorous and unanimous opposition of the Western members, declares that the UN must be informed of any changes in the status of non-self-governing territories; the assembly enumerates factors to aid the UN in determining if a territory has attained a full measure of self-government. Moreover, the Committee on Information from Non-Self-Governing Territories is renewed for three years.

December 12 The Netherlands informs the secretary-general that it will submit no further information on the Netherlands Antilles and Surinam.

December 16 General Assembly adopts a code of ethics for journalists, and approves a draft convention on the international right of correction, which entitles signatories to correct news dispatches containing false information. Over the solid opposition of the Western members, a General Assembly majority composed of the Soviet bloc, Latin America, Middle Eastern, and Asian countries recommends that all nations uphold the principle of self-determination of peoples. All members responsible for the administration of non-self-governing territories must prepare them for independence and transmit information to the UN on measures being taken to advance self-government in territories under their authority.

December 17 UNESCO announces that it will undertake a scientific history of mankind, to be compiled by 1,000 international scholars. General Assembly resolution condemns Albania, Bulgaria, Czechoslovakia, and Romania for continuing to hold Greek children; it asks the International Red Cross to continue repatriation efforts. Following a lengthy debate, the General Assembly can only appeal to France and Tunisia to negotiate an end to their differences because the Western–Latin bloc impedes any stronger action. The act of federation between Eritrea and Ethiopia is approved by the assembly and removed from its agenda.

December 18 General Assembly fails to agree on any proposal regarding the internationalization of Jerusalem. Lie requests the International Red Cross to facilitate repatriation of all sick and wounded POWs in Korea.

December 19   General Assembly resolution urges negotiations between France and Morocco, but France refuses to participate in the vote.

December 20   General Assembly urges that a peace treaty with Austria be rapidly concluded. General Assembly creates a sixteen-member committee to study the problem of defining aggression. The Convention on the Political Rights of Women, which grants women the unrestricted right to compete for and hold any public office and to discharge any public function established by national law, is adopted by the assembly. Chinese and Korean authorities accuse UN command of "mass murder" of prisoners at the Pongam prison camp. A Soviet request that the General Assembly condemn the action is defeated by a vote of 45–5 with 10 abstentions.

December 21   General Assembly recommends bilateral and multilateral agreements to eliminate racial and religious discrimination. A special committee to study the factors that should apply to the admission of new members to the UN is created. The assembly also declares Japan, Jordan, Laos, and Vietnam to be "peace-loving states," deserving of admission.

December 23   The Security Council criticizes India and Pakistan for failing to demilitarize Kashmir and calls for immediate troop reductions. India declares it will not be bound by the council's action.

December 30   Secretary-general reports that 753 treaties have been registered with the Secretariat during 1952.

1953

January 9   U.S. presidential executive order authorizes FBI investigation of American Secretariat personnel. Under heavy United States pressure, Lie allows interrogation and fingerprinting of American employees at UN headquarters.

January 19   Meeting in New York, the UN Population Commission sets the agenda for the upcoming World Population Conference in Rome. In a letter to Lie, the United States announces its refusal to transmit information about Puerto Rico under Article 73e.

January 21   Lie appoints a special committee of nine members to consider the details of a UN fund for economic development.

January 22   The UN Mixed Armistice Commission for Palestine reports a steady increase in truce violations.

January 23   Foreign ministers of India and Pakistan agree to meet in Geneva under the auspices of the UN representative.

January 31   Lie reports he had transmitted 468 claims for the indemnification of Nazi death-camp survivors to the Federal Republic of Germany.

February 2   Sixty-nine nations pledge a total of $22.3 million to the Expanded Programme of Technical Assistance.

February 6–14   Economic Commission for Asia and the Far East meets in Bandung, Indonesia.

February 25   General Assembly rejects a Soviet proposal that North Korea be invited to participate in the debate on Korea.

March 5   Joseph Stalin dies suddenly. Relying on signed statements by two U.S. Air Force officers, the USSR again accuses the United States of bacteriological warfare in Korea.

March 9   India accuses South Africa of implementing the Group Areas Act in violation of General Assembly resolutions condemning racial separation.

March 10   Defending his personnel policies before a hostile General Assembly, Lie says his part in mass dismissals of American UN employees was to preserve the political independence of the Secretariat.

March 11   General Assembly urges member governments to fulfill their pledges to the UN Korean Reconstruction Agency.

March 13–June 15   Special Committee on the Admission of New Members fails to break the Great Powers' deadlock over admissions.

March 16   In a letter to the General Assembly, fourteen Middle East and Asian members accuse France of forcibly suppressing Tunisia's national liberation movement.

March 17   Following an acrimonious debate, the General Assembly agrees to extend the life of the Collective Measures Committee for one year. Reaffirming its previous appeals to the governments of Albania, Poland, Hungary, Romania, Bulgaria, and Czechoslovakia, the assembly urges repatriation of all Greek soldiers taken to these countries during the Greek civil war.

March 19 UNICEF meets in New York to consider emergency aid for children victimized by natural disasters in Greece and Japan.

March 20 In a letter to Lie, South Africa denies UN jurisdiction over the treatment of its Indian nationals.

March 23 Arab states complain to the UN that Israel is using Arab refugees' property to finance resettlement of Jewish settlers.

March 25 Burma accuses Nationalist China of aggression because 12,000 of its troops, who had fled there following the Communist victory of 1949, have refused to surrender to Burmese authorities.

March 27 Repudiating the confessions of U.S. Air Force officers, the United States denies all charges of bacteriological warfare in Korea. UN representative reports that India and Pakistan are unwilling to agree on the number of troops that will remain in Kashmir or on the appointment of a plebiscite administrator.

March 28 Chinese and North Korean delegation agrees to the exchange of sick and wounded prisoners of war. Chinese Prime Minister Chou En-lai agrees to the resumption of armistice negotiations on March 30.

March 30 UN Commission on Narcotic Drugs meets in New York to consider the codification of all international agreements in a single narcotics convention. Over the strenuous objections of South Africa, the General Assembly appoints a three-member commission of inquiry to study race relations in South Africa.

April 1 Guatemala accuses the United States of interfering in its domestic affairs, but the Security Council refuses to consider the complaint.

April 2 United States informs the Security Council that Bikini atoll in the Trust Territory of the Pacific Islands is now closed for security reasons; hydrogen bomb tests begin.

April 7 In a brief but emotional statement to the General Assembly, Lie sums up his administrative accomplishments and welcomes Sweden's Dag Hammarskjöld as his successor.

April 8   General Assembly continues to advocate balanced reductions in all armed forces and the elimination of all weapons of mass destruction; it renews the Disarmament Commission.

April 14   World Bank reports that a total of $475 million in loans were made in the preceding year, the highest yearly total thus far.

April 15   General Assembly approves drawing up a protocol on uniform road signs and signals.

April 16   Before the American Society of Newspaper Editors, Eisenhower supports internationally supervised worldwide disarmament and pledges a portion of savings to a development fund for the emerging nations.

April 16–23   ECOSOC considers the world economic survey, which reveals a wide gap in living standards between advanced and backward nations.

April 18   General Assembly orders an impartial investigation into charges that the UN command has engaged in bacteriological warfare. By unanimous vote, the General Assembly orders the removal of all Nationalist Chinese forces from Burma.

April 26   After a six-month impasse over the repatriation of war prisoners, armistice talks resume in Kaesong. In a radio address from his home in Forest Hills, New York, Lie bids farewell to the United Nations. The secretary-general laments the failure of the UN to preserve the peace but praises the efforts of the specialized agencies in extending the hope for a better life to millions of people.

Appendix A

United Nations Members

1945 Argentina, Australia, Belarus (Byelorussia), Belgium, Bolivia, Brazil, Canada, Chile, China, Colombia, Costa Rica, Cuba, Czechoslovakia,* Denmark, Dominican Republic, Ecuador, Egypt, El Salvador, Ethiopia, France, Greece, Guatemala, Haiti, Honduras, India, Iran, Iraq, Lebanon, Liberia, Luxembourg, Mexico, Netherlands, New Zealand, Nicaragua, Norway, Panama, Paraguay, Peru, Philippines, Poland, Russian Federation,‡ Saudi Arabia, South Africa, Syrian Arab Republic,† Turkey, Ukraine, United Kingdom of Great Britain and Northern Ireland, United States of America, Uruguay, Venezuela, Socialist Federal Republic of Yugoslavia§

1946 Afghanistan, Iceland, Sweden, Thailand

1947 Pakistan, Yemen″

1948 Myanmar

1949 Israel

1950 Indonesia

1955 Albania, Austria, Bulgaria, Cambodia, Finland, Hungary, Ireland, Italy, Jordan, Lao People's Democratic Republic, Libyan Arab Jamahiriya, Nepal, Portugal, Romania, Spain, Sri Lanka

1956 Japan, Morocco, Sudan, Tunisia

1957 Ghana, Federation of Malaya (Malaysia)#

1958 Guinea

1960 Benin, Burkina Faso, Cameroon, Central African Republic, Chad, Congo, Côte d'Ivoire, Cyprus, Democratic Republic of the Congo, Gabon, Madagascar, Mali, Niger, Nigeria, Senegal, Somalia, Togo

1961 Mauritania, Mongolia, Sierra Leone, Tanganyika (United Republic of Tanzania)**

1962 Algeria, Burundi, Jamaica, Rwanda, Trinidad and Tobago, Uganda

1963 Kenya, Kuwait, Zanzibar (United Republic of Tanzania)**

1964 Malawi, Malta, Zambia

1965 Gambia, Maldives, Singapore#

1966 Barbados, Guyana, Lesotho

208 *Appendix A*

1967 Democratic Yemen"
1968 Equatorial Guinea, Mauritius, Swaziland
1970 Fiji
1971 Bahrain, Bhutan, Oman, Qatar, United Arab Emirates
1973 Bahamas, German Democratic Republic and Federal Republic of Germany (Germany)
1974 Bangladesh, Grenada, Guinea-Bissau
1975 Cape Verde, Comoros, Mozambique, Papua New Guinea, Sao Tome and Principe, Suriname
1976 Angola, Samoa, Seychelles
1977 Djibouti, Vietnam
1978 Dominica, Solomon Islands
1979 Saint Lucia
1980 Saint Vincent and the Grenadines, Zimbabwe
1981 Antigua and Barbuda, Belize, Vanuatu
1983 Saint Kitts and Nevis
1984 Brunei Darussalam
1990 Liechtenstein, Namibia
1991 Democratic People's Republic of Korea, Estonia, Federated States of Micronesia, Latvia, Lithuania, Marshall Islands, Republic of Korea
1992 Armenia, Azerbaijan, Bosnia and Herzegovina,§ Croatia,§ Georgia, Kazakhstan, Kyrgyzstan, Republic of Moldova, San Marino, Slovenia,§ Tajikistan, Turkmenistan, Uzbekistan
1993 Andorra, Czech Republic,* Eritrea, Monaco, Slovak Republic,* The former Yugoslav Republic of Macedonia§
1994 Palau
1999 Kiribati, Nauru, Tonga
2000 Tuvalu, Federal Republic of Yugoslavia§

---

* Czechoslovakia dissolved (1992) to create two independent member states: Czech Republic and Slovak Republic.
† Egypt and Syria were original members under the union, United Arab Republic. Syria assumed its independent status in 1961. In 1971 the United Arab Republic changed its name to the Arab Republic of Egypt.
‡ Union of Soviet Socialist Republics dissolved to into eleven member countries, most of which became UN member states.
§ The Socialist Federal Republic of Yugoslavia dissolved to create independent member states, Bosnia and Herzegovina, Croatia, Slovenia, former Yugoslav Republic of Macedonia, and Federal Republic of Yugoslavia.
" Yemen and Democratic Yemen merged in 1990 and represent a unified state in the UN under the name "Yemen."
Formerly part of the Federation of Malaya, Singapore became an independent state as well as a member of the UN.
** Tanganyika and Zanzibar united to create the United Republic of Tanganyika and Zanzibar and became UN member under the new name (1964); now United Republic of Tanzania.

Appendix B

Excerpt from the Charter of the United Nations

CHAPTER XV

Article 97

The Secretariat shall comprise a Secretary-General and such staff as the Organization may require. The Secretary-General shall be appointed by the General Assembly upon the recommendation of the Security Council. He shall be the chief administrative officer of the Organization.

Article 98

The Secretary-General shall act in that capacity in all meetings of the General Assembly, of the Security Council, of the Economic and Social Council, and of the Trusteeship Council, and shall perform such other functions as are entrusted to him by these organs. The Secretary-General shall make an annual report to the General Assembly on the work of the Organization.

Article 99

The Secretary-General may bring to the attention of the Security Council any matter which in his opinion may threaten the maintenance of international peace and security.

Article 100

1. In the performance of their duties the Secretary-General and the staff shall not seek or receive instructions from any government or from any other authority external to the Organization. They shall refrain from any action which might reflect on their position as international officials responsible only to the Organization.
2. Each member of the United Nations undertakes to respect the exclusively international character of the responsibilities of the Secretary-General and the staff and not to seek to influence them in the discharge of their responsibilities.

Article 101

1. The staff shall be appointed by the Secretary-General under regulations established by the General Assembly.
2. Appropriate staffs shall be permanently assigned to the Economic and Social council, the Trusteeship Council, and, as required, to other organs of the United Nations. These staffs shall form a part of the Secretariat.
3. The paramount consideration in the employment of the staff and in the determination of the conditions of service shall be the necessity of securing the highest standards of efficiency, competence, and integrity. Due regard shall be paid to the importance of recruiting the staff on as wide a geographical basis as possible.

From the *Charter of the United Nations and Statute of the International Court of Justice*, Department of Public Information, United Nations, 2000.

Bibliography

Alger, Chadwick F. "Personal Contact in Intergovernmental Organizations." In *The United Nations and Its Functions*, edited by Robert W. Gregg and Michael Barkun. Princeton, N.J.: Van Nostrand, 1968. Exaggerated appraisal of the value of corridor diplomacy at the UN on the reduction of world tensions.

Alker, Hayward R., and Bruce M. Russett. *World Politics in the General Assembly*. New Haven, Conn.: Yale University Press, 1965. Study of bloc politics in the General Assembly.

Asher, Robert E. "Multilateral versus Bilateral Aid: An Old Controversy Revisited." *International Organization* (Autumn 1962): 697–719. Valuable discussion; especially helpful in understanding U.S. reluctance to channel aid through UN programs.

———. *The United Nations and the Promotion of General Welfare*. Washington, D.C.: Brookings Institution, 1957. Positive assessment of the UN's social and economic activities.

Bailey, Sydney D. *The Secretariat of the United Nations*. New York: Carnegie Endowment for International Peace, 1962. Technical analysis of the structure and legal responsibilities of the Secretariat. Good introductory treatment.

———. *The General Assembly of the United Nations: A Study of Procedure and Practice*. New York: Praeger, 1964. Excellent introductory text.

Ball, J. H. *Collective Security: The Why and How*. Boston: World Peace Foundation, 1943. Idealistic assessment of the prospects for world peace.

Ball, Margaret M. "Bloc Voting in the General Assembly." *International Organization* (Spring 1951): 3–31. Ball documents the adverse effect of bloc voting on the General Assembly.

Barr, Stringfellow. *Citizens of the World*. Garden City, N.Y.: Doubleday, 1952. Idealistic appeal for world government based on popular consent.

Bechhoefer, Bernard C. *Postwar Negotiations for Arms Control*. Washington, D.C.: Brookings Institution, 1961.

Bennett, A. Leroy. *International Organizations.* Englewood Cliffs, N.J.: Prentice Hall, 1977. Useful, short, introductory text.

Bentwich, Norman. *Israel.* London: Elek, 1952.

Berger, Carl. *The Korean Knot.* Philadelphia: University of Pennsylvania Press, 1957. Useful examination of post–World War II Korea.

Black, Charles E. "Greece and the United Nations." *Political Science Quarterly* (December 1948): 551–68.

Blaisdell, Donald R. *International Organization.* New York: Ronald Press, 1966. Standard, readable text, but Claude and Goodrich should be read first.

Bloomfield, Lincoln P. *The United Nations and U.S. Foreign Policy.* Boston: Little Brown, 1960. Bloomfield analyzes the potential benefits and limitations of the UN for the furtherance of U.S. interests; cynical, but honest.

———. "Law, Politics, and International Disputes." *International Conciliation* (January 1958): 257–316.

Boyd, Andrew. *Fifteen Men on a Powder Keg.* New York: Stein and Day, 1971. Valuable short story of the Security Council.

Boyer, W. W., and N. Akra. "The United States and the Admission of Communist China." *Political Science Quarterly* (September 1961): 332–53. History of U.S. maneuvers to exclude Peking from the United Nations.

Brennan, David G., ed. *Arms Control, Disarmament, and National Security.* New York: Braziller, 1961. Useful anthology.

Brierly, James L. *The Law of Nations.* Oxford: Clarendon Press, 1963. The best short work on international law. A must. Brierly argues persuasively that states undertake legal obligations under international law despite the absence of central enforcement.

———. *The Covenant and the Charter.* New York: Macmillan, 1947. Excellent, readable analysis by one of the giants in the field of international law.

Brown, B. H. *Chinese Representation: A Case Study in the United Nations' Political Affairs.* New York: Woodrow Wilson Foundation, 1955.

Carr, E. H. *Nationalism and After.* London: Macmillan, 1945. Excellent treatment by one of the best writers on this subject.

Carroll, Faye. *South–West Africa and the United Nations.* Lexington: University of Kentucky Press, 1967. Comprehensive study of this troubled mandate.

Cavers, D. F. "Arms Control in the United Nations: A Decade of Disagreement." *Bulletin of the Atomic Scientists* (April 1956): 105–11. Useful treatment of various disarmament proposals that have come before the United Nations.

Cecil, Lord Robert. *A Great Experiment.* New York: Oxford University Press, 1941.

Chase, Eugene P. *The United Nations in Action.* New York: McGraw-Hill, 1950.

Chowdhuri, R. N. *International Mandates and Trusteeship Systems: A Comparative Study.* The Hague: Martinus-Nijhoff, 1950.

Churchill, Winston. *The Grand Alliance.* Boston: Houghton Mifflin, 1950.

Clark, Grenville. *A Plan for Peace.* New York: Harper, 1950.

Clark, Mark. *From the Danube to the Yalu.* New York: Harper, 1954. Critical analysis of U.S. postwar policy in the Far East.

Claude, Inis L. *Power and International Relations.* New York: Random House, 1962. Excellent treatment of various theories of balance of power politics.

————. *Swords Into Plowshares.* New York: Random House, 1956. Classic early work that critically analyzes the various organs of the United Nations and their functions.

————. *The Changing United Nations.* New York: Random House, 1967. Claude argues that with the end of its role in collective security, the UN has become a powerful voice for the promotion of international norms.

————. "United Nations Use of Military Force." *Journal of Conflict Resolution* (June 1963): 119–29.

Clausewitz, Karl von. *On War.* New York: Random House, 1956. Theoretical treatment of war and its causes.

Clay, Lucius. *Decision in Germany.* New York: Doubleday, 1950. The Berlin blockade through the eyes of one of the key players.

Cohen, Benjamin V. *The United Nations: Constitutional Developments, Growth, and Possibilities.* Cambridge, Mass.: Harvard University Press, 1961. Cohen argues that the charter has been sufficiently flexible to accommodate new political conditions.

Cohen, Israel. *The Zionist Movement.* London: Frederick Muller, 1945.

Collins, James F. "The United Nations and Indonesia." *International Conciliation* (March 1950): 115–200.

Conwell-Evans, T. P. *The League Council in Action.* London: Oxford University Press, 1929.

Coplin, William. *The Functions of International Law.* Chicago: Rand McNally, 1966. Coplin argues that conflict in the United Nations serves as an outlet for violence.

Corbett, Percy E. *The Growth of World Law.* Princeton, N.J.: Princeton University Press, 1971. Good standard text, but begin with Brierly.

Cordier, Andrew W., and Wilder Foote. *The Public Papers of the Secretaries-General of the United Nations, Vol. 1, Trygve Lie 1946–1953.* New York: Columbia University Press, 1969.

Coster, D. W. "The Interim Committee of the General Assembly: An Appraisal." *International Organization* (August 1949): 444–58. Useful examination of a generally neglected subject.

Cox, Robert W., ed. *International organization: World Politics.* London: Macmillan, 1969.

Dallek, Robert. *Franklin D. Roosevelt and American Foreign Policy, 1932–1945.* New York: Oxford University Press, 1979. Valuable account of FDR's campaign to break the hold of isolationism on U.S. foreign policy.

Dallin, Alexander. *The Soviet Union at the United Nations.* New York: Praeger, 1962. Seminal work on the evolution of Soviet attitudes toward international organization.

Davis, Harriet E., ed. *Pioneers in World Order*. New York: Columbia University Press, 1944.

Davison, W. Phillips. *The Berlin Blockade*. Princeton, N.J.: Princeton University Press, 1958. Excellent account of the background and settlement of this crisis.

Dougherty, J. E. "The Disarmament Debate: A Review of Current Literature." *Orbis* (Fall 1961): 342–59. Valuable survey of the theories that have dominated this important debate.

Eagleton, Clyde. "The Attempt to Define Aggression." *International Conciliation* (November 1930): 581–650. Penetrating analysis of a complex and elusive concept.

———. "The Case of Hyderabad Before the Security Council." *The American Journal of International Law* (April 1950): 277–302. The best treatment of this case in print.

———. "The Charter Adopted at San Francisco." *American Political Science Review* (October 1945): 934–42. Excellent account of the forming of the charter by one of the leading writers in the field.

Eichelberger, Clark M. *Organizing for Peace: A Personal History of the Founding of the United Nations*. New York: Harper and Row, 1977. Especially useful for an understanding of the dynamics and personalities of the peace movement in the United States.

Emerson, Rupert. *From Empire to Nation*. Cambridge, Mass.: Harvard University Press, 1950. Excellent study of the anticolonial movement and the best start to develop an understanding of this subject.

———. "Reflections in the Indonesian Cause." *World Politics* (October 1948): 59–81. Good, short account of UN role in bringing about Indonesian independence.

Evatt, Herbert. *The United Nations*. Cambridge, Mass.: Harvard University Press, 1948. Short, thoughtful and hopeful essay on the prospects for world peace through the United Nations by a statesman who participated in the drafting of the charter.

Feis, Herbert. *China Tangle*. Princeton, N.J.: Princeton University Press, 1953. Seminal account of U.S. policy during World War II and immediately after.

Finger, Seymour M., and John Mugno. *The Politics of Staffing the United Nations Secretariat*. New York: Ralph Bunche Institute, 1974.

Finkelstein, Lawrence S. "The United Nations in a Changing World." *UN Monthly Chronicle* (March 1965): 41–46. Excellent short analysis of the early political evolution of the United Nations.

Finkelstein, Marina S., and Lawrence S. Finkelstein, eds. *Collective Security*. San Francisco: Chandler Publishing, 1966. Informative anthology on the theory and historical development of collective security. Good starting point for study of the subject.

Fischer, John. *Master-Plan USA*. New York: Harper, 1951. Useful analysis of the application of the policy of containment to various parts of the world.

Gaddis, John L. *The United States and the Origins of the Cold War: 1941–1947*.

New York: Columbia University Press, 1972. Excellent revisionist examination of U.S. responsibility for the onset of the Cold War.

Garcia-Granados, Jorge. *The Birth of Israel.* New York: Knopf, 1949. Good study, but adds nothing new.

Godwin, Geoffrey L. *Britain and the United Nations.* New York: Manhattan Publishing Co., 1957. Valuable source for understanding British policy in the UN.

Goldman, Eric. *The Crucial Decade.* New York: Harper, 1951. Excellent treatment of changing postwar attitudes in the United States.

Good, Robert C. "The United States and the Colonial Debate" In *Alliance Policy in the Cold War,* edited by Arnold Wolfers. Baltimore: Johns Hopkins, 1953. Good study of U.S. ambivalence about decolonization.

Goodrich, Leland M. "Collective Measures Against Aggression." *International Conciliation* (October 1953): 131–92. Analysis of UN response to aggression in Korea.

———. "Geographical Distribution of the Staff of the UN Secretariat." *International Organization* (Summer 1962): 465–82.

———. "The Maintenance of International Peace and Security." *International Organization* (Summer 1965). Goodrich argues that charter provisions on collective security are not an improvement over the League's.

———. "The United Nations and Domestic Jurisdiction." *International Organization.* (February 1949). Brilliant analysis of conflicting interpretations of the domestic jurisdiction provisions of the charter.

Goodrich, Leland M., and Edvard Hambro. *Charter of the United Nations, Commentary and Documents.* Boston: World Peace Foundation, 1949. Authors analyze the origin and legal meaning of each charter provision. The best work on this subject.

Goodrich, Leland M., and Anne P. Simons. *The United Nations and the Maintenance of Peace and Security.* Washington, D.C.: Brookings Institution, 1955. Highly legalistic treatment of the subject; lucid and informative.

Gordenker, Leon. *The UN Secretary-General and the Maintenance of Peace.* New York: Columbia University Press, 1967. Gordenker criticizes Trygve Lie for ignoring the political limits of his office.

Graebner, Norma. *The New Isolationism.* New York: Ronald Press, 1956. Examination of neo-isolationist policies and anticommunist hysteria in the United States following the Korean War.

Gregg, Lester. "U.N. Economic, Social and Technical Activities." In *The United Nations: Past, Present and Future,* ed. James Barrows. New York: Free Press, 1972. Excellent, surprisingly comprehensive treatment.

Grey, Arthur L. Jr. "The Thirty-Eighth Parallel." *Foreign Affairs* (April 1951): 482–87.

Haas, Ernst B. "The Attempt to Terminate Colonialism: Acceptance of the United Nations' Trusteeship System." *International Organization* (November 952): 521–36.

————. *Beyond the Nation-State: Functionalism and International Organization.* Stanford, Calif.: Stanford University Press, 1964. Best study in print of the functional approach to world peace.

————. "Types of Collective Security: An Example of Operational Concepts." *American Political Science Review* (March 1955): 40–62. Informative, but very technical treatment of collective security with special emphasis on Russo–American conflicts.

Hadwen, John G., and Johan Kaufman. *How United Nations Decisions Are Made.* New York: Oceana Publications, 1962. Useful analysis of political coalition-building in various organs of the UN.

Hall, H. Duncan. *Mandates, Dependencies and Trusteeship.* Washington, D.C.: Carnegie Endowment for International Peace, 1948. Comprehensive, good introductory text.

Halpern, Manfred. *The Politics of Social Change in the Middle East and North Africa.* Princeton, N.J.: Princeton University Press, 1965.

Hartmann, Frederick H. *The Relations of Nations.* New York: Macmillan, 1962. Standard, very readable text.

Higgins, Rosalyn. *The Development of International Law Through the Political Organs of the United Nations.* London: Oxford University Press, 1963. Higgins argues that decisions of the UN form the basis for legal obligations by states.

Holcome, Arthur, ed. *Organizing Peace in the Nuclear Age.* New York: New York University Press, 1959. Good selection of readings about the impact of national policy on the United Nations.

Houston, John A. *Latin America and the United Nations.* New York: Carnegie Endowment for International Peace, 1956. Houston analyzes the policy of the largest voting bloc in the United Nations. Essential reading.

Hovet, Thomas. *Bloc Politics in the United Nations.* Cambridge, Mass.: Harvard University Press, 1960. Quantitative analysis of the evolution of the major voting blocs in the General Assembly. The standard text on this subject.

Hull, Cordell. *The Memoirs of Cordell Hull,* vols. 1 and 2. New York: Macmillan, 1948. Essential reading for an understanding of the developing commitment of the United States to the creation of the United Nations.

Huntington, Samuel P. *The Soldier and the State.* Cambridge, Mass.: Harvard University Press, 1957. Provocative analysis of civil–military relations in the United States. Huntington traces military policy to evolving social values.

Hurewitz, J. C. "The United Nations Conciliation Commission for Palestine." *International Organization* (November 1953): 482–97.

Hyde, James N. "Peaceful Settlement." *International Conciliation* (October 1948): 531–74.

Jackson, Elmore. *Meeting of Minds.* New York: McGraw-Hill, 1952. Jackson argues that the tendency of the UN to postpone showdowns is not, as many observers believe, a good thing.

Jacobson, Harold K. "The United Nations and Colonialism: A Tentative

Appraisal." *International Organization* (Winter 1962): 36–56. Jacobson credits the UN with hastening the end of colonialism.

———. *The USSR and the UN's Economic and Social Activities*. South Bend, Ind.: University of Notre Dame Press, 1963. Traces reasons for change in Soviet policy from total isolation to active support for some UN programs.

Jenks, Wilfred C. *Social Justice in the Law of Nations: The ILO Impact After Fifty Years*. London: Oxford University Press, 1970.

Jimenez de Arechaga, Eduardo. *Voting and the Handling of Disputes in the Security Council*. New York: Carnegie Endowment for International Peace, 1950. Critical analysis of the veto on the council's capacity to resolve conflict.

Johnston, Walter, ed. *The Yalta Conference*. New York: Doubleday, 1949. Informative accounts of this highly controversial meeting.

Kaplan, Morton, ed. *The Revolution in World Politics*. New York: John Wiley, 1962.

Kay, David. "The Impact of the African States in the United Nations." *International Organization* (Winter 1969): 20–47.

Kelsen, Hans. *The Law of the United Nations: A Critical Analysis of Its Fundamental Problems*. New York: Frederick A. Praeger, 1964. Brilliant but often obscure analysis of the legal obligations undertaken by states under the charter. Not for beginners.

Keohane, Richard. "Political Influence in the General Assembly." *International Conciliation* (March 1966).

Kirk, G., and L. Chamberlain. "The Organization of the San Francisco Conference." *Political Science Quarterly* (June 1945): 321–42.

Kissinger, Henry A. *Nuclear Weapons and Foreign Policy*. New York: Harper, 1957. Harsh criticism of U.S. reliance on the doctrine of massive retaliation.

Koestler, Arthur. *Promise and Fulfillment: Palestine 1917–1949*. London: Macmillan, 1949. Beautifully written, pro-Zionist, anti-British account of the creation of the state of Israel.

Koo, Wellington Jr. *Voting Procedures in International Political Organizations*. New York: Columbia University Press, 1947.

Korey, William. "The Key to Human Rights—Implementation." *International Conciliation* (November 1968).

Kunz, Josef L. "Chapter XI of the United Nations' Charter in Action." *American Journal of International Law* (January 1954): 103–10. Legal defense of anticolonial politics in the UN.

Laqueue, Walter. *A History of Zionism*. London: Weidenfeld and Nicolson, 1972. Well-documented, comprehensive study that ends with the creation of Israel in 1948.

Larus, Joel, ed. *From Collective Security to Preventive Diplomacy*. New York: John Wiley, 1965. Valuable anthology; especially helpful in understanding the changing role of the secretary-general.

Lauterpacht, Sir Hersch. *The Development of International Law by the International Court*. New York: Praeger, 1958.

Lawson, Ruth C., ed. *International Regional Organizations.* New York: Praeger, 1962. Good anthology on the development and politics of regional organizations.

Lee, Clark G., and Richard Henschel. *Douglas MacArthur.* New York: Holt, Rinehart, and Winston, 1952.

Leonard, L. "The United Nations and Palestine." *International Conciliation* (October 1949): 607–786. Good, short account of the partition plan and its aftermath.

Liang, Yuen-Li. "Abstention and Absence of a Permanent Member in Relation to the Voting Procedure in the Security Council." *American Journal of International Law* (October 1950): 694–708.

Lie, Trygve. *In the Cause of Peace.* New York: Macmillan, 1955. Lie's own account of his years as secretary-general, a rich source of information.

Lissitzyn, Oliver J. *The International Court of Justice.* New York: Carnegie Endowment for International Peace, 1951. Excellent text.

Loewenheim, Francis L. et al. *Roosevelt and Churchill: Their Secret Wartime Correspondence.* New York: E. P. Dutton, 1975. A must for an understanding of Anglo-American wartime collaboration.

Loewenstein, Karl. "Sovereignty and International Cooperation." *American Journal of International Law* (April 1954): 222–44. Excellent study of the theoretical and practical contradictions of collective security.

Loveday, Alexander. *Reflections on International Administration.* New York: Oxford University Press, 1956.

Lowenstein, Allard K. *Brutal Mandate.* New York: Macmillan, 1962. Fine, detailed account of South–West African mandate.

Luard, Evan, ed. *The Evolution of International Organizations.* London: Thames and Hudson, 1966.

Mangone, Gerard J. *The Idea and Practice of World Government.* New York: Columbia University Press, 1951. Excellent survey of this subject.

———, ed. *UN Administration of Economic and Social Programs.* New York: Columbia University Press, 1966. Excellent volume of readings covering all aspects of the subject.

Martin, Peter. "Peacekeeping and the United Nations—the Broader View." *International Affairs* (April 1964): 191–204.

Meyer, Cord. *Peace or Anarchy.* Boston: Little Brown, 1947. Brilliant critique of the shortcomings in the charter's approach to peace.

Mitrany, David. *A Working Peace System.* Chicago: Quadrangle Books, 1966. Idealistic view of the UN.

Moldaver, Arlette. "Repertoire of the Veto in the Security Council: 1946–56." *International Organization* (Spring 1957): 261–74. Concise analysis of early Soviet use of the veto.

Murray, James N. *The United Nations Trusteeship System.* Urbana: University of Illinois Press, 1957.

Nicholas, Harold G. *The United Nations as a Political Institution.* New York:

Oxford University Press, 1963. The best account of the United Nations in print with a particularly insightful comparison of the UN Charter and League Covenant.

Padelford, Norman J. "Politics and Change in the Security Council." *International Organization* (Summer 1960): 227–46. Good study of evolving patterns of influence within the council.

———. "The Use of the Veto." *International Organization* (June 1948): Padelford argues that Soviet vetoes are cast essentially to protect vital interests and that the West accomplishes the same result through its voting majority in the council.

Plano, John C., and Robert E. Riggs. *Forging World Order: The Politics of International Organization.* New York: Macmillan, 1967. Somewhat confusing analysis of the political patterns that have developed within the organization.

Rees, David. *Korea: The Limited War.* New York: St. Martin's Press, 1964. Adds little to other standard treatments of the Korean War.

Riches, Cromwell A. *Majority Rule in International Organization.* Baltimore: Johns Hopkins, 1940.

Riggs, Robert E. *Politics in the United Nations: A Study of United States Influence in the General Assembly.* Urbana: University of Illinois Press, 1958. Excellent study of U.S. pressure tactics in the General Assembly.

Roun, H. "The International Court of Justice and Domestic Jurisdiction." *International Organization* (February 1954): 36–44.

Rovine, Arthur W. *The First Fifty Years: The Secretary-General in World Politics.* Leiden: Sijthoff, 1970. Very useful analysis of the office with short biographies of the men who served up until 1970.

Rowe, Edward T. "The Emerging Anti-Colonial Consensus in the United Nations." *Journal of Conflict Resolution* (September 1964): 209–30. Quantitative analysis of growing anticolonial sentiment in the General Assembly.

Rudzinski, Aleksander W. "Admission of New Members: The United Nations and the League of Nations." *International Conciliation* (May 1961). Excellent comparative analysis.

Rushbrook-Williams, L. F. "Inside Kashmir." *International Affairs* (January 1957): 26–35.

Russell, Ruth B. "Changing Patterns of Constitutional Development." *International Organization* (Summer 1965): 410–25. Russell argues that the charter has been amended through informal political interpretation and adapted to changing world conditions.

Russell, Ruth, and Jeanette Muther. *A History of the United Nations: The Role of the United States, 1940–45.* Washington, D.C.: Brookings Institution, 1958.

Sady, Emil. *The United Nations and Dependent Peoples.* Washington, D.C.: Brookings Institution, 1956. Comprehensive, sympathetic account of the early development of the anticolonial movement at the United Nations.

Scheinman, Lawrence, and David Wilkinson, eds. *International Law and Polit-*

ical Crisis. Boston: Little Brown, 1968. Authors agree that international law minimizes the prospects of violence in international disputes.

Schuman, Frederick L. *The Commonwealth of Man.* New York: Knopf, 1952. Excellent study of the problem of world government.

Schwebel, Stephen. *The Secretary-General of the United Nations: His Political Powers and Practice.* Cambridge, Mass.: Harvard University Press, 1952. Very technical, but essential treatment of the office with a valuable comparison of powers under the charter and covenant.

Seton-Watson, Hugh. *Neither War Nor Peace.* New York: Praeger, 1960. Brilliant examination of the political conditions that prevailed following World War II.

Sewell, James P. *Functionalism and World Politics.* Princeton, N.J.: Princeton University Press, 1966. Comprehensive treatment of the subject.

Sharp, Walter R. *The United Nations Economic and Social Council.* New York: Columbia University Press, 1969.

Shotwell, James T. *War as an Instrument of National Policy.* New York: Harcourt, Brace, 1949.

Spanier, John W. *The Truman-MacArthur Controversy and the Korean War.* New York: Norton, 1965. Excellent account of the Korean War and defense of Truman's decision to dismiss MacArthur.

Spiro, Herbert J. *World Politics: The Global System.* Homewood, Ill.: Dorsey Press, 1966. Analysis of the similarities between the UN and national governmental institutions.

Stein, Eric. *Some Implications of Expanding United Nations Membership.* New York: Carnegie Endowment for International Peace, 1956. Comprehensive critique of the principle of universality.

Stoessinger, John G., ed. *Financing the United Nations.* Washington, D.C.: Brookings Institution, 1964. Informative readings on various UN activities.

————. *The United Nations and the Superpowers.* New York: Random House, 1977. Stoessinger argues that the veto has not weakened the United Nations

Sweetser, Arthur. *The League of Nations at Work.* New York: Macmillan, 1920.

Taylor, Alastair M. *Indonesian Independence and the United Nations.* Ithaca, N.Y.: Cornell University Press, 1960. Extremely detailed and informative; the best book on the subject.

Truman, Harry S. *Memoirs. Volume I, Years of Decision. Volume II, Years of Trial and Hope.* New York: Doubleday, 1956. An essential source for an understanding of the period.

Tung, William L. *International Organization Under the United Nations System.* New York: Thomas Y. Crowell, 1969. Somewhat superficial treatment of the structure and functions of the United Nations.

Ulam, Adam B. *Expansion and Coexistence: The History of Soviet Foreign Policy: 1917–67.* New York: Praeger, 1968. Comprehensive, very readable account of the evolution of Soviet foreign policy from the early days of isolation to the emergence of the Soviet Union as a major power.

Van Dyke, Vernon. *Human Rights, the United States and World Community.* New York: Oxford University Press, 1970. Comprehensive study of evolving U.S. attitudes toward UN development of human rights standards.

Wainhouse, David W. *Remnants of Empire: The United Nations and the End of Colonialism.* New York: Harper and Row, 1964.

Ward, Barbara. *The Rich Nations and the Poor Nations.* New York: W. W. Norton, 1962.

Winchmore, Charles. "The Secretariat: Retrospect and Prospect." *International Organization* (Summer 1965).

Wohlgemuth, Patricia. "The Portuguese Territories and the United Nations." *International Conciliation* (November 1963): 7–68. Useful study of Portuguese defiance of UN authority over decolonization.

Wolfers, Arnold. "Collective Security and the War in Korea." *Yale Review* (Summer 1954). Wolfers argues persuasively that U.S. policy in Korea was dictated not by support for collective security but by containment politics.

———. *Discord and Collaboration.* Baltimore: Johns Hopkins, 1962. Wolfers views the UN as a source of legal and moral norms that bind nations together.

Wright, Quincy. *Mandates Under the League of Nations.* Chicago: University of Chicago Press, 1930. The best book on this subject in print.

Yates, Paul L. *So Bold an Aim: Ten Years of International Cooperation Toward Freedom from Want.* Rome: Food and Agriculture Organization, 1955. Comprehensive account of FAO efforts to alleviate hunger.

Yeselson, Abraham, and Anthony Gaglione. *A Dangerous Place: The United Nations as a Weapon in World Politics.* New York: Grossman, 1974.

Zimmern, Alfred. *The League of Nations and the Rule of Law, 1918–1935.* London: Macmillan, 1936.

Index

Note: References to the United Nations organizations and functions are scattered through the index (e.g., "Security Council, UN," "Atomic Energy Commission, UN," and "disease, fighting"). References to committees, commissions, conferences, and conventions can be found under key words in title (e.g., "Human Rights, UN Commission on")

Acheson, Dean, 31–32, 46, 65, 140
Acheson-Lilienthal proposal, 31–33, 144
Afghanistan, 27, 145, 148
African National Congress (ANC), 196
Albania, 26, 36, 147, 149, 160, 167
Allied Control Council, 41, 144
Anglo-American Conference, 136
Annual Report of the UN, 45, 145, 151, 157, 171
Appeal for Children, UN, 161
Arab Higher Committee, 50–51
arms reduction, military, 29, 32–35, 168, 174, 179, 189, 205
Articles of UN Charter: Article 26, 29; Article 42, 27; Article 43, 27, 28; Article 47, 28; Article 51, 11, 110, 155; Article 55, 93; Article 73e, 86; Article 97, 209; Article 98, 45, 209; Article 99, 44, 67, 122, 146, 209; Article 100, 210; Article 101, 211

association agreements, 154
Atlantic Alliance, 190
Atlantic Charter, 3, 134
Atlee, Clement, 30–31
Atomic Energy Commission, UN, 31, 34, 141, 142, 148, 168, 177, 189
atomic weaponry, 29–35, 141, 168, 174, 179
Austin, Warren, 52, 178
Austria, 151, 154, 161
Avenol, Joseph, 131
Azerbaijan, 21–25

Balfour Declaration, 49
Balkan Commission of Investigation, 35–36, 127
Balkans, UN Special Committee on the (UNSCOB), 160, 188
Ball, Joseph, 135
Baruch Plan, 32–34, 145, 150, 160, 189
Benes, Eduard, 37
Ben Gurion, David, 52, 156

Berle, Adolph, 36

Berlin blockade, 39–42, 155, 157, 159, 163

Bernadotte, Count Folke, 53, 159, 160, 170

Bevin, Ernest, 22, 40

Brussels Pact, 155

Bulgaria, 27, 36, 146, 147, 151, 160

Bunche, Ralph, 54, 161

Burma, 27, 156, 204

Burton, Harold, 135

Byrnes, James, 22, 23, 46

Caroline islands, 149

Ceylon, 158, 161

Charter, UN: approval of, 140, 141; Chapter VII provisions, 41; Chapter XI, 86, 87; Chapter XV excerpts, 209–10; drafting of, 8–11; excerpt from, 209–10; military force provisions, 27–28. *See also* Articles of UN Charter

Chile, 37–38

China: charges US aggression, 173; Korean intervention, 175, 179; Mao's triumph in, 162, 166, 179; membership in UN, 58–61, 63–64, 168, 188; rinderpest vaccination, 100–101

cholera, 102

Chou En-lai, 58, 204

chronology of UN: 1939, 131–32; 1940, 132–33; 1941, 133–34; 1942, 134–35; 1943, 135–36; 1944, 136–38; 1945, 138–41; 1946, 141–48; 1947, 148–54; 1948, 154–61; 1949, 162–67; 1950, 168–77; 1951, 177–89; 1952, 189–202; 1953, 202–5

Churchill, Winston, 3, 20, 135, 143

civil aviation, 137

Clark, Mark, 194

Cold War politics: bloc politics in General Assembly, 126–27;

impact on UN function, 119–21; and membership applications, 26–27, 120, 152; origins of, 19–20; pursuit of national political goals, 127–30; and Secretary-General's function, 121–25

Collective Measures Committee, 77, 188, 191, 203

colonialism, 83–88

Columbia, 166

Committee of Twelve, Disarmament Commission, 177, 179, 187

communism, containment of, 35–39, 120–21

Communist International (Comintern), Third, 136

Conant, James B., 132

Concert of Europe, 109

Conciliation Commission for Palestine, UN, 161, 165, 185

conflict mediation, 110–11

Consular Commission, 151, 153

Conventional Armaments, Commission for, 149, 177

Coordination, UN Committee of, 69

Corfu Channel dispute, 149, 150, 167

Costa Rica, 162

Council for Mutual Economic Assistance (COMECON), 163

Council of Europe, 146, 163

Council of Foreign Ministers, 41, 139, 147

Covenant on Economic, Social, and Cultural Rights, 81

Czechoslovakia, 37–39, 155, 156

Declaration of Death and Missing Persons, Convention on the, 175

Declaration of the United Nations, 3, 134

Declaration on the Rights of the Aged, 161

Defend America by Aiding the Allies, Committee to (CDA), 2
dependent peoples, emancipation of, 83–88
diplomacy, 110, 124, 127, 146
diplomatic immunity, 164
disarmament, 29, 32–35, 168, 174, 179, 189, 205
Disarmament Commission, 177, 179, 188, 190, 192, 205
disease, fighting, 101–3, 172
Dixon, Sir Owen, 179
Drummond, Sir Eric, 44
Dulles, John Foster, 194
Dumbarton Oaks proposals, 5–6, 137

East Africa, 158
East Germany, 39–42, 166, 170
Economic and Social Council (ECOSOC): Ad Hoc Committee on Slavery, 82; Commission on Narcotic Drugs, 149, 158, 159; Economic Commission for Asia and the Far East, 149, 180, 191, 203; Economic Commission for Europe, 147, 150, 183; Economic Commission for Latin America, 149, 183; Economic Commission for the Middle East, 153, 186; established, 9, 89, 142; Expanded Programme of Technical Assistance, 93, 98, 166, 177, 180, 185, 189, 197; growth of, 99; human rights debates, 184, 192; immigration policies, 197; limitations, 89–90; national employment policy remarks, 185; Subcommission on Economic Reconstruction of Devastated Areas, 145; SUNFED proposal, 91, 93–99, 190; Technical Assistance Board, 198
economic development, 93–99, 168–69

economic equity, 181
Eden, Sir Anthony, 4
Educational, Scientific, and Cultural Organization, UN (UNESCO), 102–6, 141, 145, 195; International Institute for Intellectual Cooperation, 146
educational programs, 104–5
Egypt, 102, 151, 162, 174
Einstein, Albert, 61, 132
Entezam, Nasrolla, 177
Eritrea, 196, 197, 201
Ethiopia, 196, 197, 201
European Coal and Steel Community (Schuman Plan), 195
Evatt, Herbert, 9

famine relief, 191
Feller, Abraham H., 199
field observers, panel of UN, 164, 166
Finland, 27, 132, 154, 161
First Quebec Conference (1943), 4
flag adopted, UN, 153
Food and Agriculture, Conference on, 136
Food and Agriculture Organization (FAO), 100–101, 136, 139, 145, 185, 188, 191, 194
Forrestal, James C., 30
Four Power Control Council, 40, 155
Four Power Declaration, 5
France, 60, 155, 193, 198, 201, 203
Fraser, Peter, 9
freedom of information, 83, 155, 172, 193, 199
Freedom of Information, Conference on, 83, 155
Freedom of Information, Convention on, 172

General Assembly, UN: bloc politics, 126–27;

General Assembly (*Continued*)
   expanded powers of, 75–76;
   first convened, 12–13, 141, 142;
   first special session convened,
   156; "Little Assembly" (Interim
   Committee on Peace and
   Security), 36–37, 76, 152; moral
   force of resolutions, 125–26,
   127–28; reliance on, by members,
   106–7, 125; Western dominance
   of, 77
genocide, 82, 147
George, David Lloyd, 84
Germany, 39–42, 131–40, 144, 148,
   186, 188
Ghavam, Ahmed, 23
Good Offices Committees, 115, 116,
   151, 179, 200
Graham, Frank
Great Britain: Corfu Channel
   dispute, 149, 150, 167; Malta/
   Pitcairn Islands, 162; Palestinian
   Mandate, 49–51, 54; troops in
   Greece and Indonesia, 23
Greece: British troops in, 23, 142;
   outside interference in, 35–39,
   144, 145–46, 147, 150, 152, 160,
   176
Grew, Joseph, 139
Gromyko, Andrei, 23–24, 33, 46, 186
guard, UN, 56–57, 157, 159, 164, 167
Gurmane, M.A., 182

Hatch, Carl, 135
Hatta, Mohammed, 116
headquarters of UN, 16–17, 143,
   147, 150, 158
health issues, 101–3
Hickerson, John C., 65
Hill, Lester, 135
Hoover, Herbert, 179
Hopkins, Harry, 3, 8
Hughes, William, 126
Hull, Cordell, 2–3, 4–5, 10–11, 138

human rights, 78–83, 150, 166, 176,
   184
Human Rights, UN Commission
   on, 78, 149, 150, 169, 182, 192,
   194, 195
Hungary, 27, 138, 146, 150, 151, 154
Hyderabad, 158, 159, 161

Iceland, 27, 145, 148
India, 162, 168, 179, 182, 189
India and Pakistan, UN
   Commission on (UNCIP), 155
Indochinese War, 147
Indonesia: admitted to UN, 27, 117;
   British troops in, 23;
   Commission for Indonesia, UN,
   116, 162; independence conflict,
   113–17, 143, 151, 161; Renville
   Accords, 115–16, 155
Indonesia, UN Commission for,
   116, 162
Information from Non-Self-
   Governing Territories,
   Committee on, 86–87, 88, 153,
   160, 162, 194, 199, 201
International Children's Emergency
   Fund, UN (UNICEF), 104, 161,
   176, 204
International Civil Aviation,
   Convention on, 137
International Court of Justice, 142,
   144, 156, 159, 163
International High Frequency
   Broadcasting Conference, 159
International Institute for
   Intellectual Cooperation, 146
International Labor Organization
   (ILO), 145
International Law Commission,
   154
International Military Tribunal for
   the Far East (IMTFE), 142
International Monetary Fund (IMF),
   137, 154, 165, 180

International Penal and Penitentiary Commission, 176
International Red Cross, 178
International Refugee Organization (IRO), 143, 148, 185, 196
International Rice Commission, 101
International Telecommunication Union, 154
International Transmission of News, Draft Convention on the, 163
Iran: nationalization of oil interests, 182, 198; Soviet troops in, 21–25, 142, 143, 144, 147
Ireland, 26, 145, 154, 161
Israel, 27, 52–55, 156, 160, 162, 163, 165, 173, 183, 196. *See also* Palestine
Italian colonies, 166
Italy, 27, 151, 154, 161, 192

Japan, 139–40, 180, 185, 198
Jerusalem, 166, 169, 201
Jordan, 26, 145, 154, 161, 183

Kashmir, 110, 158, 168, 173, 181, 182, 189, 191, 197
Kennan, George F., 151
Kerr, Sir Archibald Clark, 113
King, Mackenzie, 30, 31
Korean conflict: aftermath, 73–74, 111; cease-fire and truce, 73; Cease-Fire Committee, 177; Chinese intervention, 175, 182; Commission on Korea, UN, 65, 154, 161, 166; history of division, 64, 158; Korean Reconstruction Agency, UN (UNKRA), 176; "Legal Aspects of Security Council Action in Korea," 68; Lie's role in, 66–67, 68–69, 123–24; North Korea invades South Korea, 65, 170; Panmunjom armistice talks, 197; peace negotiations at Kaesong,

184, 193, 205; POWs, 178, 190, 200, 201; "Suggested Terms of Settlement of the Korean Question," 70; UN membership, 162, 163, 199; UN response, 66–70, 152, 172, 174; UN-supervised elections held, 64–65
Korean Reconstruction Agency, UN (UNKRA), 176

League of Nations, 1, 10, 84–85, 144
Lebanon, 143
"Legal Aspects of Security Council Action in Korea," 68
Lend-Lease Act, 133, 138
Libya, 166, 175, 187, 189
Lie, Trygve: annual reports, 45, 145, 151, 157, 171, 186; antagonizes East and West, 121–23; Berlin blockade crisis, 42, 43, 55; biography of, 13–16; Chinese participation on Security Council, 58, 61, 63–64, 169; chosen first Secretary-General, 12–13, 142; critical of unilateral Western actions, 46–47; final addresses, 204, 205; on Iranian complaint, 45–46, 144; and Korean conflict, 66–67, 68–69, 70, 123–24, 171, 183; Palestinian partition, 47, 55, 124, 156; portrayed as "Moscow's Man," 25; private beliefs interfere with role, 123–25; reappointment of, 71–74, 174; Twenty-Year Peace Plan, 43–44, 61–64, 69–70, 124, 169, 175, 176, 187; UN world-role shaped by, 55–57
Lilienthal, David E., 31–32
literacy projects, 104–5, 167
"Little Assembly" (Interim Committee on Peace and Security), 36–37, 76, 152, 153, 165
London Conference, 155

MacArthur, Douglas, 172, 173, 179, 181, 186

Macedonia, 36

Malan, Daniel François, 156

malaria, 102, 172, 185

Malik, Jacob, 59

mandates system, 84–85, 144

Mariana islands, 149

Marshall, George, 36, 150

Marshall islands, 149

Marshall Plan, 39–40, 90–91, 150

Masaryk, Jan, 37

McNaughton, Andrew George Latta, 168

Mehta, Mrs. Hampa, 79

membership, UN: Chinese membership, 58–61, 63–64; debates over, 26–27, 120, 146, 153, 156, 187, 191, 202, 203; Korea membership, 162, 163, 199; Lie advocates universal, 60–61, 152; list of all, 207–8; original membership, 7; veto use to block, 112, 151–52, 165

military force/requirements debate, 27–29, 56–57, 157

Military Staff Committee, 28, 29, 142–43, 149, 150, 157

Mixed Armistice Commission for Palestine, 168

Molotov, Vyacheslav, 5, 131

Monetary and Financial Conference, UN (1944), 137

Mongolia, 26, 145

Moscow Conference (1943), 4–5

Mossadegh, Mohammed, 198

Mountbatten, Lord Louis, 113

national self-interest, 125–26

Nauru, 153

Nehru, Jawaharlal, 117

Netherlands, and Indonesian independence, 113–21

Neutrality Act, 131, 132

Nicaragua, 162

Non Self-Governing Territories, Special Committee on, 167

North Atlantic Treaty Organization (NATO), 57, 157, 163, 193

North Korea. *See* Korean conflict

Norwegian Labour Party, 13–14

Norwegian Trade Union Youth Organization, 13

opium, 180

Pakistan, 27, 151, 153, 162, 168, 179, 182, 189

Palestine: Arab-Israeli War, 52–54, 157, 161; armistice agreement violations, 191, 192, 194, 198, 203; Conciliation Commission for Palestine, UN, 161, 165, 185, 188; Lie supports, 47, 55, 124; Mandate, 49–51, 54, 156; Mixed Armistice Commission for Palestine, 168, 198, 203; Palestine Commission, 51–52, 154; Palestine Truce commission, 156; refugees, 200; Truce Supervision organization, 180, 198; trusteeship proposal, 52, 159; UNSCOP report, 50–51

Palestine, UN Special Committee on (UNSCOP), 50–51, 150

Panama Canal Zone, 165

Papanek, Jan, 37

Paris Peace Conference, 145

Peace and Security, Interim Committee on, 36–37, 76, 152, 153, 165

peacekeeping role/issues, 10, 109–11

Peace Observation Committee, 76–77, 191

Peace Through Deeds Resolution, 175

Pearl Harbor, 134

Pearson, Lester, 12–13, 177

Peru, 166
pesticides, 165
Point Four Program (U.S.), 95, 162, 166
Poland, 131, 137, 154, 170
Political Rights of Women, Convention on the, 82, 202
politics. *See* Cold War politics
Population Commission, UN, 202
Portugal, 26, 145, 154, 161
Potsdam Conference, 139, 140
poverty, combating, 100–103
Preparatory Commission, 12, 16–17
Prevention and Punishment of the Crime of Genocide, Convention on the, 82, 161
Problems of Foreign Relations (U.S. State Dept.), Advisory Committee on, 2–3
Protocol on Narcotic Drugs, 167
Provisional International Civil Aviation Organization (PICAO), 137

Rao, Vijendra K.R.V., 94
Rau, Benagal, 177
Red Cross, International, 178
refugees: Committee on Refugees and Displaced Persons, UN, 144; High Commissioner for Refugees, Office of the UN, 177, 179, 194; International Refugee Organization (IRO), 143, 148, 185, 192; Palestinian, rights of, 200; Relief and Works Agency for Palestinian Refugees in the Near East, UN (UNRWA), 55, 160, 167, 174, 184; Relief for Palestinian Refugees Organization, UN (UNRPR), 160
Refugees, Office of the UN High Commissioner for, 177, 179, 194
Refugees and Displaced Persons, UN Committee on, 144

regional autonomy/defense pacts, 10–11, 57–58
Relief and Rehabilitation Administration, UN (UNRRA), 136, 148
Relief and Works Agency for Palestinian Refugees in the Near East, UN (UNRWA), 55, 160, 167, 174, 184
Relief for Palestinian Refugees Organization, UN (UNRPR), 160
Renville Accords, 115–16, 155
reparations, 163
Reston, James, 61
Rhodes, 162
Ridgway, Matthew B., 182
Rockefeller family, 17, 147
Romania, 27, 143, 146, 147, 151
Roosevelt, Eleanor, 79, 149
Roosevelt, Franklin Delano: Atlantic Charter meeting, 3; "Four Freedoms" speech, 2, 133; vision for international organization, 44; in WWII, 132, 133, 134, 138
Russia. *See* Soviet Union (USSR)

San Francisco (United Nations Conference) (1945), 8–11, 138
Santa Cruz, Hernan, 94
Secretary-General, UN Office of the: Cold War effect on, 121–25; historical antecedents for role of, 44–45; political independence of, 72–73; role in advising/commenting on Security Council actions, 46; Secretariat personnel, 199, 202, 203; selecting first Secretary-General, 12–13
Security Council, UN: Berlin crisis' impact on, 42; China's participation on, 58–61, 63–64, 68; creation of, 6–7;

Security Council, UN (*Continued*)
    Czechoslovakian debate, 38–39;
    dominance of, 77–78; early
    power struggles, 21, 24–25;
    expanded to fifteen members,
    118; Indonesian matter before,
    113–17; "Legal Aspects of
    Security Council Action in
    Korea," 68; Soviet absence from,
    59, 68, 170–71, 172; summit
    diplomacy of, 62; veto power in,
    7, 8, 10, 25–26, 27, 33, 36, 111–12,
    118–19
self-determination, 192, 195
Shotwell, James T., 1
Siam (Thailand), 145, 150
Sino-Soviet Treaty of Friendship,
    172, 173
Sixth General Assembly, 95
slavery, 82, 181
Slavery, Ad Hoc Committee on, 82
Smuts, Jan, 9, 84
Somaliland, 166, 169
South Africa: Ad Hoc Committee
    on South-West Africa, 180, 183,
    200; African National Congress,
    196; apartheid, 156, 178, 198, 200;
    Indian nationals in, 157–58, 164,
    171, 176, 178, 181, 190, 200, 204;
    race relations in, 204; South-West
    Africa issue, 153, 167, 180, 183,
    186, 188, 191, 200
South Korea. *See* Korean conflict
South-West Africa, Ad Hoc
    Committee on, 180, 183, 200
Soviet Union (USSR): atomic
    weapons policy, 32–35, 165;
    Berlin blockade, 39–42; Cold
    War politics in UN, 119–21; and
    Czechoslovakia, 36–39;
    denounces Japanese peace
    accords, 185; ECOSOC
    participation, 89–90; free
    elections in satellites, 147, 149;

human rights philosophy, 78–79;
    "Little Assembly" created to
    circumvent, 36–37, 152; military
    requirements debate, 28; non-
    recognition of Lie as Secretary
    General, 73; peace treaties, 146;
    Security Council boycott, 59, 68,
    170–71, 172; Security Council
    return, 70, 172; support for
    international organization, 4–5;
    troops in Iran, 21–25; veto use in
    Security Council, 7, 8, 10, 25–26,
    27, 33, 36, 111–12, 119; war
    propaganda proposal, 174; in
    WWII, 131, 132, 133, 135
Spaak, Paul-Henri, 12, 14, 141, 180
Spain, 143, 144, 145, 147, 164
Special United Nations Fund for
    Economic Development
    (SUNFED), 91, 93–99
Stalin, Joseph, 203; on Twenty-Year
    Peace Plan, 63; views of
    international organization, 6
Stalingrad, 135
Status of Women, UN Commission
    on the, 82, 162, 170, 182, 184, 193
Stettinius, Edward, 8
Stevenson, Adlai, 178
Study of Peace, UN Commission for
    the, 1–2
Suez Canal, 183, 185
"Suggested Terms of Settlement of
    the Korean Question," 70
Sukarno, Achmed, 116, 172
Sweden, 27, 145, 148
Syngman Rhee, 64–65
Syria, 143, 165

Taft, Robert, 178, 182
technical assistance, 99, 101, 148,
    176, 190; Expanded Programme
    of Technical Assistance, 93, 98,
    166, 177, 180, 185, 189, 197;
    Technical Assistance Board, 198;

Technical Assistance Conference, UN, 170
Territories, Non-Self-Governing, 86–87, 88, 153, 160, 162, 163, 167, 176, 201
Thailand, 27, 145, 150
Togoland, 178, 184
Tojo, Hideki, 134
trade unions, 180
Transjordan, 151
Treaty of Dunkirk, 149
Trieste, 47, 148, 154, 158, 163
Truce Supervision Organization, UN (UNTSO), 54
Truman, Harry S., 30–31, 35–36, 65–66, 179, 182
Truman Doctrine, 35, 149
Trusteeship Council, 85–86, 86, 148, 150, 162, 178, 184
trusteeship system, 7–8, 54, 85–86, 147
Tunisia, 193, 194, 196, 197, 198, 201, 203
Twenty-Year Peace Plan, 43–44, 61–64, 69–70, 124, 169, 175, 176, 187

Union of Soviet Socialist Republics (USSR). *See* Soviet Union (USSR)
United Nations Conference (San Francisco) (1945), 8–11, 138
United Nations Day, 153
United States: ECOSOC participation, 90–91; foreign aid issues, 90–91; Indonesian independence, 117–18; international organization support, 2–3, 135, 136; Japanese peace treaty, 180, 186; military requirements debate, 28, 32; Mutual Security Act, 187; Security Council conflicts with USSR, 26–27, 120–21; SUNFED opposition, 96–97; and UN Korean policy, 65–67, 69–70, 171, 174, 179; U.S. citizens as

Secretariat personnel, 199, 202, 203; uses Assembly to condemn Soviet policy, 76–78; Vandenberg Amendment, 157
Uniting for Peace Resolution, 76–78, 111, 174, 175, 183, 188
Universal Declaration of Human Rights, 79–81, 150, 161, 176
Universal Postal Union, 154, 157

Vandenberg Amendment, 30
venereal diseases, 103
veto use in Security Council, 7, 8, 10, 25–26, 27, 33, 36, 111–12, 118–19, 151
Vietnam, 189
Vishinsky, Andrei, 36
von Ribbentrop, Joachim, 131, 137

war propaganda, 37
Welles, Sumner, 3–4
West Africa, 162
West Germany, 39–40, 163
White, William Allen, 131
Wilson, Woodrow, 84, 126
women's equality issues, 82, 162, 170, 184–85, 193, 195, 202
Woods, John T., 187
World Bank, 137, 152, 154, 180
World Food Survey, 100
World Health Organization (WHO), 101–3, 148, 154
World Meteorological Organization, 181
World War II chronology, 131–40

Yalta Conference (1945), 7–8
Yearbook on Human Rights, 158, 190
Yemen, 27, 151, 153
Yugoslavia, 35–36, 147, 160, 182, 188, 189

Zellerback, David, 96–97
Zorin, Valerian, 38

About the Author

Anthony G. Gaglione was a professor of political science at East Stroudsburg University (East Stroudsburg, Pennsylvania) from 1968 until his sudden death in June 1995. He completed his academic work at Rutgers University (New Jersey), specializing in the United Nations, constitutional law, and international law. He published many articles as well as a book about the United Nations: *A Dangerous Place, The United Nations as a Weapon in World Politics,* which he co-authored with Abraham Yeselsen. Dr. Gaglione delivered papers at professional conferences on the topic of the United Nations and also appeared on television as an expert to discuss both U.S. foreign policy and the uses of the United Nations by member states.

Dr. Gaglione devoted much of his time to community children, coaching local high school baseball teams as well as a countywide summer baseball league for teenagers. He drew his expertise in this field not only from his interest in the "national pastime" but also from the years he spent playing professional baseball with the Brooklyn Dodgers organization before and after his service in the U.S. Army.

A portion of the obituary his family wrote about him following his death in 1995 stated, "Tony Gaglione succeeded in his life goals. He was an extraordinary husband and father, teacher, and resource in the community, on topics that included areas beyond his formal education, such as woodworking, the making of fine furniture, and wines of the world. He gave freely of his time, knowledge, expertise, and materials. He was a very kind, loving, and generous man. He influenced so many young people in positive directions, and taught them how to analyze information, and how to live a productive, rewarding life."

A scholarship in his name has been established at East Stroudsburg University for students of political science.

Beverly H. Gaglione
February 19, 2001